The Coventry Motor Industry

The Coventry Motor Industry

Birth To Renaissance?

David Thoms and Tom Donnelly

Routledge
Taylor & Francis Group

LONDON AND NEW YORK

First published 2000 by Ashgate Publishing

Reissued 2018 by Routledge
2 Park Square, Milton Park, Abingdon, Oxon OX14 4RN
711 Third Avenue, New York, NY 10017, USA

Routledge is an imprint of the Taylor & Francis Group, an informa business

A Library of Congress record exists under LC control number: 99053974

ISBN 13: 978-1-138-73926-0 (hbk)
ISBN 13: 978-1-138-73900-0 (pbk)
ISBN 13: 978-1-315-18419-7 (ebk)

Contents

List of Tables

Foreword

Coventry is synonymous with both the creation and relative decline of the British motor car industry. Our purpose in writing this volume is to explore the relationship between the car industry in this specific local context and the wider economic, social and political environment. The book analyses the emergence and early dominance of Coventry's motor manufacturers, the rise of volume production in the 1930s and the instabilities of the post-war era. Specific chapters deal with the industry's response to the demands created by the two world wars. A number of themes run throughout the book including the structure of the industry and the relationship between its various sectors, resource provision, management and labour relations, and the nature of and response to market demand. The book represents a substantially revised version of *The Motor Car Industry in Coventry Since the 1890s* which was published by Croom Helm in 1985. Use has been made of primary and secondary material which has become available since the original volume appeared, while the analysis has been extended to incorporate recent developments in the history of Coventry's motor vehicle industry.

We remain grateful to colleagues in our respective universities, in the various record offices and motor-vehicle companies who have assisted our research in a variety of ways, and to our friends and families for their support. Particular thanks are due to Ann Holton, Muriel Morgan and Sheila Petticrew for wrestling with our vain attempts at word processing and turning this into a meaningful document. Publication of this volume was assisted by a grant from the Peugeot Heritage Trust.

Chapter 1

The Coventry Motor-Car Industry: Parameters and Significance

The foundations of British motor-vehicle production were laid in Coventry in the 1890s as the city moved away from its traditional industries of textiles and watchmaking towards the manufacture of cars and their components. Daimler, Rover, Standard, Siddeley and Riley are among the famous marques associated with Coventry from its early car-making days and, although competition soon arrived from other parts of the country, for a short time the city represented in essence the British motor industry. Coventry's rapid industrial expansion in the late nineteenth and early twentieth centuries was also associated with electrical and aeronautical engineering, machine tools and artificial fibres, producing a cluster of enterprises based on relatively high levels of science and technology.

The reasons for Coventry's chequered experience during this period centre upon the replacement of the ailing crafts of silk weaving and watchmaking as the principal sources of income and employment by the new engineering products of cycles, motor vehicles and machine tools. By 1911 the vehicle and metal industries together absorbed just over 41 per cent of Coventry's occupied population, while watchmaking and silk weaving, which for most of the nineteenth century had dominated the labour market, accounted for less than 6 per cent of the total. These changes were accompanied by a rise in the scale and complexity of production. Although factory organisation was found in textiles and watchmaking, both industries relied heavily upon relatively small-scale enterprises. Many of the early cycle firms were also modest in their resources and output, but with the expansion of demand and greater capitalisation the industry became dominated by a number of very large firms such as Rudge Whitworth whose 2,700 employees in 1906 were responsible for the manufacture of 75,000 cycles.[1] By 1914 volume production had modified traditional work patterns, though in most areas, including motor vehicles, the specialised skills of the craftsman had not yet been superseded by the more routine activities of the assembly-line worker.

The social impact of Coventry's relatively late industrial revolution further illustrates the exceptional speed and magnitude of change. After a reversal in the 1860s, the earlier pattern of steady population growth reasserted itself. In 1901 the city's inhabitants numbered 69,978 but by 1911 the largest recorded decennial increase of 52 per cent had taken the total to 106,349. During the 1890s, inward migration became a significant factor in Coventry's demographic experience, but between 1901 and 1911 it emerged as the dominant element with some 67 per cent of the population increase of that period being accounted for by immigration from outside Warwickshire. The nearby counties of Worcestershire and Northamptonshire were major contributors, though some people were attracted from more distant locations, including almost 3,000 from London.[2] One of the consequences of this phenomenon was that it helped to produce a relatively young population, which no doubt influenced other social trends, such as marriage and birth rates, both of which were above the national average in 1911.

The peak year of the cycle boom in 1896 brought a flood of immigrants to Coventry and an immediate housing crisis. According to the city's Medical Officer of Health, 'Houses could not be built fast enough to accommodate the inrush.'[3] The city's electric tramway helped to ease the problem by facilitating the development of outlying areas, such as Foleshill, and by 1906 the building rate had improved substantially, reaching around 800 houses per annum compared with less than 200 a decade earlier. Nevertheless, the acceleration of population growth in the early twentieth century meant that Coventry's relatively small-scale building contractors found difficulty in keeping pace with the rising demand for inexpensive property, and one result of this was that many hundreds of workmen were obliged to lodge in the city during the week, returning home for Sundays. Although overcrowding remained a problem in 1914, it was largely confined to the central areas where it was exacerbated by the narrow medieval streets which restricted the ventilation and natural lighting of the houses. On the outskirts, to the north-east of the city, where most building work had been concentrated, relatively prosperous artisans rented or were purchasing accommodation which was officially regarded as of good standard. The 1890s saw a considerable increase in the provision of mortgages and between 1896 and 1914, for example, the the total advances held by the Coventry Permanent Economic Building Society increased from £12,106 to £102,166.[4] Yet, with the industrial expansion and population growth of the war years and beyond, inadequate supply remained a continuing feature of Coventry's housing market.

Similar difficulties plagued education as the schools bulged under the impact of a rapidly expanding child population. When the Local Education Authority assumed its responsibilities in 1903 it was already disadvantaged by the laxity of its predecessor, the Coventry School Board, which had been slow to respond to the new pressures, but the problem was compounded by the development of the peripheral areas where school building had not been designed to cope with the heavy demand which appeared after the turn of the century.[5] Only three of the authority's thirteen elementary schools were said to be free from overcrowding in 1908 and by the outbreak of war the Board of Education estimated that some 28 per cent of Coventry children were handicapped in this way, with the area to the north of the city being a particular worry. Although the LEA was penalised for its overcrowded elementary provision, board officials recognised that serious efforts were being made to rectify the deficiencies, and appreciated that Coventry's phenomenal growth rate rendered it virtually impossible to devise an effective school-building programme.[6]

Although the local authority was slow to respond to Coventry's housing shortage, important steps were taken to ameliorate other concerns in the decade before the First World War. Environmental health was gradually improved and by 1910 this was said to have contributed significantly to the city's declining death rate. Maternal and infant health care received particular attention, with the appointment in 1901 of a woman health visitor and in 1905 the introduction of a limited scheme of school medical inspection. Under pressure from the local branch of the Women's Co-operative Guild, Coventry was one of the first cities in Britain to establish an infant welfare clinic in 1915.[7]

Despite only a limited development of trade union organisation in the pre-war period, Coventry wages were generally good, certainly compared with rates of pay traditionally available in the textile industry.[8] Incomes were vulnerable to periods of unemployment resulting from trade fluctuations and the seasonal nature of work in the cycle and motor industries, but the Medical Officer of Health's comment in 1910 that Coventry children were well nourished and that this was due to the city's commercial prosperity is indicative of a broad rise in living standards.[9] The general work environment seems to have benefited from the structural changes in employment. It was reported in 1890 that in the new industries 'the artisan works under conditions more favourable to health than the watchmaker or weaver did'.[10] Apart from Courtaulds's viscose plant where employees could be obliged to work in an unpleasant and even dangerous atmosphere, factory conditions some twenty years later did not cause any serious concern. The new generation of Coventry workers were not only better paid than their predecessors, but in general by 1914 enjoyed substantially improved living and working conditions and, according to *The Times*, were soon to demonstrate a greater sense of industrial pride than could be found anywhere else in the country.[11]

When representatives of the Reform League visited Coventry in 1868 they reported that 'Party feeling runs very high in the Borough, nearly every man being an active Politician.'[12] This was given a new twist from the 1880s by the city's accelerated economic development and the general spread of interest in socialist ideas. Traditional working-class support for the Liberal position was shaken by the commercial treaty with France in 1860 which was widely held responsible for the downfall of the silk ribbon industry, but by the early twentieth century support was growing for more radical politics reflected in the formation in 1902 of the Coventry Labour Representation Committee. Although the first election success arrived in 1905, it was not until 1937 that Labour gained control of the city council, though in the intervening period it came to exercise considerable influence over local affairs. The new business community also became involved in municipal politics and when George

Singer, the cycle and motor manufacturer, became mayor in 1891 his election was indicative of the growing dominance of the new economic order.

The crisis in the silk ribbon industry following the removal of tariff protection revealed the inability of Coventry producers to meet the challenge of Swiss and French manufacturers whose competitive prices and attractive designs enabled them to capture a major share of the British market.[13]   The advancement of factory production had been inhibited in Coventry by local craft traditions, while the unattractive economic climate after 1860 deterred businessmen from investing the capital required for modernisation. For a brief period in the late nineteenth century watchmaking became Coventry's principal source of employment, but eventually it, too, was eclipsed by foreign competition as American and Swiss firms, using mass-production techniques, came to monopolize the market for inexpensive timepieces, which was growing quickly in the 1870s.[14]

The cycle industry provided a timely, if fortuitous, solution to Coventry's economic predicament. The pioneering work of the Coventry Machinists Company, formed in 1869, laid the foundations of the British cycle industry. Apart from its technical and production achievements, the firm became the starting point for many of Coventry's leading cycle manufacturers, including George Singer and John and Thomas Bayliss. The origins of Coventry's economic and social transformation are varied and complex, but the growth of the cycle industry was enormously influential in the diversification of the industrial base, for it was the pivot of a development block incorporating machine tools and motor vehicles which underpinned the city's prosperity during the formative years of the new century.

Coventry's occupied population almost doubled during the interwar period, confirming the city's promise as one of Britain's most dynamic growth areas and contrasting sharply with the manifestations of industrial decline in many other parts of the country. Immigration continued to supplement the natural population increase, though by the 1920s migrants were drawn from more distant locations than earlier in the century, including substantial numbers from Wales, Scotland and the northern counties. In addition, it was claimed in 1929 that some 27,000 workers commuted daily to Coventry, mainly from Birmingham.[15] Although job security continued to be threatened by trade and seasonal factors, the general economic expansion ensured that favourable employment prospects and relatively high wages remained a powerful attraction to labour. By 1939 Coventry's population stood at 220,000 compared with 136,000 in 1919, giving it the distinction of the fastest-growing city in Britain during this period.

The tension which accompanied rapid economic and social change was again apparent in housing and education. Demand for residential property remained high around the city's northern fringes where many of the major engineering firms were situated, but new areas of growth like Stoke, which had developed swiftly during the First World War, placed additional strain upon the limited resources of the building industry. Construction increased steadily during the interwar years, aided in part by a more positive approach from the local authority, seen mainly in the form of municipal housing. Land was acquired at Radford in 1923 for the first corporation estate which by the late 1930s contained almost 2,500 houses, making it one of the most densely populated districts in the city. Coventry also enjoyed an exceptionally high rate of owner occupation. Between 1932 and 1938 over 18,000 privately financed houses were built in the city, dwarfing the public provision for that period.[16] Yet the supply of both private and council housing was persistently outstripped by demand and employers complained frequently that this rendered it more difficult to attract suitable manpower to the city.

The provision of school buildings remained an issue throughout the interwar period and in 1938 one of His Majesty's Inspectors commented that 'the rapid growth and development of the City made the Public Elementary School accommodation problems bewilderingly complex.'[17] However, increasingly, the problem of overcrowded schools spread from the elementary to the secondary sector fuelled by growing public interest in more advanced education as well as the continued upsurge in population. In 1925 the secondary allocation was about 1,400 places below the Board of Education's target and the real shortfall was probably far greater than this. The LEA responded by introducing a selective central school and a limited number of elementary 'higher tops', but plans for a major building initiative did not begin to take shape until the later 1930s when Stoke Park School was rebuilt and land was acquired for the construction of Caludon Castle Boys' School. Technical education experienced similar pressures as a growing number of employers and their workers came to appreciate the benefits of college-based training. In January 1933 some 3,000 technical students petitioned the local authority for improved training facilities but, although an impressive new college was opened in 1936, the additional accommodation quickly proved inadequate for by the end of the following year over thirty classes were forced to meet in neighbouring outposts, while enrolments in engineering had been suspended due to excess demand.[18]

In the interwar period Courtaulds's expansion programmes and the diversification into new products by some old-established firms, including J. and J. Cash, helped to boost job prospects but could not prevent a further decline in the textile industry's share of total employment. The relative importance of the cycle industry, so important to Coventry's industrial regeneration in the 1890s, also diminished as the leading manufacturers turned to motor vehicles. By 1939 Standard and Rootes were among the 'big six' in the industry, while the engine division of the Morris organisation, the market leader, was also Coventry based. Alfred Herbert dominated the local machine-tool industry, though Coventry Guage and Tool, and Wickmans also enjoyed a national reputation. During the 1930s all three subsequently expanded their capacity and production in order to cope with bulging order books.

The emergence of the aeronautical engineering industry was related to Coventry's involvement in the First World War when several of the leading motor firms went over to the production of airframes, aero-engines or both. The Siddeley company is particularly important in this respect for, unlike other motor manufacturers, it continued to develop its aircraft production after 1918. This was because its highly successful fighter plane, the Puma, remained in demand until well into the 1920s, but also because John Siddeley believed that the market for both civil and military aircraft was likely to be an expanding and profitable one. The General Electric Company's links with Coventry may also be traced to the First World War when one of its subsidiaries opened a factory at Copsewood Grange for the production of magnetos. A new building was erected in 1920 for the manufacture of telephone equipment and by the end of the 1930s GEC was one of the city's largest employers and the basis of its profile within the electrical engineering industry.

Pre-war links were also maintained in the 1920s by the continuing increase in the size and complexity of the business unit and the virtual disappearance of the traditional workshops and toyshops of nineteenth-century Coventry. By 1939 Courtaulds and the principal motor car assemblers each employed around 5,000 workers, while in electrical engineering GEC and British Thompson Houston had a combined labour force of almost 10,000. Mergers and takeovers became commonplace, especially in the motor industry, while the structure of management followed the national trend in becoming more specialised and professional. With the greater capitalisation and the growth of subsidiary organisations, ownership and control continued to become more broadly dispersed. Additions to plant, the spread of new production methods and increases in output were other indications of Coventry's growing industrial maturity.[19]

Changes in the nature and scale of production, particularly the spread of assembly-line techniques, profoundly influenced working conditions, including occupational status, wage payments and the general pattern of the working day. Coventry's reputation in the 1920s and 1930s as a boom town derived in part from the relatively high wages paid to its skilled industrial labour force. Yet mass production and the opportunity to earn bonus payments conveyed particular benefits to unskilled and semi-skilled workers. Indeed, some skilled men deliberately chose production work in order to increase their weekly pay, so that in some respects skill counted for rather less in Coventry than in some other parts of the country. Within the context of a buoyant labour market, even the slow growth of trade unions among the unskilled could not seriously undermine their financial prospects.

The rise in real incomes was reflected in changing leisure pursuits. Although going to a club or pub for a drink and social engagement remained perhaps the major pastime of Coventry factory workers in the twentieth century, the interwar period witnessed the rise of the annual seaside holiday and the growing popularity of dance bands. Many of the best dance halls were provided by employers, and a number of firms saw the development of leisure facilities as a way of maintaining the support and co-operation of their employees. This may well have applied to George Singer when he established works cycling, cricket and football clubs, the latter forming the basis of what was to become Coventry City Football Club.[20] Works bands became common in the 1920s and 1930s, while Standard eventually even developed its own holiday camp. It has been noted that while participation in leisure activities in Coventry mirrored that of other large towns in the 1930s, the city was distinctive in the way that it catered for its skilled and semi-skilled workers. According to Crump, 'These people with good wages, had access to the leading sports and social clubs, with their new pavilions and refurbished ballrooms, to the super-cinemas and to commercial dance halls.'[21]

The expansion of Coventry's occupied population included a rise in the number of women workers, from 7,918 in 1901 to 23,183 in 1951. Although this was only a small increase in female employment as a percentage of the total workforce, it meant that in national terms Coventry remained a relatively good source of job opportunities for women. In 1951 women formed 37.9 per cent of Coventry's working population compared with a figure of 30.8 per cent for Britain as a whole. The trend of female employment mirrored the pattern of Coventry's industrial transition with a swing towards electronics and motor vehicles, though Courtaulds in artificial fibres and a declining number of firms in more traditional product areas continued to provide jobs for women in the textile industry. In addition, the growth of large-scale business enterprise together, perhaps, with tightness in the labour market, meant that by 1931 the proportion of women in clerical posts was some 50 per cent above the national level.[22]

The nature of Coventry's industrial development was greatly influenced by the two world wars. In 1936 the city became closely involved in the rearmament programme when John Black and William Rootes, both from the motor industry, and Alfred Herbert met with Whitehall officials to plan the construction of shadow factories in anticipation of wartime requirements. The eventual volume production of military equipment reinforced Coventry's position as one of Britain's leading centres of modern engineering and left it poised for further rapid growth in the post-war era. This was encouraged by the incoming Labour government which by 1948 had approved plans for some 707,355 square feet of new factory space in the city. As before, this expansion brought a sharp rise in the size of Coventry's occupied population so that in the decade 1951 to 1961 the rate of growth far outstripped the national average. Innovations in production methods, high wages in selected industries and multinational ownership were additional features of Coventry's industrial expansion.

Problems began to appear in the 1960s, however, as the growth in the labour force fell away and unemployment rose, reaching the exceptionally high level of 5.6 per cent in 1968. Growing local concern was demonstrated in that year by the convocation of a series of Lord Mayor's Conferences designed to examine the plight of the city's ailing economy. Yet the outlook deteriorated further in the 1970s as underlying weaknesses in the industrial fabric became more evident with additional business failures, vacant factory accommodation and a marked increase in redundancies, so that by 1980 unemployment exceeded the UK average. Between 1975 and 1982 the top fifteen employers in Coventry axed almost half of their combined labour force, with job losses by the end of the period averaging 520 a month. Coventry's industrial base was declining rapidly, a phenomenon rendered especially poignant by its contrast with the years of economic boom.[23]

The Times noted in 1959 that Coventry's economy was highly dependent upon a relatively narrow range of metal engineering products. The pitfalls of this particular form of economic concentration became increasing apparent during the next twenty years as the aircraft, motor-vehicle and machine-tool industries grappled with the vagaries of government policy and competition from firms which were often more innovatory and efficient. Hawker Siddeley ceased production at Baginton in July 1965, and because of this and other rationalisation schemes 11,000 jobs disappeared from Coventry's aviation industry between 1962 and 1967. Although employment in motor vehicles continued to increase until the early 1970s, indications of the industry's problems in Coventry appeared earlier in the form of unprofitable production, a relatively modest share of the home market and a decline in the number of independent manufacturers. The injection of government finance was necessary to sustain the Chrysler assembly plant at Ryton before its sale to Peugeot of France in 1978, while British Leyland was rescued from collapse by being taken into public ownership. Between 1975 and 1982 BL shed 19,047 workers, or almost 70 per cent of its Coventry labour force. A similar situation developed at Herbert's machine-tool plant which, after financial assistance from the National Enterprise Board, was eventually taken over by Tooling Investments in 1980. However, losses continued to mount, bringing the firm's final demise in 1983 and the sale by auction of its entire stock of machine tools and other equipment. At that time the labour force stood at 400 compared with 12,000 Herbert employees in the early 1970s.[24]

Coventry's industrial malaise reflected the wider problems of the national economy, but the Lord Mayor's Conferences in 1968 identified certain issues of special local importance. In particular, it was argued that government policies relating to defence and regional development had seriously handicapped the aircraft and motor-vehicle industries. The cancellation of the HS 681 project by the Wilson administration in 1964 was directly responsible for Hawker Siddeley's decision to close its Baginton works, while the Rootes Group had already succumbed to government pressure by opening a new assembly plant at Linwood near Glasgow rather then expand their Ryton operation. However, the particular significance of government intervention is hard to assess, especially since the Board of Trade denied that Industrial Development Certificates had been used in a way which curtailed Coventry's economic expansion. The conferences also concluded that the city was disadvantaged by its ageing and sometimes outmoded industrial stock. It was claimed that one of the reasons why efforts to attract the new science-based industries had largely failed was that existing capacity was not readily adaptable to their needs. This was important, but in many respects more fundamental was the problem of underinvestment in existing activities, which hampered productivity, depressed profits and further restricted the introduction of new capital. Not only was the industrial base limited, but it was also noted in 1968 that Coventry had failed to attract and develop a significant service sector. The city suffered in this respect from the close proximity of Birmingham with its extensive range of financial and distribution services and public utility and local government offices.[25]

By the mid-1980s Coventry's economy demonstrated signs of revival as employment increased and new firms were attracted to the city and its environs. However, with the onset of economic recession in the early 1990s this trend was reversed so that between 1991 and 1993 employment fell by 6 per cent, some four points above the national average.[26] Yet the underlying strength of the local economy soon brought further job opportunities, until progress was undermined by the impact of an increasingly unstable international economy. Although Coventry's recent economic vicissitudes appear roughly to mirror national patterns, they do disguise important local variations, including the growth of the service sector. During the recession of the early 1990s, for example, employment opportunities in banking, finance and insurance rose sharply, helping to ensure that the growth of Coventry's service sector as a whole outstripped the national average. Similarly, the establishment of the University of Warwick Science Park, the Westwood Business Park and other related initiatives helped manufacturing industry to take full advantage of the economic upswing of the late 1980s, allowing Coventry to boast 'one of the highest concentrations of leading-edge businesses in Europe'.[27] These changes had a significant impact upon the labour force, particularly in creating employment opportunities for highly-trained and skilled workers in the advanced technology sectors. In addition, the gap between the level of female and male employment became very narrow with a number of areas beyond manufacturing and construction being dominated by women, many of whom worked part-time.

At first glance, motor-vehicle manufacture may appear to be a less dominant force within Coventry's economy in the 1990s than in the pre-war years. The 1950s and 1960s witnessed considerable change as specialist producers ceased production, Lea-Francis, Armstrong-Siddeley and Alvis manufactured their last cars respectively in 1954, 1960 and 1967, while the volume makers were subject to a period of takeover.[28] By 1980 motor-car production was controlled by BL (formerly British Leyland) and Talbot (successor to Rootes and Chrysler), while the changes of recent years have created a situation where the only volume producer of standard cars in the city is Peugeot, Rover (once part of BL and bought by BMW in 1994) having ceased production in Coventry. Two important and successful specialist firms remain in the shape of Jaguar, the luxury car firm purchased by Ford in 1987, and London Taxis International, manufacturers of taxicabs. The only other major vehicle manufacturers, Massey Ferguson (tractors) and Alvis (armoured vehicles), are not involved in car production.

The rise and subsequent near demise of Coventry's car industry is reflected in the city's changing physical profile as motor works came and went. To begin with, many firms simply converted existing buildings to the manufacture of cars, with Daimler's occupation of a four-storey former cotton mill in Sandy Lane being an early and one of the most important examples. As production increased and investment funds became available car production came increasingly to be concentrated in purpose-built accommodation. In 1908, for example, the Daimler company purchased additional land close to the Coventry to Nuneaton railway line for the construction of workshops which were said to have 'established a new scale for car factories in the city'.[29] New systems of production and larger outputs required more space so that motor manufacturers took the opportunity to move beyond the city centre where land was at less of a premium. Thus, the impressive Humber factory in Folly Lane (Stoke) was opened in 1908 to be followed in the interwar period by Standard's large new site at Canley on the northern edge of the city. What is now the Peugeot works at Ryton, and Daimler's factory in Browns Lane, were constructed as shadow factories on greenfield sites peripheral to the city. Although these plants remain in production, many other car factories have been demolished in recent years, including the landmark Standard and Alvis works, to make way for shopping centres and other commercial ventures. Together with the ring road, which has been so important in determining the constrained nature of Coventry's traditional commercial hub, it is perhaps appropriate that these initiatives should have so influenced the architecture of the city which was the midwife to Britain's motor-car industry.

Yet car-making remains important within Coventry's economy as a source of employment and income generation. In 1997 (at the time of writing the latest figures available) Jaguar (4,206) and Peugeot (3,673) were the second- and third-largest employers in the city, together accounting for some 6 per cent of the total labour force. In addition, however, Coventry houses a number of firms who source the major car manufacturers, as well as other firms in aerospace and defence, with a wide range of component products. Research by the economic division of Coventry City Council in 1994 identified some thirty-seven local suppliers of components to the automotive industry, ranging from engine parts (Coventry Apex) and car seats (Callow and Maddox) to robotic automation systems (Fanuc Robotics) and machine tools (Marrill Engineering).[30] Like the assemblers, many of these firms are foreign owned and controlled, indicating the attraction of the Coventry region as a centre for motor-vehicle related investment. Despite the departure of its manufacturing base from the city, Rover continues to be a particularly important source of orders for components manufactured in Coventry. Although relatively small scale in terms of the employment opportunities which it creates, component manufacture has a particular importance within the local economy since it benefits from a relatively broad-based and therefore less volatile market than car assembly, and in many cases has important linkages with a variety of high technology industries.

The foundations of the British motor industry were laid in Coventry in the 1890s and, for a short time in the early twentieth century, the city justified its sobriquet of the British Detroit. The reasons for this phenomenon in Britain's industrial history are many and varied. The availability of capital and labour, and technology transfers from cycles and watchmaking were important, but so, too, was the nature of the entrepreneurial base, a significant proportion of which proved sufficiently prescient and flexible to mobilise the key factors of production. But Coventry's business community operated in a wider context so that rising middle-class incomes, a growing taste for mobility and the influence of war provided the background against which the development of motor-car manufacture in the city was made possible.

Although its relative importance as a centre of the motor industry has declined as major firms have failed or left the city and ownership, as with car manufacture as a whole, has been concentrated overseas, Coventry retains a significant and vibrant car-making sector. With the benefit of hindsight, Coventry's central role in the development of motor-vehicle technology and systems of manufacture can be appreciated, while in helping to spawn the horseless carriage the city set in motion a social, cultural and economic revolution in which the car dominates our public space and helps to define the parameters and quality of our private lives.

Notes

[1]   S.B. Saul, 'The Engineering Industry', in D.H. Aldcroft (ed.) *The Development of British Industry and Foreign Competition 1875–1914* (Allen and Unwin, London, 1968), p. 215.
[2]   Census Report, 1911, birthplace details, vol. 9, Cmd. 7017, table 2.
[3]   Medical Offier of Health for Coventry, Annual Report (Coventry, 1898), p. 7.
[4]   M. Davis, *Every Man His Own Landlord* (Coventry Building Society, Coventry, 1985), p. 21.

[5]   Public Record Office (PRO), Ed. 16/318, Report of a meeting between representatives of the LEA and the Board of Education, 6 November 1912.

[6]   PRO, Ed. 16/318, HA to Richardson, 10 February 1915.

[7]   M. Lodge, 'How we ran the welfare', *Health Visitor*, vol. 56 (1983), p. 244.

[8]   E.H. Hunt, *Regional Wage Variations in Britain 1850–1914* (Clarendon Press, Oxford, 1973), pp. 160–61.

[9]   Medical Officer of Health for Coventry, *Annual Report* (1910), p. 90.

[10]   Medical Officer of Health for Coventry, *Annual Report* (1890), p. 11.

[11]   *The Times*, 17 January 1916.

[12]   Bishopgate Institute, Reform League, Report by Hales and Brighty, 1868.

[13]   P. Searby, 'Lists of Prices in the Coventry Silk Industry, 1800–1860', *Bulletin of the Society for the Study of Labour History* (1973), pp. 48–53.

[14]   R.A. Church, 'Nineteenth Century Clock Technology in Britain, the United States and Switzerland', *Economic History Review*, 2nd series, vol. XXVIII, no. 4 (1975), pp. 621–2.

[15]   C. Saunders, *Seasonal Variations in Employment* (Longmans, London, 1936), p. 98 (footnote); *Birmingham Gazette*, 3 November 1937.

[16]   Davis, *Every Man His Own Landlord*, p. 70.

[17]   PRO, Ed. 60/557, T.W. Southern to G.L. Thornton, 13 October 1938.

[18]   K. Richardson, *Twentieth Century Coventry*, (Coventry City Council, Coventry, 1972), pp. 251–6.

[19]   Ibid., pp. 32–64

[20]   K. Atkinson, *The Singer Story*, (Veloce, Godmanstone, 1996), pp. 19–20; see also, D. Brassington, R. Dean and D. Chalk, *Singers to Sky Blues* (Buckingham, Sporting and Leisure Press, 1986).

[21]   J. Crump, 'Recreation in Coventry Between the Wars' in B. Lancaster and T. Mason, *Life and Labour in a 20th Century City: The Experience of Coventry* (Cryfield Press, Coventry, n.d.), p. 280; see also, P. Thompson, 'Imagination and Passivity in Leisure; Coventry Car Workers and their Families from the 1920s to the 1990s', in D.W. Thoms, L. Holden and T. Claydon (eds), *The Motor Car and Popular Culture in the 20th Century* (Ashgate, Aldershot, 1998).

[22]   A. Friedman, *Industry and Labour*, (Macmillan, London, 1977), pp. 202–4.

[23]   Richardson, *Twentieth Century Coventry*, pp. 142–3.

[24]   S. Taylor, 'Unemployment in the West Midlands', in B. Crick (ed.), *Unemployment*, (Methuen, London, 1981), pp. 74–3; 'Redundancies in Coventry', *Coventry Quarterly Monitor of the Economy*, no. 3 (1980).

[25]   Richardson, *Twentieth Century Coventry*, pp. 127–53.

[26]   *Coventry Facts and Figures* (Coventry City Council, Coventry, 1997), p. 33.

[27]   Ibid., p. 30.

[28]   *Coventry Evening Telegraphy*, 16 January 1996.

[29]   *Coventry Car Factories. A Centenary Guide* (Coventry City Council, Coventry, 1995), p. 5.

[30]   S. Smith, *Challenges and Opportunities for the Automotive Component Sector in Coventry in the 1990s* (Coventry City Council, Coventry, 1994).

Chapter 2

Origins: From Cycles To Cars

Coventry joined the industrial revolution at a relatively late stage, for until the latter part of the nineteenth century the city's industrial structure was based upon traditional crafts, the most important of which were ribbon weaving and watchmaking. The rise of imported products following the removal of tariff protection in 1860 revealed that Coventry's silk-ribbon manufacturers were unable to compete with their Swiss and French counterparts in either price or design. This particular dip in the economic cycle brought unemployment and substantial migration from the city. By 1867 half of Hillfields was said to have become depopulated with row upon row of houses standing vacant.[1] For those who remained there was often little alternative but to resort to Poor Relief or help from one of the city's numerous charities.[2]

Watchmaking provided an alternative source of employment for those with the appropriate skills, or the adaptability to acquire them but it, too, succumbed to foreign competition as Swiss and American manufacturers, using mass-production techniques, came to dominate the market for cheap watches, which was growing quickly in the 1870s. By 1914 Coventry's two largest watchmaking concerns, Rotherhams and the Coventry Watch Movement Company, had diversified into the manufacture of cycle and motor-car components, while the remainder of the industry, still controlled by small-scale producers, formed a relatively insignificant part of the city's economic structure. Yet, by the close of the century, Coventry was enjoying a renewed period of economic prosperity based upon the cycle and infant motor-vehicle industries. In 1916 one visitor from the United States referred to the 'briskness in the very air of the place', comparing the rate of industrial expansion favourably with that of Detroit, one of America's boom cities.[3] This represented a remarkable economic transformation which had been condensed into little more than two decades of prodigious effort.

Cycle manufacture was central to Coventry's renaissance from a city characterised by economic conservatism and decline to one of the leading centres of the new industries of the twentieth century. The importance of the relationship between cycles and cars was captured by W. O. Bentley's experience when, as a young man, he toured the country in search of orders for his own agency. It was only in the Midlands that he experienced any real hostility, noting that for 'some reason the fact that I had not "come up through bicycles" seemed to stick in a few of the Midlanders' throats'.[4] Although a number of major firms such as Daimler, Standard and Alvis were formed as motor-vehicle enterprises, a majority of the city's leading car-makers, and certainly the pioneers, had their origins in cycles. These included Humber, Rover, Swift and Singer, which together accounted for around 75 per cent of Coventry's motor-vehicle output in 1913.[5] The Riley family demonstrated an exceptional level of continuity in moving from textiles to cycles, motorcycles and eventually cars. Calcott Brothers followed a similar pattern of development, acquiring a large factory in Gosford Street, before the firm's collapse in 1926. Clarke, Cluley and Company, another old-established cycle manufacturer, entered the car market but with only short-term success, while many smaller firms appear to have faltered during the initial period of research and development. Triumph, which opened its cycle factory in 1890, delayed making cars until 1913, while the giant Rudge-Whitworth concern eschewed involvement with the industry altogether, though both firms maintained a strong and successful interest in motorcycles. William Hillman and Lea-Francis Cars Limited also had roots in the cycle business and, although they produced only a modest number of cars before 1914, both ultimately achieved considerable distinction within the industry. Lea-Francis is particularly interesting because its history demonstrates that the transition from cycles to cars was far from the natural linear progression which some studies imply since the firm entered, left and rejoined the industry on four separate occasions.[6] Similarly, J.K. Starley, one of the earliest cycle manufacturers to produce a prototype motor vehicle and the founder of the Rover company, adopted an ambivalent position which delayed his firm's entry to the car industry until after his death in 1901.

The Coventry cycle industry effectively began in 1869 when James Starley and others formed the Coventry Machinists Company. This firm had evolved from an enterprise established earlier in the century to build sewing machines, but a relatively weak market for these, coupled with Starley's technical inventiveness, brought reconstruction and diversification into cycles.[7] The company's success soon attracted further entrants to the industry, including in 1871 Haynes and Jeffries, the first specialist cycle-manufacturing operation in Coventry.[8] A decade later the city housed sixteen cycle-makers, with the number increasingly steadily despite the fluctuating nature of the trade. By 1890 the industry was expanding quickly, reflected in the construction of new factories and a growing army of labour. However, a trade boom in the 1890s encouraged particularly rapid growth, with the number of manufacturers peaking at some seventy-five firms in 1898.[9] Coventry's role as the principal centre of cycle production diminished in the early twentieth century as several of the smaller companies ceased trading and many of the larger ones became more concerned with the construction of motor vehicles.

The decline of the traditional crafts of silk weaving and watchmaking help to explain Coventry's prominence as the focus of the early cycle-making industry. As one of the city's principal motor companies, Riley appears unique in progressing successfully from textiles to cycles before becoming involved in the manufacture of cars. In 1890 William Riley added to the family's ribbon-weaving business by purchasing the cycle firm of Bonnick and Company. Six years later this became the basis of the Riley Cycle Company, at which point the family severed its connections with the textile trade.[10] Watchmaking was a more fertile source of recruitment to the cycle industry than textiles, especially in the 1890s when a number of firms moved in this direction, including James Hawley and Sons, one of the largest watchmaking concerns in Coventry. Yet many of the industry's leading pioneers were not Coventry born, nor had they close links with either silk weaving or watchmaking. James Starley, for example, was employed by the marine engineers Penns of Greenwich before moving to Coventry, while his nephew J.K. Starley, the inventor of the Rover Safety Bicycle, was born in London to a family of market gardeners. The Machinists Company employed a number of individuals who later ranked among Coventry's leading cycle entrepreneurs, including George Singer, William Hillman and Thomas Bayliss, but all of these were immigrants from other parts of the country. Thomas Bayliss was a native of Birmingham where he had worked in the small-arms industry, while Hillman and Singer, both particularly interesting because of their connections with motor vehicles, had trained as engineers in London. Similarly, the Humber and Rudge cycle companies moved to Coventry after their respective origins in Nottingham and Wolverhampton, while Triumph was the creation of Siegfried Bettman, a London cycle agent of Bavarian ancestry.[11]

The presence of a suitable workforce was almost certainly a major attraction when James Starley and his financial backers established their sewing-machine business in Coventry. Labour made redundant from textiles and other traditional crafts was important in servicing the manpower needs of the infant cycle industry. As one contemporary observed, 'The cycle shops were asylums for weavers, watchmakers, and others down on their luck.'[12] During the initial stages of development most cycle manufacturers designed and made their own tools so that the precision engineering skills associated with some aspects of Coventry's traditional industries were in high demand. The example of George Freeman illustrates one line of progression. Born in 1842, Freeman trained as a loom builder before joining the Machinists Company, where he remained for some years, eventually ending his career as a toolmaker with Rudge-Whitworth.[13] It was reported in 1896 that 'Of the residents nearly all artisans who were capable of turning their hands to the new industries have gone over from the watch and ribbon trades.'[14] At the same time the flow of apprentices into textiles and watchmaking had fallen to insignificant levels. From its early days the Coventry Machinists employed workers from London and Birmingham, but these men were said to be 'hopelessly at sea on the fine delicate work required by the sewing machine manufacturers'.[15] Perhaps this was merely the prejudice of one Coventrian. In any event, by the 1890s the manpower requirements of the cycle trade could not be satisfied locally so that workers were increasingly brought in from outside the city, and in this respect Coventry's proximity to the West Midlands industrial conurbation was a particular asset. Despite occasional manpower shortages in the 1890s, the generally favourable nature of Coventry's labour market, combined with the introduction of suitable classes in the local technical school, represented a positive factor in the overall growth of the cycle industry and, by implication, the motor trade too.[16]

Although many of Coventry's cycle pioneers came from outside the city, much of the industry's finance, particularly in the early stages of development, was provided locally. This was partly an attempt to profit from the new areas of economic growth, but reflected also the relative unattractiveness of traditional capital outlets in textiles and watchmaking. Strenuous efforts to attract funds were made by the directors of the Coventry Watch Movement Company when it was formed in 1889, but with very little success, so that plans to install modern American machinery were soon abandoned.[17] Again, in 1891, the company's attempt to raise £4,000 through the issue of preference shares proved abortive, with less than half that amount being taken up.[18] The failure of Coventry's textile manufacturers to respond successfully to foreign competition after 1860 with a vigorous programme of factory building and technical modernisation was another indication of the reluctance of investors to risk their capital at a time when prospects were so uncertain.

Many small cycle firms functioned with very limited financial resources, facilitated in part by the availability of redundant textile workshops which could no doubt be rented fairly cheaply. Such important cycle firms as Rover, Centaur and Wareman and Hazelwood started with modest rented accommodation formerly occupied by weavers. In addition, the buying-out of components and low output levels minimised labour and other costs, though anything more than a small assembly operation could require substantial capital for the purchase of plant and machinery. In common with other spheres of economic activity, partnerships were used to link money with technical initiative. The firm of J.K. Starley and William Sutton, which was formed in 1873, enjoyed considerable success for its Meteor Works in West Orchard, producing a highly popular tricycle as well as the famous 'safety' bicycle. Most of the finance seems to have been supplied by Sutton, a keen cyclist who made his money from Coventry's haberdashery trade.[19] The partnership of Hillman and Herbert also united money and technical ability to form the engineering firm of Automachinery, though on this occasion the finance emanated from beyond the city. Although only twenty-six when Automachinery was formed in 1875, William Hillman already possessed substantial technical experience having worked for Messrs Penns the marine engineers, the Coventry Machinists, and also joined forces briefly with James Starley to manufacture cycles on their own account. William Herbert, the elder brother of Alfred, drew his funds from the family building and farming interests in Leicestershire. Automachinery was originally concerned with the manufacture of cycle parts, sewing machines and roller skates, but an additional partner, George Beverley Cooper, later provided fresh injections of capital which stimulated further expansion. In 1896 the cycle part of the business, which by then included the production of complete machines, was separated to become the New Premier Cycle Company. With a labour force of 600 and an output of 33,000 bicycles, this was claimed to be one of the largest firms of its kind in the world. Automachinery retained its independent identity, specialising in the manufacture of bearings.[20]

Although new partnerships continued to be formed, the final two decades of the nineteenth century were characterised by the reconstruction of Coventry's larger cycle firms into private and public companies, though with local capital often still prominent. For example, Thomas Mercer, one of Coventry's leading participants in the watchmaking trade, not only invested in the Quinton Cycle Company when it was formed in 1891, but also became its managing director.[21] George Woodcock, a wealthy Coventry solicitor with family banking and hotel connections in the city, was involved in some of the most interesting company flotations of this period. In 1880 Woodcock gained control of the Wolverhampton cycle firm of Daniel Rudge which he then merged with his own Coventry Cycle Company. Woodcock's cycle interests were extended in 1885 when he received financial assistance from business contacts in Coventry and Birmingham to create the new enterprise of Daniel Rudge and Company which, following another amalgamation in 1893, became Rudge-Whitworth and Co. Ltd.[22] By the 1890s Coventry's principal cycle manufacturers attracted funds from many different parts of the country, but the availability of local capital was of crucial importance to the industry's development during the key decades of the 1870s and 1880s.

The Coventry cycle industry rapidly developed its own growth momentum. In explaining why he left the Machinists Company in 1872, Thomas Bayliss recalled that 'there was such a demand for bicycles that it was a favour to get an order executed under about three months, and the makers did not appear to trouble themselves about extending their output'.[23] Once it discovered a product with wide market appeal, even a firm with very modest resources could grow quickly. As Bayliss noted, 'We commenced making the "Excelsior" bicycle in a small way, and it soon had such a run that we found it impossible to keep pace with the demand, and very soon we were compelled to take larger premises.'[24] Wareman and Hazelwood was another successful enterprise which soon outgrew its original accommodation. Like Bayliss, John Warman left the Machinists Company to establish his own business and, after a series of unproductive partnerships, eventually joined forces with James Hazelwood, whose knowledge of the local metal trades helped to bring the firm its success.[25] In 1889 Wareman and Hazelwood received an order for 4,000 cycles, the largest single purchase made from any Coventry firm at that time, thus securing its position as one of the industry's market leaders.[26]

The inventiveness of many of Coventry's early cycle manufacturers extended the market and promoted growth. James Starley's tricycle and his nephew's 'safety' bicycle opened this mode of transport to a wider clientele than merely athletic young men. The 'ordinary' or penny-farthing bicycle required considerable strength to operate successfully, while the tricycle was suitable for an entirely new set of customers. As one journalist commented in 1880, the tricycle increasingly found favour among 'men of declining years, clergymen, and members of other professions and lastly, but not least, the fair sex, to all of whom the attainment of a high rate of speed, and the possible chances of a "smash", are at the same time uncomfortable and inappropriate'.[27] The introduction by the Centaur Company in 1881 of a machine designed to accommodate four passengers was an attempt to capitalise on the same market.[28] However, it was the marriage in 1888 of the diamond-framed 'safety' bicycle with Dunlop's pneumatic tyre which brought the cycle its wide popular appeal and precipitated the industry's rapid expansion during the 1890s. Yet the Starleys were not the only manufacturers to achieve major technical or commercial innovations, either in the production of whole machines or their components, and this is one reason why Coventry attracted so many aspirant cycle-makers. The competitive nature of the trade, stimulated by the practice of introducing revised models for the new season, ensured that changes relating to technical specification and design occurred with great frequency. Intelligence received in a variety of ways made it possible for many smaller firms, without the resources to develop their own technical advances, to benefit from the work of others. Copying was a major problem for the more innovative concerns and, while patents offered some protection, the costs of registration and defending them in the courts deterred some firms from making full use of this device.

Many Coventry cycle-makers bought substantial quantities of components from manufacturers in other parts of the country. In 1903, for example, the Riley Cycle Company alone purchased 18,000,000 ball bearing from Hoffmanns of Chelmsford.[29] Other volume imports included steel tubing, springs, paints and enamels, lamps, tyres and rims, but most of these came from firms in Birmingham and other nearby centres of the light metal and engineering trades. Coventry's nearness to Birmingham, coupled with the good railway link between the two engineering centres, was important in facilitating the growth of its cycle industry, but was also a significant influence in restricting the size of the city's own components sector. Despite this qualification, Coventry became well known for the manufacture of frames, bearings, saddles and tyres, as well as other parts used in cycle assembly and this contributed to the industry's overall growth and significance within the city. By 1896 some forty-nine separate Coventry firms were said to have been engaged in one or more areas of production directly related to the cycle trade.[30]

Component production grew in part from Coventry's old-established industries. Some enterprising weavers made string guards for bicycles in order to supplement their incomes from the declining textile trades, while saddle-making was a natural progression from the traditional leather goods industries.[31] In 1896 Middlemores, whose links with the leather trades went back to the eighteenth century and who were already famous for their saddles, acquired a defunct ribbon warehouse in the city, part of which they used for making mudguards, gear cases and other cycle accessories.[32] Diversification involving broader change also occurred. In the early 1890s chains were one of the few cycle parts not made in Coventry, but this deficiency was remedied in 1896 when Alick Hill moved from watchmaking to set up the Coventry Chain Company. At first the business functioned on a small scale, sharing steam power at its Dale Street works with an adjacent firm of carpet cleaners, but the company expanded quickly, raising more money by going public, extending its output to include cycle free-wheels and eventually moving into purpose-built accommodation at Spon End.[33] A further example of diversification in the same direction concerns the Coventry Watch Movement Company which by 1903 had moved into cycle parts and a range of other light-engineering products.

When Automachinery was established in 1875 it was largely for the purpose of manufacturing cycle components, with William Hillman designing and making the equipment for cutting ball bearings from wire.[34] Many other firms were also set up in Coventry specifically to service the needs of the cycle industry. Bluemel Brothers arrived at Wolston, on the southern outskirts of the city, in 1891 and soon developed a successful home and export business in cycle accessories, including celluloid handlebar coverings and mudguards. In 1897 the small Northampton firm of A.E. Dover established a depot in St Nicholas Street Coventry employing some fifty workmen to make and fit detachable gear cases, and by 1901 the city housed three firms which specialised in this aspect of the cycle trade.[35] One of the most important of the new concerns attracted to Coventry by the cycle boom of the 1890s was the Dunlop Pneumatic Company. Although initially the firm assembled pneumatic tyres from bought out components, it soon extended its operations to incorporate all the stages of manufacture.[36] However, in the early twentieth century the company transferred its tyre business to Fort Dunlop on the edge of Birmingham, though it renewed its association with Coventry in 1906 through the purchase of a rim- and wheel-making company in the city.[37]

The growth of the cycle industry also encouraged firms at the heavier end of the engineering and metal trades to settle in Coventry. The trade directories recorded the presence of a specialist electroplating and enamelling business in the city for the first time in 1892, while five years later Webster and Bennett, engineers and machine-tool makers, established the Atlas Works in West Orchard, the traditional home of the Coventry cycle industry. Thomas Smith began his stamping works at Darlaston in the 1880s before extending his operation to Coventry in 1896 in the misplaced hope, as it transpired, of profiting from the city's cycle boom.[38] Alfred Herbert was to become the best known of the engineering arrivals during this period. He appeared in Coventry in 1887 to assume the post of works manager to Coles and Mathews, steam-engine builders. In the following year Herbert and William Hubbard, an old friend from his engineering apprenticeship days in Leicester, took over the firm and began making rim-bending and other machinery suitable for use in the cycle industry. Hubbard soon left the partnership, partly because he was fortunate enough to acquire the UK agency for a French patent for weldless steel tubing, a commodity much in demand in the late 1880s because of its application to the manufacture of the 'safety' bicycle.[39] Herbert's family provided valuable assistance in promoting his engineering and business career, particularly his elder brother William, one of the founders of Automachinery and later the New Premier Cycle Company. William Herbert appears to have been instrumental in securing Alfred's purchase of Coles and Mathews for he arranged for Mathews, who owned the business, to obtain an alternative and, apparently more attractive, source of income. It was also William Herbert who introduced his brother to the French owners of the lucrative steel-tubing patent.[40] William Herbert's cycle interests provided an important source of demand for Alfred's products, and when the firm became a limited company in 1894 William appeared as one of the principal shareholders. Alfred Herbert's machine-tool company expanded rapidly, demonstrated by rising profits and a labour force in 1914 of 2,000, which made it the largest employer in the industry.[41]

Many firms from a variety of backgrounds which had supplied components to the cycle industry, also branched into motor products. One of these was the Coventry Watch Movement Company which had been formed in 1889 by several of the city's leading watchmakers as a quasi-co-operative. The company's purpose was to produce watch movements in quantity in order to release the local industry from its dependence upon traditional suppliers in Prescot who had formed a syndicate to push up prices. During the 1890s the firm was handicapped by inadequate supplies of capital and skilled labour and by the growth of foreign competition. Sales were never high enough to justify the application of mass-production techniques, particularly because the craft practices of the Coventry watchmakers required a wide range of watch movements, so that productivity remained at a relatively low level. A trade depression brought a sharp fall in profits and a search for new product areas. In 1903 the company began to produce significant quantities of cycle and motor parts and accessories, including lubricators, radiator tubes, spark-plugs and contact breakers.[42] The new products found a ready market so that by 1912 approximately two-thirds of the company's output went to the motor-vehicle and electrical engineering industries. Hawleys and Rotherhams were other major Coventry watchmaking concerns whose diversification into cycle and motor components paralleled that of the Watch Movement Company. Perhaps the most significant individual Coventry watchmaker to branch into motor vehicles was Alfred White, for the firm he created with Peter Poppe at the end of the nineteenth century became widely respected for its engines, carburettors and other components. Indeed, White achieved recognition in the industry for his work in pioneering the machining of parts to interchangeable limits.[43]

Other trades, apart from watchmaking, contributed to the growth of the Coventry motor industry. Having been founded in 1879, Blakemore and Sons of Godiva Street was one of the oldest sheet-metal firms to become involved in manufacturing such products as wings, panels, fuel tanks and under-shielding. The Coventry Plating Company, set up in 1898, was a slightly later arrival but it, too, quickly became heavily dependent upon the motor industry, specialising in radiators. On a smaller scale, Broadhursts had entered the Coventry hardware trade in the 1880s, but with the growth of car output soon moved into the manufacture of tool kits, motor lamps and other accessories. Coachbuilding was one of Coventry's old established industries, with seven firms being engaged in the trade in 1881. One of these, Messrs Hollick, constructed the body for J.K. Starley's electrically-propelled tricar built at the Meteor Works in 1888 and probably the first motor vehicle to be built in Coventry. The Hollick family eventually became one of the most important firms in the motor-body side of the industry. The coach-building firm of Thomas Pass was set up in 1850, and half a century later with its founder still in control it, too, was beginning to take advantage of the opportunities in the car industry. In common with other areas of component manufacture, new coach-building firms were also attracted to Coventry. One significant example, which again illustrates the importance of the city's geographical proximity to Birmingham, was Hawkins and Peake. Hawkins arrived from Birmingham in 1895, taking over the small and ailing coach-building firm of M.T. Hobley. According to Hawkins, 'Hobley was more interested in amateur opera than his work so of course his business did not proceed very long.'[44] In 1898 Hawkins was joined by Peake and two years later the firm concentrated solely upon the manufacture of bodies for motor vehicles. At first the partners supplied several different car-assemblers, including Humber, but from 1904 most of their output went to Rover.

The links between the cycle and motor-vehicle industries are perhaps most obvious in the technical field. In particular, it is significant that nearly all of the cycle firms which became successful car-makers also developed a substantial interest in motor cycles. Apart from the financial attractions of this kind of diversification, motor cycles posed new engineering problems concerned with the generation and transmission of power which were applicable to four-wheeled vehicles. The Riley Cycle Company provides an interesting example of one pattern of technical progression. Although the company's first car, designed in 1898, failed to enter production, the firm quickly developed an important business in motor cycles and tricars, the latter being a motorised version of the three-wheeled cycle which had been a Coventry specialism since the 1880s. The Riley tricar ceased production in 1907 as the firm switched to conventional motor vehicles to meet changing market conditions. A number of companies also experimented with cyclecars, a variant on the motorcycle and sidecar involving a lightweight body and low-powered engine. These vehicles were described as 'little more than a coffin-like box fitted with four wheels and seating two persons tandemwise'.[45] The majority of cyclecars had a belt or chain drive, the most popular, the Coventry-made Humbrette, was shaft driven. The technical simplicity of these machines also meant that many enthusiasts were able to convert motorcycles into cyclecars. Their popularity with manufacturers emanated from market demand, but also from the fact that they could be built using plant originally designed for the production of pedal cycles.

Apart from promoting the application of petrol engines to road vehicles, the cycle industry contributed significantly to the development and use of a wide variety of components, including wheels, ball bearings, brakes, lighting and chains, while experiments with gears were particularly important in solving problems concerned with the transmission of power in motor vehicles. The Quadrant Cycle Company developed a bicycle gear which was applied so successfully to cars that in 1908 a subsidiary was created to exploit its marketability.[46] Engineering innovations were encouraged by the frequent design changes introduced by the cycle firms to maintain or improve their market share, and some firms introduced special facilities for research and development. In 1902, for example, Rudge-Whitworth invested in research laboratories for testing the materials used in the construction of their cycles.

Despite Starley's experiments with his electrically-driven tricar, most leading personalities in the cycle industry were probably more interested in the transmission of power than its generation. Once major exception was the Riley Cycle Company where the founder's sons built and tested petrol engines, establishing a separate business in 1903 to manufacture their products. However, the cycle firms which became major car-assemblers purchased complete engines or their components from outside suppliers, or employed specialist engineers. By the early twentieth century White and Poppe sold their engines to Swift, Singer and other companies, while Rover relied heavily upon the technical skills of Edmund Lewis, recruited from Daimler at the end of 1903. In the initial stages of development it was often cheaper for the cycle firms, particularly the small ones, to buy out rather than design and manufacture their own engines, indicated by the fact that in 1901 the Motor Manufacturing Company supplied thirty-six firms in this way.[47] The Coventry partnership of Payne and Bates was formed in 1897 and is interesting because the firm not only designed and made its internal combustion engines, but was also exceptional in progressing from this background to the manufacture of cars. After serving an apprenticeship at his father's steam-engine works at Thrapston in Northamptonshire, Walter Payne established himself in Godiva Street in 1890 where his principal concern was the manufacture of small stationary gas engines. Payne was an engineer of some ability, reputedly producing the first petrol engine made in Coventry in the mid-1890s. An injection of cash into the business by George Bates, his wife's uncle, enabled Payne to develop this interest and also to expand into finished motor vehicles.

The partnership and its car-making business did not survive for very long, but Payne continued to manufacture car and other engines until his death in 1934.[48]

Apart from their engineering contribution to the motor industry, the Coventry cycle firms helped to set the pattern for production and business methods. By 1913 Humber, Swift, Rover and Singer, together with Rover and Standard, enjoyed relatively high levels of output, requiring considerable expertise in the management of labour and materials, as well as production methods. The cycle industry experienced similar needs from an early date. Bayliss Thomas and Company was one of the few Coventry firms to manufacture 2,000 cycles in 1878, but by 1896 the Swift and Humber companies had an average weekly output of 700 and 2,000 cycles respectively. When the Coventry cycle firm Settle and Company was formed in 1880 it immediately adopted the principle of interchangeable parts but, under pressure from foreign competition, this practice was taken a stage further by Rudge-Whitworth, enabling the company's output to dwarf that of its competitors by the early twentieth century. Similarly, Rover, which was particularly important in this respect because of its direct links with motor manufacture, also 'moved toward a system of flow production'.[49] The use of components made by outside specialists, a technique employed by James Starley during his pioneering days in the trade, was an important feature of cycle manufacture which was carried forward into some parts of the motor industry. The pace at which these production methods were applied varied between different car firms, but their introduction depended in part upon experience gained in cycle manufacture. More generally, the employment of hire purchase and advertising to promote sales, together with the build-up of agency and other business contacts, helped to smooth the transition from the cycle to the motor-vehicle business.

Although the profit motive was a powerful factor in stimulating the principal cycle firms to expand into motor vehicles, the trade recession of the late 1890s rendered inevitable a search for alternative sources of income. For example, when Humber's finances went into the red in 1899 the company felt obliged to begin experimental work on cars, financed in part by a bank loan secured on the personal guarantee of the managing director.[50] Singer's annual report for 1904 was more positive in tone, but still reflected the uncertain nature of the cycle trade, the directors expressing the hope that the introduction of motor manufacture 'will strengthen the profit earning capacity of the Company'.[51]

The recession in the bicycle industry was the result of growing competition from foreign producers, in both home and export markets, and a decline in the popularity of cycling among the wealthier classes. French and German cycle output rose markedly during the 1890s and by 1897 UK exports to both countries had fallen sharply. A similar pattern emerged in the United States where tariff protection and growing home demand brought the local cycle industry a period of unprecedented expansion in the early 1890s and a consequent decline in the share of the market held by British manufacturers. By the early twentieth century the American cycle industry had made substantial advances into British domestic and colonial markets, while in Europe, German manufacturers were gaining a commanding position. The UK was still the world's leading exporter of cycles and cycle parts in 1897 but three years later it had slipped to third place, behind the USA and Germany.[52] Although the relative position of British cycle firms improved in the decade before the First World War, there continued to be years of sharp reversal when the number of bankruptcies climbed steeply.

The more competitive environment of the late 1890s affected Coventry's cycle firms in a number of ways, but was marked generally by falling sales, profits and dividends. Although there are no output figures for the Coventry trade as a whole, the number of machines despatched from the city via the London and North-Western Railway provides an indication of the general trend, with the total for completed bicycles falling from 63,000 in 1896 to 30,677 in 1900.[53] By the turn of the century many of the major cycle companies were recording serious trading deficits, including New Premier, Calcott Bros and Bayliss Thomas. For some, the reversal of fortune was quite dramatic. In 1897 New Premier returned a profit before dividends of £78,133, but by 1900 this had degenerated into a loss of just over £3,000.[54] New Premier, together with other cycle companies, was forced to absorb losses over a three- or four-year period and only Rudge-Whitworth and Swift of the larger manufacturers appear to have escaped falling into deficit.

The impact of poor trading results was exacerbated by the boom of the mid-1890s which brought the formation of many large public companies and a record demand for bicycle shares. The Coventry Herald noted on 25 April 1996 that on one occasion 'the local brokers never had such a day for transactions'.[55] This was followed by a general increase in factory space and machinery, some of which fell into disuse when orders declined. As the chairman of Bayliss Thomas remarked in 1898, 'Nearly every firm had largely increased its plant.'[56] An exceptional, but interesting, example was Humber, whose premises were destroyed by a serious fire in 1896. However, new accommodation provided the firm with what was claimed to be 'the largest and best equipped Cycle Manufacturing Works in England'.[57] Many of the new companies created during the boom followed unsound business practices. Several of them were overcapitalised as the promotors sought to take their profit, while excessive valuations for goodwill and patent rights drained resources which might have been more usefully employed in other ways, as well representing a drag on income. The profligate issue of debentures was also attacked by shareholders for squeezing profits and making it more difficult to expand sales through price reductions. The problem, however, was that debentures were often used to secure the bank loans which were essential to provide working capital during the dull part of the season when the income stream was limited. The small partnership or one-man business was also adversely affected by falling sales and income, though in this instance the problem was often one of too little rather than too much capital, particularly since by the late 1890s the banks were becoming less accommodating towards cycle firms of almost any description. As one Coventry bank manager noted in 1900, 'It is very difficult indeed for us to get our Directors to look at a cycle a/c unless we are absolutely secured.'[58]

Economies were introduced to combat falling profits. Savings were made in plant and staffing, while company directors, sometimes under considerable pressure from shareholders, accepted reduced fees. Debentures were attacked through redemption and conversion schemes and outside investments were reassessed for their profitability. Yet these measures could not prevent business failures. From a peak of seventy-five in 1898, the number of Coventry-based cycle firms declined to forty-nine in 1912, only sixteen of which had survived from the earlier period. There were some spectacular bankruptcies, including a number of Coventry's largest and most respected firms, such as Bayliss Thomas, Centaur, Coventry Cross and the Progress Cycle Company.[59] Component manufacturers were also affected by the recession. For example, Dunlop reported that in the eighteen months to October 1899, 441 of its customers in the cycle trade had crashed, resulting in heavy losses from bad debts and a considerable amount of litigation.[60] The Coventry firm of Gallois, Brown and Company, which failed in 1898, may have been one of these. The company probably manufactured a few cycles, but its main business was as polishers, platers, enamellers, braziers and wheel-makers. The firm's collapse was due to a combination of falling orders and under-capitalisation, for it was revealed at the bankruptcy proceedings that the four partners had contributed a total of only £40 to the business.[61] A rather larger concern, that of Alfred Herbert, had anticipated problems in the cycle industry and had deliberately spread into other areas of manufacture. The manager of the Coventry branch of the Midland Bank informed head office in February 1898 that 'their General Engineering Business is expanding largely and they are not depending to any material extent upon the cycle trade, they had contemplated a reaction in that department, & have moved accordingly'. He added, perceptively, that 'Personally I think there is a brilliant future for A. Herbert Ltd.'[62] Thomas Smith's stamping business was less fortunate. Soon after the company arrived in Coventry in 1896 it was met by the onset of depression and this was compounded by changes in the technology of cycle manufacture which resulted in a decline in orders to drop-forgers. Smith was therefore obliged to seek other outlets for his firm's services, including coach-builders and makers of agricultural machinery.

Because of their involvement in overseas markets, many of the principal Coventry cycle firms were particularly vulnerable to the threat posed by foreign competitors. By the 1890s Bayliss Thomas and the Coventry Machinists had important agencies in the United States and both were affected by the growth of competition from domestic producers. The American subsidiary of the Machinists Company suffered losses of £20,000 in 1893–94 and £27,000 in 1894–95.[63] At the same period the bulk of the Bayliss Thomas output went to

America and significantly by 1895 their bankers regarded the firm as a high-risk enterprise, imposing stringent conditions upon overdraft facilities. The company was also adversely affected by trading conditions in continental Europe, with stock held abroad increasing as sales dwindled. In addition, the Boer War created serious problems for those firms, such as Singer and New Centaur, with a heavy commitment in the South African market.

It was inevitable that increased competition should cut into sales, but the scale of the problem which confronted Coventry's leading cycle manufacturers was indicative of serious underlying weaknesses in the industry. In particular, many firms specialised in cycles which were high in quality but relatively expensive compared with American machines. It became increasingly difficult for these enterprises to compete abroad, but they also suffered in the domestic market, which came to be dominated by lower-income consumers. In September 1899 the Riley directors attributed the company's trading losses for the financial year to 'decreased turnover in consequence of not having catered sufficiently for the public at popular prices'.[64] Rudge-Whitworth was the first Coventry firm to appreciate the importance of catering for the lower end of the market when in July 1897 it slashed the price of its Special and Standard models. Its example was eventually followed by a number of other companies, though some manufacturers, like Singer, were reluctant entrants to the market for inexpensive cycles after experiencing several years of falling profits. Others, including Bayliss Thomas and Coventry Cross, were firmly wedded to traditional practices and failed because they were unwilling to respond to the new competitive environment. Ironically, price reductions by some of the major Coventry cycle firms were of critical importance in undermining the position of several of their colleagues in the local trade.

Cheap but reliable British cycles helped to repel American competition during the early part of the twentieth century and restore some of the industry's prosperity. However, the reasons why some Coventry firms adjusted successfully while others faltered remains unclear. It has been suggested that differences in the quality of management may explain why Rudge-Whitworth adjusted its product range in a smooth and profitable manner while other firms struggled to survive.[65] It seems possible that the city's craft traditions may have engendered a measure of economic conservatism, reinforced, perhaps, by the fact that even at the end of the nineteenth century many of Coventry's leading cycle-makers remained first generation entrepreneurs, with a background in engineering rather than business methods. As the company's new chairman said of George Singer in 1909, 'he was not a businessman'.[66] An attempt by some local manufacturers to set a price ring in 1900 was a clear indication of conservative attitudes, though its failure also demonstrated the strength of the cycle trade's more progressive elements. Yet it is understandable that the financial rewards of the traditional bicycle industry should have retarded product innovation. As the directors of the New Centaur Company explained in 1899, they 'felt justified in pursuing the same policy as had hitherto proved so successful', and added that the firm's works and experience were particularly well suited to the production of high-grade machines.[67] Even when it became clear that the future was with the popular end of the market, some relatively new entrants to the trade, notably Lea-Francis, retained faith in high quality, high price bicycles. This particular firm's products were consistently the most expensive machines at the London Cycle Show during the early years of the twentieth century, with a reputation for quality workmanship and construction standards maintained regardless of cost.[68]

Profits, together with existing plant and equipment, accumulated from the cycle trade facilitated research and development as well as the actual production of motor cars. In 1903 the Swift Company, originally the Coventry Machinists, claimed to have allocated £10,000, or almost one-third of its net profit for that year, to motor-vehicle development.[69] Investment of this order was possible because of the company's successful entry into the market for inexpensive cycles. By contrast, the losses sustained by the more conservative firms, like Bayliss Thomas and Coventry Progress, made it difficult for them to support similar research activity, though their failure to adjust to the new situation in the cycle business may have been indicative of a more general lack of entrepreneurial drive and foresight. However, some cycle-makers who persisted with high-quality machines did experiment with cars and, for example, in 1900 the Progress Company invested in new buildings and equipment for this purpose, but with only modest success. One of the dangerous imponderables for firms seeking to diversify in this way was the expense involved, particularly when moving beyond the experimental stage and into vehicle production. It was at this point that the proceeds from the cycle trade could be used to cover losses in other areas. Thus, in 1906 the Singer Company suffered a deficit of £8,000 on its motor business, but this was more than matched by a profit of £11,000 on cycles.[70] Similarly, the subsidiary established by Lea-Francis in 1903 to begin development work on motor vehicles proved a costly failure and when it collapsed in 1909 its debts were met by the parent cycle company.[71] Lea-Francis did eventually enjoy some success in the construction of motor cycles and cars and, interestingly, their reputation for quality products seems to have played a part in this.

Whether diversification into motor cars proved financially rewarding depended to some extent upon timing. The more successful firms by 1913, Swift, Singer, Rover and Calcott Bros, were relatively late into the field and it may be that these concerns benefited from the pioneer work of others, as well as initiating production at a time when the market for motor cars was expanding. When Calcott Bros began car production in earnest they quickly benefited from the growing demand for light vehicles and by 1914 were said to be 'doing very well indeed'.[72] The point of transition from cycles to cars depended upon a variety of factors, but one significant consideration was profitability. While Swift and Rover continued to sell cycles in sufficient numbers to maintain a satisfactory balance sheet there was relatively little incentive to move into cars, at least until the industry's prospects seemed reasonably assured. Ironically, the success of Rudge-Whitworth in cycles may have been one of the reasons why the company never progressed to car production.

Although no single bicycle firm was representative of the industry as a whole, the Rover Company provides a useful illustration of the circumstances surrounding the transition from cycles to cars. The original partnership between J.K. Starley and William Sutton, referred to earlier, was dissolved in 1888. A new business was formed under Starley's management and in 1896 this was reconstructed to become the Rover Cycle Company Limited, with a capital of £150,000. This was rather too much in relation to the firm's assets, a fact eventually recognised by the board when a year after Starley's death it reduced the capital of the company by one-half. Starley was reported to have received some £50,000 from this flotation, much of which he invested in railway stock.[73] However, he retained one-fifth of the shares in the new company and stayed on as its managing director. Starley died in 1901 when the management of the company fell to its secretary, Harry Smith, first as general manager and then as managing director.

Under the guidance of Starley and Smith the Rover Company maintained a respectable financial profile and in particular managed to avoid the serious losses incurred by the majority of Coventry's cycle firms at the turn of the century.[74] Profits declined and a small deficit was recorded in 1904, but in general Rover fared well in relation to most of its competitors, with both sales and dividends remaining fairly buoyant. The company's steady progress was partly attributable to its speed in introducing a relatively cheap cycle for the mass market. This was the Meteor, which appeared in 1898, making Rover the first company to follow the example of Rudge-Whitworth in cutting prices to repel foreign competition. The Meteor was supported by a vigorous advertising campaign and a new sales drive in Europe and Australia. In addition, a bank loan was obtained to allow the company to manufacture and store machines during the winter months, in order to meet the sales boom which developed with the onset of the new season. This was an important initiative since trade had been lost in the past because stocks had been insufficient to satisfy consumer demand. Starley's support for the marketing strategy of the late 1890s is demonstrated by the personal guarantees which he provided as security for the company's overdraft. Yet he was a cautious businessman, pursuing a strategy of modest expansion rather than attempting to emulate the spectacular growth achieved by some companies during the boom years. In particular, the company appears to have refrained from becoming over-committed to one market. In addition, insurance was held to compensate for bad debts, while dividends were restricted in order to enable the company to accumulate a reserve fund. Care was also taken to negotiate favourable discounts from component and other servicing companies.

In 1898 Rover registered patents for a motor-gearing mechanism and in the following year a small number of Peugeot motorcycles were imported for research purposes. However, the decision to manufacture motorcycles was delayed until October 1902, and car production did not begin until the summer of 1904. The transition to motor vehicles was made possible by the company's success in catering for the popular end of the bicycle trade, although the fierce competition of 1904 and the consequent budget deficit gave an additional stimulus to diversification. Particularly significant in the new price war was the decision taken by the Swift Company in 1904 to undercut other manufacturers by placing an 8-guinea machine on the market, a reduction of some 20 per cent on its basic model. The Rover Company's bankers speculated accurately that 'this will prove a very disturbing influence in the trade & we should think conduce to a further weeding out of many small makers'.[75]

However, the key element in the company's decision to begin motor-vehicle production was Harry Smith's elevation to senior management. Although Starley had developed an electric tricar, he was reluctant to take the company into the new industry. The reasons for this are unclear, though he appears to have been uncertain about the efficiency of petrol-driven engines as a source of motive power.[76] However, it also seems possible that by the turn of the century his personal interest in the firm's activities had waned, and that he was simply not prepared to take the time-consuming initiatives which diversification involved. By 1900 Starley had sold most of his shares in Rover, using the money to speculate in other companies and to refurbish his house.[77] The minutes of directors meetings and the records of the company's bankers reveal Smith to have been a resourceful and energetic businessman, determined to exploit the firm's potential by taking it into the motor-vehicle market. Almost as soon as he assumed his new responsibilities, Smith began reducing production costs by substituting machines for labour. This was achieved through the purchase of second-hand equipment acquired from a Yorkshire firm which had gone into liquidation. In order to benefit from economies of scale, Smith negotiated a contract in 1902 for volume sales of bicycles to the War Office and at the same time sought to exploit the domestic retail market more intensively through an expansion of the company's depots. In advocating the manufacture of motor vehicles, Smith encountered stiff opposition from some Rover directors. The board rejected his initial request for permission to build motor vehicles, but Smith's persistence was rewarded in December 1902 when development work was allowed to begin. Smith advised the board in January of the following year that the extension of the company's manufacturing activities necessitated additional factory space, adding that 'while he felt it would be best if we could ignore this trade, he did not see how we could do so in face of the fact that many of our oldest customers & best Retail Customers as well as the agents were urging us to put a Motor Bicycle on the market'.[78] The speed at which the company subsequently progressed to car manufacture leaves little doubt that Smith was using the lever of customer demand to push through a policy of motor-vehicle development to which he was fully committed. More accommodation was duly acquired and the first Rover motorcycle went into production. However, difficulty in obtaining regular supplies of suitable engines was soon experienced and in May 1903 the company decided to manufacture its own power unit. This was an important step, for it significantly extended the firm's technical and commercial links with the motor industry, rendering it more likely that car production would follow. Despite the continued opposition of some directors, who objected to the company's involvement with the motor trade in any form, the decision to begin making cars was taken by the board in June 1904. Once again the personal influence of Harry Smith was of critical importance, for some six months earlier he had secured the services of Edmund Lewis from Daimler to design the first Rover car. Lewis's 1,300 cc Rover 8, which was assembled in the works canteen, was an immediate commercial success and initiated a permanent realignment of the company's manufacturing profile.

Although bicycle manufacturers were the principal source of recruitment to Coventry's motor industry, the arrival of the Daimler Motor Company in 1896 was particularly important in establishing the city's early reputation as the home of car production in Britain. The Daimler Company was formed specifically to take advantage of the opportunities offered by the infant motor industry and was the first firm to produce cars in significant numbers. By the spring of 1897, about a year after it was registered, the company was said to employ 160 workmen building some fifty vehicles.[79] Despite serious financial problems and boardroom squabbles, the company continued to expand, building up a reputation for high-quality workmanship. When the Prince of Wales purchased three Daimler cars in 1900 he immediately raised the status of the firm's products and this was given a further twist two years later when the company received the Royal Warrant. Yet, perhaps Daimler's most significant contribution to the development of the car industry in Coventry was as a source of experienced manpower, and this applied to both the design and production stages of motor-vehicle engineering. There was a very considerable migration of labour from Daimler to other local car firms in the period before 1914, reflecting the company's distinctive role in the history of the industry as well as its control over a number of important motor patents. In addition, Daimler supplied other firms with components, and the Coventry manufacturers were particularly well placed to take advantage of this. The editor of the *Motor* was exaggerating when in 1905 he claimed that the Daimler Company represented 'virtually the history of the trade', but his observation contained sufficient truth to help explain why the foundations of the British motor industry were laid in Coventry.[80]

The Daimler Motor Company was formed in February 1896 as a subsidiary of the British Motor syndicate. This organisation, which had been set up in the previous year, was the brainchild of Harry Lawson, a company promoter notorious for his shady business deals. The syndicate's purpose was to acquire the original German Daimler and other significant motor patents in order to gain a monopoly position which could be exploited through licence and royalty fees. Although this practice was ended by a court decision in 1901, it did give the syndicate and, at a price, the Daimler Company, a special role in the start of the British motor industry.

The siting of the Daimler factory in Coventry is usually attributed to the chance factor of suitable accommodation in the shape of a disused cotton mill on the Foleshill Road. Harry Lawson informed shareholders in May 1896 that: 'we did not wish to build works because it would take too long, so we visited various works in the country which were for sale. We went to Cheltenham and Birmingham, in both of which places there were motor works for sale. At last we went to Coventry and saw what we believed to be an almost perfect place for manufacturing these machines.'[81] The Coventry site, part of which was soon sold to other Lawson promotions, comprised some 12 acres, housed a number of buildings and benefited from close proximity to good railway and inland waterway facilities. These features, together with Coventry's manpower resources and the servicing capacity of its engineering and component industries, were no doubt important factors in Lawson's calculations, but it is difficult to accept that other available sites did not have similar or better advantages. Although he was born in London and spent much of his early life in Brighton, Lawson knew Coventry well and had many business contacts and personal friends in the city, and it is within this context that the location of the Daimler operation should be interpreted.

Lawson first arrived in Coventry in the 1870s to work in the cycle industry and he retained his connections with the city through his involvement in a series of company promotions which included, among others, Rudge, Humber, the Great Horseless Carriage Company and the New Beeston Cycle and Motor Company, the latter two sharing the Daimler site. He appears to have been an engineer and designer of some distinction, inventing a 'safety' bicycle which pre-dated that of J. K. Starley, but which failed to enjoy the same commercial success. Lawson subsequently went to considerable pains to achieve recognition as the inventor of the 'safety' cycle, a claim supported by several prominent members of the trade, including Henry Sturmey, the editor of the *Cyclist* and later the *Autocar*. Sturmey's friendship with Lawson was important for in addition to investing quite heavily in Daimler, he became one of its first directors, chairing the early board meetings when Lawson was otherwise engaged. Sturmey was probably Lawson's chief ally in the creation of the Daimler company, using the pages of the *Autocar* to endorse the firm's activities, cite its prospects and defend the personal character of its founder. Such influential support was critical to the company's successful flotation since Lawson was regularly attacked by the press for his company promotion schemes, many of which were said to have been designed to dupe gullible investors. One of his sternest critics noted that, although Lawson was relatively new to business, many of his promotions 'have been buried and almost forgotten, except by the surviving sufferers; others have been reconstructed over and over again, and have at last got free from the control of their author, while in some instances there have been mysterious disappearances'.[82]

Part of Lawson's genius was his appreciation of the commercial value of good publicity and a talent for spotting suitable openings, a skill acquired perhaps from his period at the end of the 1870s as sales manager with the Rudge Cycle Company and his association with another notorious company speculator, Terah Hooley. Lawson's inventiveness in this direction was evident in February 1896 when, in reference to the disposal of Daimler shares, he excitedly informed one of his business colleagues that 'Since leaving you just now, I noticed these expensive premises on the Viaduct, with a glorious front and shop window being wasted. Why not placard it from top to bottom with "Daimler Motor Co Ltd" and have a clerk in the show-room and let the issue take place here. My Daimler Motor Carriage will stand in the window and I will create such a sensation as has never been created in London before.'[83] Some four months later Lawson arranged a grand tour of the Daimler and Humber works in Coventry, complete with a motor-vehicle demonstration, for an invited party of some sixty London journalists, while his most enduring publicity initiative, the London to Brighton rally, took place in November 1896. Lawson's prescience is indicated by his press statement proclaiming the Brighton run an outstanding success and issued some days before the event actually occurred.[84]

In locating the Daimler factor in Coventry, Lawson became well placed to exploit the advertising potential of the *Autocar* and also to use Henry Sturmey to oversee the company's activities, leaving him free to negotiate other business deals. An additional benefit of the Coventry site was that it enabled Lawson to consolidate geographically his interests in the motor business, particularly with regard to the Humber Company. The New Beeston Company was formed to exploit recently-acquired French Motor patents, but was short-lived, while the Great Horseless Carriage Company, reconstructed several times, lasted until 1910. Daimler and Humber survived to become major elements in the British motor industry, though by the beginning of the twentieth century Lawson's connections with both companies had ended. Harry Lawson was also heavily involved in the promotion of electric tramways and this led to a conviction for fraud in 1904 and a one-year prison sentence with hard labour.[85]

There were other reasons why newly-created firms, such as Daimler and Standard, should choose to locate in Coventry. When the Daimler Company was formed the motor industry was still in the experimental stage and Lawson probably had some reservations about the likely success of the initial launch. By establishing the company in Coventry he immediately associated Daimler with the city's reputation as a successful and profitable centre of the cycle industry, an activity which had close and obvious links with the manufacture of motor vehicles. In addition, cycle production had generated an engineering labour force and a components sector, both of which could be applied to car production. Coventry's banks were acquainted with problems common to both the cycle and motor industries, particularly the requirement for working capital during the off season. When Daimler first moved to Coventry there was considerable competition among the local banks to secure the firm's custom, but with the slump in the cycle trade at the end of the century interest in the motor industry increased since it was an obvious outlet for funds. The manager of the Coventry branch of the London and Midland Bank was probably fairly typical when he advised his managing director in 1900 that trade being 'exceedingly flat just now' he was hoping to develop links with the motor firms.[86] Because of its recent industrial history, this kind of financial support was probably more easily forthcoming in Coventry than it would have been in many other parts of the country.

The provenance of Coventry's motor industry carried important implications for the character and speed of its subsequent development. In particular, the link with cycle manufacture explains why so many of the early motor firms were Coventry-based and why the majority of these were very small. In addition to the exceptionally large number of cycle-makers in the city, profits from this trade helped to prolong experimental work with cars which without a similar spreading of risks might have come to an earlier conclusion. Yet by combining car and cycle manufacture some firms were probably less fully committed to motor vehicles, and hence developed this side of their business more slowly than would have been the case with greater specialisation. Frequent model changes and the resilience in some quarters of handicraft methods of construction were legacies of the cycle trade which may have restricted the overall growth of the motor-vehicle industry in Coventry. Moreover, some firms, notably Daimler and Humber, were handicapped by the activities of speculators like Harry Lawson which left them grossly overcapitalised. These considerations meant that by 1914 the city remained the centre of motor manufacture in a numerical sense, even though many individual firms were of relatively minor significance. Nevertheless, the period before the First World War was one of remarkable change in the Coventry motor industry, a time of exceptional prosperity for some, but of lost opportunities for others.

Notes

[1] *Coventry Herald*, 4 June 1897.
[2] See, P. Searby, 'The Relief of the Poor in Coventry, 1830–1863', *Historical Journal*, vol. XX, no. 2 (1977).
[3] *The Times*, 17 January 1916.
[4] W.O. Bentley, *An Autobiography* (Hutchinson, London, 1958), p. 60.

[5]   Computed from figures in S.B. Saul, 'The Motor Industry in Britain to 1914', *Business History*, vol. V (1962), p. 25.

[6]   Richardson, *Twentieth Century Coventry*, p. 46.

[7]   G. Williamson, *Wheels Within Wheels*, (Geoffrey Bles, London, 1966), pp. 46–8.

[8]   *Cyclist*, 6 November 1901.

[9]   J. Lowe, *A Guide to Sources in the History of the Cycle and Motor Industries in Coventry, 1880–1939*, (Coventry Polytechnic, Coventry, 1982), p. 6.

[10]   E.H. Reeves, *The Riley Romance* (the Company, Coventry, 1930), p. 9.

[11]   Richardson, *Twentieth Century Coventry*, pp. 35–6. For an interesting account of Bettmann's life and work, see S. Morewood, *Pioneers and Inheritors: Top Management in the Coventry Motor Industry 1896–1972* (Coventry Polytechnic, Coventry, 1990).

[12]   E.W. Cooper, *Fifty Years Reminiscences* (the author, Coventry, 1928), p. 28.

[13]   *The Rudge Record*, vol. 1, no. 9 (1909), p. 135.

[14]   Medical Officer of Health for Coventry, *Annual Report* (Coventry, 1896), p. 3.

[15]   Cooper, *Reminiscences*, p. 15.

[16]   C.H.D'E. Leppington, 'The Evolution of an Industrial Town', *Economic Journal*, vol. 17 (1907), p. 355.

[17]   Coventry Record Office (CRO), Coventry Watch Movement Company (CWM), Minutes of the Annual General Meeting, 14 May 1889.

[18]   CRO, CWM, Directors' Minutes, 11 August 1891.

[19]   Williamson, *Wheels*, p. 101.

[20]   J. Lane, *Register of Business Records of Coventry and Related Areas*, (Lanchester Polytechnic, Coventry, 1977), p. 6.

[21]   *Coventry Times*, 4 November 1891. The only British-built entrant to the 1896 London to Brighton run was a product of the Quinton Works in Parkside, though by that time the factory was occupied by Lawson's New Beeston Cycle Company, *Coventry Car Factories*, p. 2.

[22]   B. Reynolds, *Rudge* (Haynes, Yeovil, 1977), pp. 14–18.

[23]   *Cycle Record*, 25 January 1890.

[24]   Ibid.

[25]   *American Referee*, 24 July 1891.

[26]   R.F. Prosser, 'Coventry: A Study in Urban Continuity', unpublished MA thesis, University of Birmingham, p. 81.

[27]   *Cyclist*, 21 January 1880.

[28]   *Cycle Record*, 1 January 1890.

[29]   Essex Record Office, Hoffmann Mss, Riley Cycle Company to Hoffmann Mfg Co. Ltd, 17 December 1903.

[30]   H. Perkin, 'The History of the Cycle Industry in Coventry, 1869–1914', Lanchester Polytechnic BA Modern Studies Geography Project, 1979, pp. 25–6.

[31]   Armstrong-Siddeley, *The Evening and the Morning* (the company, Coventry, 1956), p. 5.

[32]   *Coventry Herald*, 22 May 1896.

[33]   B.H. Tripp, *Renold Chains* (Allen and Unwin, London, 1956), p. 79.

[34]   W.F. Grew, *The Cycle Industry* (Pitman, London, 1921), p. 27.

[35]   Bluemel Bros Ltd, Wolston, Dover Ltd, Minutes of the Annual General Meeting, 6 August 1897. We are grateful to the firm for allowing us access to these records.

[36]   G. Jones, 'The Growth and Performance of British Multinational Firms Before 1939; The Case of Dunlop', *Economic History Review*, 2nd series, vol. XXXVII, no. 1 (1984), p. 37; Richardson, *Twentieth Century Coventry*, p. 164.

[37]   Richardson, *Twentieth Century Coventry*, p. 57.

[38]   A. Muir, *75 Years* (Smith's Stamping, Coventry, 1958), p. 15.

[39]   R. Floud, *The British Machine Tool Industry, 1850–1914* (CUP, Cambridge, 1976), p. 43.

[40]   J.Mc.G. Davies, 'A Twentieth Century Paternalist: Alfred Herbert and the Skilled Coventry Workman', in Mason and Lancaster (eds), *Life and Labour*, p. 103.

[41]   Richardson, *Twentieth Century Coventry*, p. 34.

[42]   CRO, CWM, Mss 542; *Coventry Herald*, 19 January 1912.

[43]   Church, 'Nineteenth Century Clock Technology', p. 630.

[44]   University of London, Pollitt Papers, P/8/147, G.W. Hawkins to J. Pollitt, 28 October 1946.

[45]   E.J. Appleby, 'The Small Car, An Outline History of the Small Car', *Autocar*, 9 May 1930.

[46]   *Motor*, 30 January 1906.

[47]   *Coventry Herald*, 5 July 1901.

[48]   C. O'Gallagher, 'Payne and Bates of Coventry: Pioneer Motor Manufacturers', *Warwickshire History*, vol. 3 (1976).

[49]   W. Lewchuk, *American Technology and the British Vehicle Industry* (Cambridge University Press, Cambridge, 1987), p. 122.

[50]   CRO, Humber Balance Sheet, 31 August 1899.

[51]   CRO, Singer Balance Sheet, 11 November, 11 November 1904.

[52]   A.E. Harrison, 'The Competitiveness of the British Cycle Industry, 1890–1914', *Economic History Review*, 2nd series, vol. XXII, no. 2 (1969), pp. 291–301.

[53]   *Coventry Herald*, 27 December 1901.

[54]   CRO, New Premier Balance Sheet, 31 August 1900.

[55]   *Coventry Herald*, 25 April 1896.

[56]   *Birmingham Post*, 22 December 1898.

[57]   CRO, Humber Balance Sheet, 31 August 1897.

[58]   Midland Bank Coventry (MBC), Fo. 543, 22 February 1900. We are grateful to the Midland Bank, and in particular their archivist Mr E. Green, for allowing us access to these records.

[59]   Harrison, 'The British Cycle Industry', p. 302.

[60]   CRO, Dunlop Balance Sheet, 30 September 1899.

[61]   Lowe, 'A Guide to Sources', p. 7.

[62]   MBC, 429, 23 February 1898.

[63]   Harrison, 'The British Cycle Industry', p. 291.

[64]   CRO, Riley Balance Sheet, 30 September 1899.

[65]   Harrison, 'The British Cycle Industry', pp. 301–3.

[66]   Lloyds Bank Coventry (LBC), Fo. 55, 14 April 1909. We are grateful to Lloyds bank, and in particular their archivist Mr J.M.L. Booker, for allowing us access to these records.

[67]   CRO, New Centaur Balance Sheet, 31 July 1899.

[68]   B. Price, *The Lea-Francis Story* (Batsford, London, 1978), pp. 15–16.

[69]   CRO, Swift Balance Sheet, 31 August 1903.

[70]   LBC, 396, 4 December 1906.

[71]   Price, op. cit., p. 21.

[72]   LBC, 367, 1 January 1914.

[73]   MBC, 684, 14 October 1897.

[74]   See, J. Foreman-Peck, 'Diversification and the Growth of the Firm: The Rover Company to 1914', *Business History*, vol. XXV (1983).

[75]   MBC, 278, 6 May 1904.

[76]   Foreman-Peck, op. cit., p. 184.

[77]   MBC, 687, 6 May 1904; Foreman-Peck, op. cit., p. 189.

[78]   Rover Company Directors Minutes (RDM), 3 January 1901. We are grateful to the former BL for allowing us access to these minutes. The Rover documents are now held by the Modern Records Centre at the University of Warwick (Mss. 226/RO).

[79]   CRO, Daimler Company Shareholders Minutes (DSM), 4 March 1897.

[80]   *Motor*, 7 November 1905.

[81]   *Financial News*, 20 May 1896.

[82]   Quoted by the *Coventry Herald*, 15 October 1897.

[83]   University of London, Simms papers, 16/2, H.J. Lawson, to F.R. Simms, 5 February 1896. Simms acquired the Daimler patents in 1893 and sold them to the British Motor Syndicate in 1895.

[84]   P. Brendon, *The Motoring Century. The Story of the Royal Automobile Club*, (Bloomsbury, London, 1997), p. 18.

[85]   Ibid., p. 30.

[86]   MBC, 201, 18 September 1900.

Chapter 3

Organisation and Growth to 1914

The growth of Coventry's motor industry in the years before the First World War was rapid, if somewhat uneven. Some twenty motor-vehicle manufacturers were based in the city by 1913 out of a total of around 113 for Britain as a whole. In the same year Coventry firms produced approximately 9,000 motor vehicles, or about 28 per cent of the national total, though all but a tiny proportion of these were accounted for by Daimler, Humber, Rover, Swift, Singer and Standard. Humber, with an output of 2,500, vehicles was the largest Coventry producer, but this output was still less than half that of Ford in Manchester, the market leader. Hillman, Maudslay and Riley were among the smaller firms and their combined output was probably less than 150 vehicles.[1]

The extension of existing factories and the building of new ones was testimony to the motor industry's growing presence in Coventry. Daimler and Humber were perhaps the most active firms in this respect. Daimler began a major construction programme in 1905 which involved new machine and erecting shops, a large body-building factory and the refurbishment of a four-storey building acquired from the liquidators of the Motor Manufacturing Company. Work on the new Humber factory in Folly Lane, soon to be renamed Humber Road, took almost two years to complete before the last of the new machinery was installed in 1908, and created something of a sensation in the city. As one motoring journalist commented in July 1907, 'The rapidity with which the new Humber works at Coventry are being erected and prepared for occupation must be an eye-opener to those who have lived in slower times. The size of the factory is simply enormous, and already a part of it is in occupation.'[2] In fact, the site covered some 22 acres which, when fully developed, contained a series of large single-storey sheds with elevated roofs together with a number of two-storey workshops. A two-storey office block was also constructed adjacent to the Humber Road.[3] When the new premises came into operation all the company's remaining plants ceased production and were closed.

Several car factories accommodated very large numbers of production workers. Coventry's motorvehicle and and cycle firms employed almost 12,000 people in 1911, or about 20 per cent of the city's occupied population. In addition, much of the remaining labour force in the engineering industry was engaged in the manufacture of components for motor vehicles. Swift, Rover and Singer were all major employers, but were dwarfed by Daimler and Humber. Daimler had some 5,000 employees in 1913, compared with 2,500–3,000 at Humber, and both firms were among the largest employers in Britain's engineering industry. The bulk of Coventry's car workers in 1913 were male and, because dilution had already occurred, probably included an exceptionally high proportion of semi-skilled employees.[4]

Although Riley abandoned the cycle trade in 1911, the major car firms with origins in bicycles combined the manufacture of both products in the pre-war period. Despite occasional losses incurred by the cycle department, Rover continued to produce bicycles until 1925, when motorcycle manufacture was also stopped. Lea-Francis experienced some difficulty in both the cycle and car markets and by 1913 the firm was chiefly occupied in making cycles. The production of pedal- and motorcycles enabled the early car firms to spread their risks, while the personal interests of the businessmen themselves may have helped to prolong involvement in the bicycle trade. Moreover, some companies had substantial sums of capital specifically allocated to cycle manufacture. Thus, when Swift began to make cars in earnest in 1906 it was in purpose-built accommodation, while a short distance away the cycle factory continued to function as a separate entity. Moreover, when the motor trade expanded Swift reallocated factory space from cycles to cars.[5]

The only major latecomer to the motor industry with a background in cycles was William Hillman. Already a millionaire and seemingly not motivated by financial gain, Hillman had a passion for motor sport and a strong personal desire to manufacture a motor car of sufficient speed and endurance to win the 1907 Isle of Man Tourist Trophy Race, the premier event of its kind in Britain. With this in mind, he recruited Louis Cotatalen from Humber and together they established a motor works in the grounds of Hillman's home, Abingdon House. Coatalen was a Breton with wide experience in the motor industry, having worked for Panhard et Levassor, De Dion Bouton and Clement-Baylard before moving to England where there were more opportunities for advancement. At Humber, Coatalen designed a highly popular and relatively inexpensive four-cylinder 12 hp car. He also gained a reputation for his work on a light and easily-constructed chassis which substantially accelerated production of the completed vehicle. Coatalen married Hillman's daughter but in 1908 he joined Sunbeam of Wolverhampton as chief designer and sold out his interests in the Coventry firm to his father-in-law. Ironically, perhaps, the Hillman Company came to enjoy a favourable reputation for its small family saloons, not the sportier machines which had lured its founder into the business. Hillman, together with Humber, was later taken over by the Rootes Group.[6]

With the exception of Harry Lawson's companies, all of the Coventry motor-vehicle manufacturers without a background in cycles began as fairly small-scale operations and those which survived, apart from Standard, Siddeley-Deasy and Maudslay, failed to achieve any substantial or long-term success. The nominal capital of the smaller firms was often extremely modest, sometimes as low as £1,000, providing insufficient resources for serious research and development. Even Crouch Cars Limited, one of the more successful of the small manufacturers of family saloons, only managed an output of some 3,000 vehicles during its entire existence from 1912 to 1927. The company developed a reputation for sound engineering, but eventually found it impossible to compete with the larger producers.[7]

Reginald Maudslay established the Standard Motor Company in a small factory in Much Park Street. After completing his school education at Marlborough, Maudslay was apprenticed to Sir John Wolfe Barry's London firm of civil engineers, where he remained until moving to Coventry in 1902. Maudslay appears to have been responsible for most of the design work of the early Standard vehicles which, to begin with, were sold mainly to family and friends. An increase in production was facilitated by a loan of £10,000 from Barclays in 1905 and by the end of that year the company had acquired additional accommodation and a labour force of around 100 workers.[8] Further injections of capital and a change of production policy to incorporate light cars brought a period of rapid expansion just before the First World War, and by 1913 Standard's output had reached 750 vehicles which made it one of the larger motor firms in Coventry.

The Maudslay Motor Company was founded in 1902 by Cyril, Charles and Walter Henry Maudslay, cousins to Reginald and great-grandsons of Henry Maudslay, the marine engineer. The firm specialised in high powered vehicles and by 1910 was concerned principally with the manufacture of 17 hp cars, which were renowned for their durability. The early design work was placed with an independent consulting engineer, Alexander Craig, who later became managing director and eventually the company's chairman. Craig also planned the Parkside factory where the firm operated until it moved to Alcester in 1945.[9] The firm also became involved in the manufacture of motor buses, some of which were sold to Coventry Corporation. After 1918, inspired in part by the success of Dennis Bros of Guildford, the company came to specialise in the production of commercial vehicles.[10]

In 1906 the newly-formed Deasy Company purchased the land and buildings formerly occupied by another motor firm, Iden, and later in the same year extended its facilities with the construction of further accommodation on the same site. Captain Deasy, a well-known racing driver who captured the world endurance record in 1903 when he drove his Rochet-Schneider from London to Glasgow in twenty-one hours, appears to have been largely a front for substantial financial interests from outside Coventry, though Lord Leigh, a substantial Warwickshire landowner, also invested heavily in the company.[11] Following disagreements with the board 'over the policy of the company' and having been stripped of most of his authority, Deasy resigned as managing director and chairman in 1907.[12] John Siddeley was recruited from Wolseley as general manger and within a few months was elevated to managing director. Siddeley brought with him other engineers from Wolseley and this injection of fresh talent, together with his own technical and sales experience, helped to rescue the floundering Deasy Company and give it a sense of direction. In particular, Siddeley rationalised production policy by extending the practice of buying-out components and at the same time discontinued the loss-making body section. He also initiated development work on a new 12 hp car, which by 1912 was selling well.[13]

The growth of the motor industry promoted the expansion of the components sector, much of which was based in the West Midlands conurbation where the traditional metalworking trades provided the basis for diversification into axles, brakes, wheels, springs and other vehicle parts and accessories.[14] Although many Coventry firms manufactured a high proportion of the parts used in the construction of their vehicles, it is clear that substantial quantities of components were purchased from specialist suppliers. Moreover, some companies provided parts for their local rivals. The 1912 Siddeley-Deasey 12 hp car was built on a Rover chassis, while Rover's own 15 hp model used a Daimler engine. This arrangements benefited both parties since it reduced research and development expenditure on a per unit basis.

Coventry's component suppliers grew with the general expansion of the motor industry and a number of new firms continued to be attracted into the business. By 1913 the city housed eight motor body-builders, a similar number of engine-makers and numerous specialist and general manufacturers of components for cars and commercial vehicles, one of the largest of which was the Motor Radiator Manufacturing Company which was responsible for perhaps 20 per cent of the industry's output of radiators.[15] However, it was relatively easy for individuals or partnerships to set up as small-scale component makers so that the typical firm was owner managed, often with strong family interests. W.S. Tyler and C.E. Hatfield, who established Coventry Motor Fittings in 1902, had both worked for some years as practical engineers with Daimler. The firm specialised in radiators, but also made bonnets, tanks, filters, gauges, fans and a variety of other vehicle parts which helped to cushion it against fluctuations in demand for individual products.[16] Another former Daimler employee who set up his own business was H. Pelham Lee, whose engineering firm became the basis of Coventry Climax, famous for its engines, and later, fork-lift trucks.[17] Morris-Lister Magnetos also had modest origins, being established in 1908 by two electrical engineers who had been on the staff of Birmingham University. Initially, the firm manufactured fine-wire coils, but later developed a large business in magnetos when German supplies were suspended with the outbreak of war in 1914. With the relatively high turnover of firms in the cycle and motor industries, suitable accommodation for new or expanding component manufacturers was normally available. Van Raden and Company was formed in the late 1890s to make accumulators but by 1908 had branched into ignitions and in the process transferred from small premises in Spon Street to the more spacious workshops in the Foleshill Road formerly occupied by Payne and Bates before they went into liquidation.[18]

Perhaps the best known of the Coventry component firms before the First World War was the engine-makers, White and Poppe of Lockhurst Lane. The partnership began making shell fuses for use in the Boer War soon after its formation in 1899, and for a time work on engines was largely forgotten. Given the importance of the firm's later contribution to the development of petrol-driven engines it is possible that this particular distraction may have been of some significance in retarding the general growth of Coventry's motor industry. By 1903 White and Poppe were again making engines, principally for motorcycles, though another profitable contract for fuses delayed a full return to this side of their work. The firm's turning point came in 1905 when Swift placed a large order for petrol engines and this was soon followed by similar purchases by other companies.[19] At the Olympia show in 1906 fifteen motor manufacturers displayed cars which were powered by White and Poppe engines. The firm had an annual output of perhaps 2,000 engines by 1913, many of which were for commercial vehicles. White and Poppe also diversified into carburettors and this quickly proved important in helping to compensate for periods when demand for engines was slack. William Morris was a particular admirer of the firm's carburettors and for a time insisted that they be fitted to any of his own products which displayed problems in this area.[20]

The links between the car firms and their component suppliers could be very close and involve considerable interdependence. In particular, some component manufacturers sold their products to a small number of companies which eventually resulted in takeovers, especially in the interwar period, to achieve vertical integration. However, there were some examples of this even before 1914, such as Rover's purchase of Hawkins and Peake, the coach-builders, in1907. In the same year Daimler made an outlay of £30,000 for an interest in the reconstructed Coventry Chain Company, finance which was used to facilitate a move to new purpose built accommodation in Spon End.[21] In return, Daimler acquired the right to appoint two directors to the board of Coventry Chain. Daimler had dealt with this firm for some years and had been impressed by the quality of its work, though significantly Percy Martin, Daimler's general manager, and Alick Hill, the managing director of Coventry Chain, were personal friends. In 1910 Daimler was itself merged with the Birmingham Small Arms Company, which had an interest in cycles and motorcycles and was keen to enter the car market.

One of the main reasons why Daimler acquired a holding in Coventry Chain was to ensure a reliable supply of suitable nuts and bolts, something which had proved difficult to achieve in the past from other suppliers. The reputation of Daimler vehicles depended to a considerable extent upon the quality of their composite parts and the company took care to ensure that these were of a satisfactory standard, demonstrated by the creation in 1902 of laboratory and workshop facilities for testing the quality of all bought-out materials.[22] In 1903 the company's purchases of engine valves from its Coventry supplier was discontinued when it was discovered that the product was defective, and so the board decided to revert to the practice of manufacturing these in its own works. In the same year, Daimler was forced into making its own taper pins for clutches when those supplied by the Steel Nut Company of Wednesbury not only arrived a month late but were of the wrong type.[23] The need for effective control over quality and supply also explains why by 1913 such major firms as Daimler, Rover and Standard had established their own workshops for the production of motor-vehicle body shells. Even an order from Siddeley-Deasy for the Rover chassis was terminated in 1911 for inadequate quality control.[24] By investing in one or more of its component suppliers a motor manufacturer could hope to achieve some control over production policy, but in addition certain financial and commercial benefits might also accrue. For example, in 1909 Siddeley-Deasy offered to place £10,000 in White and Poppe, but this was refused because the partners were unwilling to meet the price of two seats on the board, a discount on all engines supplied and preference in delivery.[25]

Despite these problems, there were many advantages to the motor companies in using components supplied by outside specialists. Capital was saved which would have been allocated, perhaps unprofitably, to research and development. In 1908 Daimler recorded a loss of almost £50,000 which was attributed in part to the poor state of the motor trade, but also to the expense of developing a new engine.[26] When Rover decided to purchase a new 15 hp Daimler engine for the 1912 season the cost came to £100 per unit. This was roughly the same amount incurred by the company in producing its own engine of the same size, but was less expensive when testing and other costs were taken into account. At that time Daimler planned to manufacture about 1,000 engines additional to its own requirements, of which between 400 and 600 were to be taken by Rover.[27] From Daimler's point of view these sales helped to spread development and production costs over a larger output than was possible had the engines been restricted to the company's own vehicles. Competition among engine-makers and other component firms also benefited the motor manufacturers by exerting downward pressure on prices. Despite buoyant trading conditions, White and Poppe recorded only a relatively small profit in 1913, principally because they had trimmed their prices to the minimum in order to secure a major contract from Morris.[28]

Component manufacturers not only bore part of the development costs of motor-vehicle production but also provided financial assistance through the holding of stocks and the granting of credit. All the car-assemblers suffered periodic shortages of working capital and this was a problem which they were sometimes able to pass back to their component suppliers. By November 1907 White and Poppe were said to hold stock valued at about £9,000 in excess of their needs, which had helped to put them on the verge of bankruptcy. The reason for this was that in response to a poor season the motor-vehicle companies had refused to take delivery of the firm's products, with orders valued at £17,000 being lost in June alone.[29] White and Poppe attempted to control the scale and length of credit which they gave to their customers. In 1909 they would only accept an order from Deasy for engines on the understanding that delivery would be accepted within a specified time. This was considered essential since the order necessitated the purchase of further plant valued at £1,000 and the holding of substantial additional raw materials.[30] Yet with competition high within the industry, component suppliers had to be careful not to set payment terms which were unreasonably onerous. Thus Van Raden suffered because the firm operated in the highly competitive electrical components business so that by 1908 its customers received interest-free credit of some £1,000 while its own bank overdraft was extended to £1,500.[31] In 1906 an order from Singer was quickly reduced to £3,000 when White and Poppe insisted on a large deposit and cash on delivery to cover the expenses of holding large quantities of brass and aluminium.[32] In April 1912 Singer again caused problems for White and Poppe when the company fell ten weeks behind on cash payments for engines.[33] Since the weekly payments amounted to £800 this meant that in effect White and Poppe were providing Singer with interest-free credit on goods valued at £8,000. In January of the same year 50 per cent of the credit provided by Charlesworth Bodies of Coventry was taken up by Singer.[34] In the early part of 1912, therefore, two of Coventry's major component firms were borrowing from their own bankers in order to service debts owed to them by the Singer Company. Without such broad financial support and perhaps that provided by other component manufacturers as well as its own bankers, it seems possible that at best Singer would not have been able to sustain the growth of output which occurred just before the First World War and at worst would itself have gone into liquidation. Perhaps in frustration, White and Poppe decided in the summer of 1912 that future orders would be processed more slowly so that stock in hand would be reduced and customers would simply have to wait longer for delivery.

The erratic growth of the British motor industry before the First World War was reflected in the high mortality rate among the constituent firms. Only just over one-quarter of the 393 motor vehicle manufacturers which set up in business at some time before 1914 survived to that date. The bulk of the new entrants to the industry in this period arrived before 1904, while the number of failures peaked between 1906 and 1910.[35] This was mirrored in Coventry where the number of motor manufacturers rose sharply in the Edwardian period, falling away after 1905 before increasing again in the three or four years before the outbreak of war. The only major new firm to emerge after 1910, Morris, was not Coventry based, though it did develop a major engine works in the city.

It was reported at the beginning of 1906 that 'All the motor car factories in Coventry are extremely busy, and many of the works are running overtime.'[36] However, the smaller producers found it difficult to cope with the price-cutting which set in later that year and even the larger firms experienced serious problems, with Humber, Daimler, Rover and Singer all recording substantial losses in 1907. In the summer of that year there were rumours of hundreds of Humber cars being stored in back yards and towards the end of

1908 one motoring correspondent lamented that price competition during the previous two years had reduced profits in the industry to vanishing point.[37] Further losses in 1908 drove Humber to the edge of bankruptcy, with sales being far too low to utilise fully the capacity of the new factory. Early in 1909 several important motor works in Coventry were said to be 'standing idle and for sale'.[38] However, 1910 saw a change of fortune for the motor industry. Daimler, which had been so hard pressed in 1907 that it had been forced to reduce the average price of its cars by £200 in an attempt to increase sales, suddenly found it difficult to satisfy demand. It was noted in April 1910 that at the two Daimler factories in Coventry 'well over 3,000 men are hard at work, and the machine shops are working day and night without a stop'.[39] In the same year expansion of motor-vehicle work at Swift led to the gradual 'encroachment of the car department upon the space hitherto used for cycle manufacture',[40] while at Standard an accommodation shortage was compounded by difficulty in obtaining components. Production in the industry as a whole rose quickly in the two years before 1914, based particularly on sales of light cars, and many of the Coventry manufacturers shared in this boom.

The growth of the Coventry motor industry to 1914 was facilitated by large inputs of capital, but often in modest allotments. Several firms which began in a small way drew financial support from local sources. For example, seventeen of the twenty-five shareholders who contributed to the Endurance Motor Company when it was launched in 1898 were listed as resident in Coventry.[41] Funds were also attracted from neighbouring areas. The Arden Motor Company was established in 1912 with nominal capital of £1,500 divided equally between an engineer and a building contractor from Coventry and another engineer from Kidderminster.[42] Birmingham was a significant source of capital for several of the smaller motor companies, while in some cases money was drawn from much further afield. When the Clarendon Motor Company was established in modest premises in Moor Street in 1902 it drew the bulk of its finances from London, though shares were held by individuals in Birmingham, Guildford and Harborne.[43] Similarly, the Endurance Company attracted assistance from investors in Kent, London and Bedford, as well as Coventry.

The majority of the smaller motor firms owed their existence to capital injected by the families, friends and business contacts of their founders. Many investors were recorded as engineers or manufacturers, reflecting links with the local or regional economy as well the particular nature of the motor industry with its dependence upon a network of related engineering activities. Thus, when the Rex Motor Company folded in 1914, having manufactured a huge variety of cars during its short existence, its chief shareholder was a 'gentleman' formerly described as a tube manufacturer from Birmingham. Two other members of the same family were the company's remaining principal subscribers, one a manufacturer resident in Birmingham and the other an engineer from Earlsdon on the outskirts of Coventry.[44] This reflected the company's antecedents which involved a merger in 1902 between Allard Cycles of Coventry and the Birmingham Motor Manufacturing and Supply Company. Much of the early capital for White and Poppe came from the White family, who were prominent members of Coventry's watch trade. Long personal friendship may also explain why William Herbert provided the money which enabled Calcott Bros to acquire new factory accommodation, almost certainly for the manufacture of motor cars.[45] By 1913 Alfred Herbert was a major shareholder in Standard, reflecting perhaps both a personal friendship with Reginald Maudslay and important business links with the company.[46] Similarly, the creation of Alvis in the post-war era depended in part upon injections of capital provided by the founder's family and friends in the Pembroke Dock area of Wales.[47] The mobilisation of capital was aided through Coventry's many clubs and societies. Most important of all, perhaps, was the Coventry and County Club formed in 1898 which soon became known as 'the unofficial headquarters of the motor industry in Coventry'.[48] This was where manufacturers could meet and do business with their suppliers and financiers in a relaxed and congenial atmosphere.

Standard provides an interesting example of the complex personal factors which could be involved in the finance of the early motor industry. When it was formed in 1903, the company's nominal capital was £5,000. Part of Reginald Maudslay's funding came from his former employer, Wolfe Barry, who contributed £3,000 to enable him to start his own business. Rustat Blake, one of Maudslay's fellow pupils with Wolfe Barry, also provided some of the firm's initial capital, while another, Alexander Gibb, later became Standard's second-largest shareholder. As the company grew, however, the need for additional finance increased and it was in these circumstances that in 1907 Maudslay lost control of Standard to Charles Friswell, who ran a well-known London-based motor-vehicle distribution agency. Maudslay became a salaried director without a share in the company's profits. However, Friswell's reign as company chairman ended in 1912 when he was bought out with money provided by Siegfried Bettman of the Triumph Cycle Company, and other of Maudslay's close associates in Coventry. The rise and fall of Friswell's association with Standard is interesting from an investment viewpoint but it also points to the connections between funding and business strategy. During Friswell's period as chairman, Standard acquired additional premises for production, repairs and servicing, moved the design process towards the more expensive end of the market and engaged in a number of important marketing initiatives, including the introduction of the Union Jack radiator badge, a motif displayed on all the firm's cars until 1930. With Maudslay in control once again the firm changed direction, moving firmly and successfully into the market for light cars.[49]

The larger motor firms raised capital through public issues. Deasy was formed in 1906 as a public company, while Standard went public in 1913 in order to secure the investment to support its new production strategy. Similarly, Rover went to the market several times to attract the capital required for expansion, including, for example, the purchase of Hawkins and Peake in 1907. The firm's capital was eventually raised to £200,000 in the pre-war period, which helped it to transfer successfully from cycles to cars. Public capital was also used to support the reconstruction of ailing firms, notably Humber and Daimler. Humber was saved from collapse during the slump of 1908 by a capital reconstruction programme supported by the company's wealthier shareholders. More impressive, perhaps, was the series of issues associated with Daimler in the early years of the century which helped to place the company on a sound footing after the dubious practices associated with the original Lawson flotation. Daimler was entirely reconstructed in 1904 and subsequent issues of debentures and preference shares allowed public confidence in the firm to develop to a point where substantial placings of ordinaries could be made. In the six years after it was reconstructed Daimler raised £81,000 in preference shares, over £100,000 in debentures and £137,000 in ordinaries.[50] These initiatives were essential in order to secure the firm's future development for at the beginning of the twentieth century it was virtually bankrupt and unable to produce cars in sufficient numbers to generate the income stream needed for survival.

Yet, undercapitalisation remained a feature of the Coventry motor industry. The bankruptcy records of the Board of Trade reveal, as one would expect, the firms with minimal resources to have been particularly vulnerable to trade and other forms of business instability. The *Motor* complained in 1907 that 'We constantly see firms starting to manufacture cars with a capital of £5,000 or £10,000. Such a sum is a mere drop in the ocean, and is almost bound to be totally lost, and not only that, but the industry suffered through a firm coming into it with inadequate capital, making a few cars at a loss, dying out and then leave the users with cars for which spares are unobtainable.'[51] The structural characteristics of motor-vehicle production in Coventry, with its many small businesses, is thus important in explaining its susceptibility to the particular problems emanating from inadequate funding. However, even many of the larger companies found their growth inhibited by low capitalisation. For example, this was a persistent problem for Standard during its formative years, eventually forcing the company to public issue in 1914, but even then its capital amounted to only £50,000, compared with £650,000 for Austin at Longbridge, 7 miles to the west of Birmingham.[52]

The relatively low level of funding of some Coventry motor companies is explained partly by the operation of the capital market. The achievement of Austin, Daimler and other firms in attracting substantial funds to motor manufacture suggests that both the institutional mechanisms and the investing public were receptive to the industry's capital requirements. Yet undersubscription did occur. The relatively small Coronet Motor Company, floated in 1903, was undersubscribed by almost £7,000 on a nominal capital of

£20,000.[53] Perhaps this explains why the company folded in 1906 after only two years of car production. On a larger scale, the Deasy Company failed to reach its full subscription which was launched in 1906, while the issue of £80,000 by the Maudslay Motor Company in 1907 was more than 60 per cent undersubscribed, with only £6,000 being taken by the general public and the rest being contributed by Cyril Maudslay and his personal associates. Indeed, Maudslay's own investment of £3,000 was made possible only with the aid of a bank loan.[54] The company subsequently experienced a serious shortage of capital which induced its management to seek assistance from a variety of quarters. In 1908 both the District and Lloyds Bank refused to grant the firm overdraft facilities of £20,000, while a request to the Midland for £15,000 was eventually scaled down by two-thirds before acceptance.[55] A few months later the firm was reported to have secured financial help from at least two major insurance companies. Deasy, however, managed to escape such traumas, mainly because it benefited from the support of wealthy business interests in Scotland, while John Siddeley apparently enjoyed the financial backing of Lionel Rothchild.[56] This meant, however, that by 1914 the firm had 'practically been financed as if it were a private business belonging to the Directors', a situation which Siddeley regarded as highly unsatisfactory, probably because of the degree of control which was exercised over the company's management.[57]

The problem of undersubscription experienced by Deasy and Maudslay was partly explained by the failure of both companies to take the precaution of arranging for their issues to be formally underwritten. This was probably due to a combination of complacency and a desire to save the commission and other expenses which underwriting involved. Yet a number of similar flotations proved equally unattractive to the investing public in 1906-1907. In May 1907 the *Motor* commented upon the ease with which American, French and German motor firms attracted capital, adding that 'even the most firmly established concern on this side is received with indifference'.[58] This was attributed to lingering public disquiet following the loss-making speculative ventures of the late 1890s, though the gathering trade slump must have contributed significantly to the uncertainty surrounding the promotion of motor-vehicle companies at that time.

A related matter was the unwillingness of pioneer entrepreneurs to accept the loss of control over their business activities which resulted from large public issues, and this was almost certainly a factor in limiting the financial resources of both Singer and Hillman. Apart from influencing company policy through the appointment of board members, shareholders might also exercise some control over management through membership of special investigating committees. In applying for credit facilities in January 1908, George Singer was said to have informed Lloyds Bank in Coventry that 'they can get more capital into the Business, but they wanted to keep in their own hands as much as possible'.[59] Similarly, William Hillman invested £2,000 in his motor company in 1907 and, apart from £1,000 from another director, he provided all the firm's additional capital before 1914, totalling more than £20,000.[60] There seems little doubt that the growth of these two companies was inhibited in their early years by the politics of boardroom management.

Many firms in the motor industry were handicapped by inadequate and uneven flows of working capital, large amounts of which could be required for the payment of wages and raw materials. In addition, the normal problem of balancing income and expenditure caused by the seasonal nature of the industry could be exacerbated by sharp fluctuations in the level of trade. At one period during the depression of 1908 Daimler held stock valued at £300,000, with a further £92,000 owed to the company by sundry debtors.[61] Expansion could create similar difficulties. Orders for White and Poppe engines totalled £5,000 in the autumn of 1908, but twelve months later this had increased to £30,000, adding significantly to the firm's long-standing liquidity problem.[62] The income stream was also affected by the nature of a company's product and the terms of sale. More expensive cars were bought on a seasonal basis, while those designed for the popular end of the market tended to be sold through the year. When demand for a particular model was high it was possible for the manufacture to require a sizeable deposit and this could help to spread the inflow of funds. This practice was largely terminated during the decline in sales of 1908 but was reintroduced once the economic cycle improved. By 1913, for example, the Calcott light car was so sought after that all vehicles had to be paid for in advance of delivery.

The financial support of the banks was often of critical importance in enabling the motor manufacturers to resolve the industry's cash-flow problems. This could be decisive for the small firms where operations were frequently conducted from such a limited resource base that the accumulation of a reserve fund was difficult or even impossible. By 1904, just two years after its creation, the Clarendon Motor Company had debts of £2,500 and although this was a relatively small sum, the firm never fully recovered and went into liquidation in 1906. The key factor in the company's eventual demise appears to have been the refusal by both Lloyds and the Midland to grant it significant overdraft facilities.[63] Conversely, the willingness of the banks to provide working capital was an important element in the survival of many small motor concerns and contributed to the particular structural characteristics of the industry in Coventry. The larger car companies also relied heavily upon the goodwill of the local financial community with assistance sometimes being acquired from a number of different banks. Although Daimler's main account in 1909 was with the Midland, the company also negotiated a loan of £10,000 from the London and Westminster bank for the purchase of tyres. John Siddeley later reminded the manager of the Coventry branch of the Midland that on the one occasion he had been refused accommodation, 'money was easily forthcoming from another Bank'.[64] Siddeley was in a relatively strong bargaining position and weaker firms sometimes found the banks less tolerant. Cyril Maudslay's request for assistance in 1908 received a decidedly frosty reception from Lloyds, the local manager noting that 'we should not be sweet on it as they would not take our advice at first, & have been to two other Banks, & now come back to us'.[65]

The banks' willingness to accommodate their customers varied according to the circumstances of the firms concerned, but the conditions under which loans were made, including advice as to what constituted financial rectitude, was a significant variable in the development of the Coventry motor industry. Financial help normally assumed the form of overdrafts and could involve considerable sums of money. In 1908 Daimler was allowed to go to £65,000, while in 1912 White and Poppe had a limit of £12,000. There seems to have been no formal arrangement for calculating the creditworthiness of particular firms. The decision to grant overdraft facilities, and the terms and conditions surrounding particular advances, depended principally upon a general assessment of the firm's prospects related in particular to cash flow, capitalization, quality of management and product strength. Although requests for major loans were made to head office, local managers enjoyed considerable authority in influencing the final decision. Managers were sometimes checked when they appeared to be treating a particular firm too generously, though on occasions they were also instructed to be more flexible with customers. In connection with the Midland's Daimler account, the Coventry branch manager was told by head office in 1908 that 'you were unduly alarmed with regard to this account, but it was of course necessary to take notice of your objections so seriously pressed upon us as you are on the spot & ought to be able to form a correct opinion. It is an important a/c, & I think that you should now let them rest.'[66]

The banks were usually unwilling to make advances for capital projects. The manager of the Coventry branch of the Midland emphasised to senior bank officials in 1908 that 'no part of the Bank's money was put into bricks and mortar'.[67] Similarly, one of the reasons why Lloyds adopted an uncompromising position with Cyril Maudslay in the same year was that his company wanted an advance for purposes of capital development. Yet exceptions to this general rule were sometimes allowed. In 1913 the Midland permitted Siddeley-Deasy to extend its overdraft to £30,000 in order to finance new extensions and additions to plant. The Coventry branch manager pointed out to head office that the company enjoyed an extremely healthy financial position, having doubled its turnover in the preceding three years, and that it also benefited from very strong capital support. It was suggested that under these circumstances the personal guarantees of the directors would not be necessary, particularly since 'Mr Siddeley has a son in Lloyds Bank & we are desirous of keeping him happy in the relationship'.[68]

Overdrafts were normally granted for a maximum of twelve months, but were renewable so long as the borrowers's prospects appeared favourable. Personal guarantees provided by board members were the most popular form of security with the financial institutions and help to explain the importance which most companies attached to recruiting men of substance as directors. The guarantees provided by Charles Friswell, which in 1908 amounted to £10,000, assisted Standard in remaining solvent during its difficult early years, although they also eventually enabled him to gain control of the company. Other, more tangible assets, could also be employed as security for bank loans. When Rover obtained an overdraft of £40,000 from the Midland in 1904 it was secured by the company's own debentures and the deeds to its property. In providing financial support the banks placed themselves in a position to advise on a wide range of commercial issues, from the viability of prospective customers to the various forms of property tenure. For example, in 1911 one Coventry motor-body firm was warned by its bankers 'to go quietly, and not lock up capital in buildings, but to get the present accommodation extended, even if not so convenient'.[69] This was a relatively small concern and such firms appear to have been particularly susceptible to bank intervention in business policy.

Debentures were also a popular method of raising finance in the early motor industry. These were fixed-interest securities which, until the Companies Act of 1929, were a particularly secure form of investment since they attracted priority in the event of a firm's liquidation. Rover, Deasy, Swift and Alvis were among the many Coventry car firms which relied heavily upon debentures in their early days. However, debentures had their disadvantages and could be a cause of instability. For example, interest payments could be so substantial as to become a major drag on resources and an impediment to development. They could also increase the risk element in a firm's financial portfolio. Thus, the Dawson Car Company was wound up in 1920 when a receiver was appointed to protect the interests of debenture holders.[70]

The insecure, often precarious financial position of many of Coventry's early car firms is important to an understanding of the industry's volatility in terms of entry and exit. Although a variety of opportunities existed for raising capital, investors were often equally nervous about the security of their money leading to the constant threat of punitive action. In addition, many small-scale firms embarked upon a phase of demand- and investment-led expansion only to find that they lacked the organisational and financial expertise to cope successfully with the problems of growth.

The ease with which labour was recruited to motor-vehicle manufacture was an important element in the industry's growth in Coventry. The transferability of skill from cycle- to car-making was important. As Leppington observed in 1907, younger workers in particular went 'in the first instance as labourers, but in this position they are very soon able to qualify themselves as skilled mechanics'.[71] The same comment also applied to a range of other trades, such as coach- and engine-building. The largest group of migrants to the city between 1901 and 1911 were from rural Warwickshire and probably had relatively little experience of employment in the engineering industry. However, over 5,000 people came from Birmingham and many others moved from areas with a similar tradition of engineering skill, especially London, Lancashire and Cheshire.

The motor firms attracted boys from both elementary and secondary schools. Bablake, one of the city's oldest foundations, found that few of its pupils moved on to university, preferring to take employment in local factories. To its credit, the school responded by providing practical instruction rooms which were large and well equipped, while much of the teaching was also said to have been of exceptionally good quality.[72] Apart from Daimler, few motor manufacturers paid very much attention to formal works training. A new technical institute was opened in 1888, but a lack of interest by both the governing authorities and the employers limited its contribution to the development of the motor industry. Evening instruction suffered from the seasonal nature of vehicle manufacture which, at certain times of the year, could involve long hours of overtime working, and by 1914 there was still no properly organised course of this type in motor-car engineering. However, the institute did develop an important part-time day provision in mechanical engineering which came to be attended by a significant number of Daimler apprentices.[73] While the inflow of skilled workers to Coventry was sufficient to meet their needs, most motor manufacturers felt no urgency in supporting a training programme, either within their own works or at the city's technical institute.

Design rather than construction was the main area of motor-vehicle development where a serious manpower shortage was apparent. Most early British cars were modified versions of French models and some contained a high proportion of foreign components. Similarly, the American-invented Silent Knight sleeve-valve engine, adapted by Frederick Lanchester, became perhaps the focus of Daimler's engineering reputation before the First World War and remained in production into the 1920s. The success of individual motor companies often depended upon the work of one or two key design engineers and the rate at which such men switched employers is indicative of the premium placed upon their services. Following employment with Daimler and Rover, Edmund Lewis became chief designer to the Deasy Company, partly in order to give the firm's products their market credibility.[74] The Coventry engineering consultancy practice of Alexander Craig was used by a number of local manufacturers, including Standard, Maudslay and Lea-Francis. One of Craig's senior assistants, Clifford Ingall, was seconded to Singer to take charge of the firm's experimental motor work and later joined the staff of Lea-Francis. Even such individuals as George Singer and Reginald Maudslay, with their considerable technical flair and experience, thus relied heavily upon the engineering skills of others.

Motor manufacturers often sought to improve labour productivity through the manipulation of working conditions and methods of reward. The introduction of piecework payments before the First World War was particularly rapid in Coventry, reflecting in part the financial advantages of incentive schemes to the car and some other engineering firms.[75] In addition to the normal practice of negotiating piecework rates between individuals or groups of men, some companies introduced a system of payment known as 'premium bonus' under which a job was timed and workers received bonuses according to the amount of time saved. This arrangement was frequently attacked by the trade unions on the grounds that only a portion of the saving reached the workers, the rest being retained by the employers, and that estimates of job times were calculated unfairly.

The minutes of the Coventry branch of the Amalgamated Society of Engineers reveal that union officials were regularly embroiled in disputes over the operation of payment by results schemes. In particular, complaint was commonly expressed that rates were imposed upon workers rather than being negotiated jointly and that pieceworkers who failed to complete a job within the specified time were required to carry forward the time lost on to the next assignment. Daimler was the scene of much controversy over the way the bonus system was used by management. The company's tinsmiths went on strike in 1907 over the introduction of a premium bonus arrangement, but were forced back on the original terms after seven weeks.[76] In the following year shop-floor meetings at Daimler identified a number of grievances, including incompetent rate-fixing, reduction of times without changes in the method of production and non-payment of bonus until the work was completed. In connection with the last point, it was noted that when bonuses were paid at the conclusion of a particularly long job, involving perhaps fifty cars, employees might have to wait months for their money.[77] Shop-floor unrest in 1908 probably reflected Daimler's response to the financial problems of that time and illustrate how company policy towards labour could be adjusted to meet changing business conditions. Another type of complaint arose in 1909 when men employed at Standard objected to reduced bonus money as a consequence of being transferred from work on 20 hp to 16 hp cars, their argument being that the vehicles were made from the same patterns and involved a similar amount of work.[78] Some eighteen months later the ASE considered a case at Humber where a foreman was alleged to have threatened and bullied his men into greater effort in order to maximise incentive payments, something which, in varying degrees, must have been a common occurrence in the early motor industry.[79]

Labour was attracted to Coventry by a combination of job availability and relatively good wages, but piece-rates and similar methods of payment helped to ensure that manufacturers secured from their workers what they considered to be value for money. The scale and regularity of employment were often closely regulated to suit the need of particular firms so that workers were laid off or put on short time during slack periods and conversely encouraged to work long hours when demand for motor vehicles approached its peak. In 1910 the five main engineering unions in Coventry arrived at an agreement with the local engineering employers association to limit overtime to fifteen hours in any one week. This meant that men could work as many as sixty-nine hours a week, perhaps over an extended period of time, and considerable pressure was sometimes applied to regard overtime as compulsory.[80] Before 1914 labour was insufficiently organised to be a formidable opponent to the motor-car companies, while the smaller firms probably benefited from the knowledge that industrial disputes could be equally calamitous for shop-floor workers and management.

Labour disputes were a response to a new effort bargain between employers and employees but they also represented the growing influence of factory mangers such as Harry Smith at Rover, John Siddeley at Deasy and Percy Martin at Daimler. The pre-war period was thus a time when production in the Coventry motor industry, at least for the larger firms, became more managed as the importance and relative independence of the skilled craftsman diminished.

More intensive use of machine tools and modifications to the organisation of production were other ways in which some Coventry motor manufacturers attempted to improve labour productivity. Edward Manville, the chairman of Daimler, claimed in 1906 that during the previous two years the company's costs per unit of output had fallen by almost 15 per cent, which he attributed to the greater use of machine tools, modifications in workshop organisation and the general application of a bonus scheme for shop-floor workers.[81] Moreover, during the ensuing three years weekly output increased from twenty-four to forty-five vehicles, reflecting investment in additional plant designed to mechanise a number of key processes.[82] These initiatives, and the overall improvement in Daimler's financial position, was largely the work of Percy Martin. Martin, who had experience of production engineering in both continental Europe and the United States, was appointed works manager in 1901 and managing director in 1906, by which time he was the company's second-largest shareholder. Under the guidance of Harry Smith, Rover pursued a similar strategy with regard to production techniques, though the company does not seem to have placed such a high degree of emphasis upon incentive payments as Daimler. However, attempts were made to regulate production in order to minimise output blockages and in 1909 machinery was installed which reduced unit wage costs by 30 per cent. A further substantial sum was invested in new equipment in 1912.[83] When the new Humber plant was opened in 1908 operations were also said to have been highly mechanised with interchangeable components as standard. These and similar capital inputs by other firms help to explain why by 1914 Coventry's labour force appears to have contained a relatively high proportion of unskilled and semi-skilled workers, and why some skilled employees had effectively been de-skilled. These processes applied to a broad range of factory work, since interchangeability meant that fewer skilled fitters were required in the assembly shops as well as in the manufacture of components.[84]

The scale of motor-vehicle production in Britain prior to the First World War, and particularly before 1912, was modest compared with the achievements of the industry's leading competitors abroad. This is explained by a variety of factors, including the technological lead enjoyed by some foreign manufacturers and the failure of the British government to protect the home market with tariff protection. But perhaps the main weakness of the British motor industry during its formative years was the emphasis which the major firms placed upon the production of high-powered expensive vehicles which necessarily had limited market appeal. The popularity of light cars from 1912 suggests that an earlier introduction of technically sound and relatively inexpensive small vehicles might well have broadened the appeal of the motoring habit and hence stimulated a more rapid expansion of the industry's output.[85]

Light cars were essentially miniature versions of the larger prototypes but with an engine capacity limited to 1500 cc. They were more comfortable and technically superior to the cyclecar and, normally retailing at less than £250, quickly found a ready market among the more affluent members of the middle classes.[86] In 1913 Ford dominated British sales of these vehicles, though the parts were imported and assembled at Trafford Park, Manchester. Some Coventry manufacturers gained a significant share in this sector of the car market, particularly Singer, Standard, Calcott Bros and Humber, while the cheapest British-made light car in 1913, the Morris Oxford, was equipped with a White and Poppe four-cylinder 1018 cc water-cooled engine.

Output of light cars grew rapidly in the two years before the outbreak of war, though the concept of a scaled-down model of the larger vehicle had been discussed at least a decade earlier. The lateness of British manufacturers to capitalise on the potential market for low-priced cars was related to the image of motoring as a luxury activity reserved for the wealthy. This view was fostered by the relevant interest groups, including some of the leading motor agents whose advice was often an important element in manufacturers' production strategies. The arrangement practised by some firms which allowed custom-made body shells to be fitted to a chosen chassis also restricted the development of standardised, cheaply-produced light cars. Yet, a variety of factors influenced the policies of individual motor vehicle companies and their apparent conservatism can only be explained through an appreciation of the particular context in which they operated.

By 1914 the reputation of the Daimler Company was based upon the manufacture of a variety of high-powered expensive motor cars, some of which generated at least 45 hp However, in 1899 the firm had developed an early version of the light car, driven by a 4 hp water-cooled engine, but with belt transmission. The Critchley light car, named after the works manager, was highly regarded and sold well, but was never intended to be a major part of the company's production activity. Indeed, the vehicle was originally designed to find use for some fifty surplus engines received from the German Daimler works at Cannstatt.[87] In 1904 a 7 hp light car was included in the Daimler range, though only a few were actually manufactured. According to the company's chairman, the reason for this was that the works was specifically designed to accommodate construction of larger vehicles. This is not a convincing explanation since, despite the subsequent acquisition of new machinery and factory space, the company failed to develop its interest in smaller vehicles. In reality, the company's reputation derived from its position in the luxury-car market. The association of the aristocracy and even royalty with the Daimler marque was a valuable commercial asset which might have been damaged by the manufacture of cheaper vehicles. This was a particularly important consideration as the luxury market became more competitive with Lanchester, Rolls-Royce and Napier all producing successful prestige cars.

The Edmund Lewis-designed 8 hp Rover car of 1905 was the most commercially successful prototype of the later, more sophisticated, versions of the light car, and was manufactured continuously in a variety of models until 1912. Lewis left the company to join Deasy soon after the Rover 8 entered production and the failure to replace him quickly with a suitably qualified engineer appears to have created problems once the original design became obsolete. This partly explains why in 1910 Rover began to purchase the Daimler Silent Knight engine and also why the company's share of total British car output fell from around 10 per cent in 1907 to 3.4 per cent in 1912.[88] The appointment of Owen Clegg as works manager in September 1910 was preceded by a period of unsettled design policy. Clegg, who had previously worked for Wolseley, was an automobile engineer of considerable ability and by the end of 1911 had designed and initiated production of the highly popular Rover 12. This light car revived the company's fortunes, but in March 1912 Clegg left Rover to join the French motor manufacturers, Darracq. The apparent delay in recruiting high-quality engineering talent after Lewis's departure is difficult to explain but was probably linked to conservatism among some Rover directors. This inertia was reflected at the beginning of 1913 when Harry Smith, the managing director, suggested that demand existed for a 'small runabout car to sell at £100 guineas'. The board rejected this proposition, arguing that the 'present car and motor cycle trades are so satisfactory and there was every indication of them keeping so for some considerable time to come to do nothing further in the matter at present'.[89]

The first Standard cars were relatively high-powered vehicles and in 1905 the company, together with Rolls-Royce and Napier, pioneered the introduction to Britain of the six-cylinder engine. This line of development was strengthed in 1907 when Charles Friswell became chairman. Friswell was a flamboyant entrepreneur, keen to emphasise the cachet attached to motoring and, like Harry Lawson, a seeker after royal patronage. His Albany Street premises in London were renowned for their good showroom accommodation and generous facilities for the comfort of prospective customers. Friswell became Standard's sole distributive agent for a time as well as the company's chairman. By 1909 Reginald Maudslay was expounding the merits of a light car designed for the popular market, but Friswell's strong preference was for larger vehicles produced in small batches, even though this was opposed by most board members. Friswell's departure in 1912 was marked in the following year by the appearance of a 9.5 hp Standard light car. This retailed originally for £185 and proved an immediate success with almost 2,000 being made up to May 1915, when production ceased as the company became fully involved in the war effort.

The growth of motor-vehicle production in Coventry before 1914 was constrained by factors similar to those which influenced the performance of the industry as a whole. However, the importance of Coventry's experience is that it demonstrates the complex nature of those influences and their significance for particular manufacturers. Thus, generalisations about the quality of management must necessarily take into account variations in the organisational structure of different firms. While company founders such as George Singer and William Hillman exercised great personal influence, other concerns were managed in a more corporate style. Rover is perhaps the best example of a company where, despite the presence of a strong personality as managing director, the board played a key role in the determination of policy, while Standard under Friswell's leadership illustrates the power of a chairman whose authority was supported by financial control. The raising of finance was often a serious problem for small firms, though even large companies experienced occasional embarrassment. However, it is clear that the seasonal nature of the industry created acute shortages of working capital rendering the manufacturers dependent upon trade credit and bank loans. The scale and complexity of these arrangements is something which the Coventry motor industry reveals to have been of outstanding importance. It also suggests that the importance of the components sector has hitherto been undervalued, both in terms of its financial and technical contribution to the growth of motor manufacture.

Lack of commercial foresight and an emphasis upon individuality and technical excellence are traditional explanations for the relatively modest progress of the British motor industry before 1914. The particular example of Coventry supports these assertions but suggests, too, that growth was prompted and retarded by the interaction of personal, financial and structural factors, the balance of which varied markedly from one firm to another.

Notes

[1]   Saul, 'The Motor Industry in Britain', pp. 23–4.
[2]   *Motor*, 8 June 1907.
[3]   *Coventry Car Factories*, p. 6.
[4]   J. Hinton, *The First Shop Stewards' Movement* (Allen and Unwin, London, 1973), p. 218.
[5]   *Motor*, 2 August 1910.
[6]   K. White, *Company Heritage* (Chrysler UK, Coventry, 1979), p. 2; *Motor*, 22 January 1907; Saul, 'The Motor Industry in Britain', p. 28.

[7]   K. Richardson, *The British Motor Industry 1896–1939*, (Macmillan, London, 1977), pp. 162–3.
[8]   J.R. Davy, *The Standard Car 1903–1963*, (Sherbourne Press, Coventry, 1964), pp. 1–16.
[9]   Price, op. cit., p. 18.
[10] LBC, 352, 20 December 1911.
[11] *Royal Automobile Club Journal*, 6 November 1914, p. 246; Atkinson, op. cit., p. 18.
[12] CRO, 1060/1/1, Deasy Company Directors Minutes, 27 May 1907.
[13] *The Evening and the Morning*, p. 22.
[14] C. Lee, *Regional Economic Growth in the United Kingdom Since the 1880s* (McGraw Hill, Maidenhead, 1971), pp. 87–8.
[15] S.E. Medlicott (ed.) *Coventry Directory 1912–13* (Spennell, Warwick, 1913), pp. 823–6; Saul, 'The Motor Industry in Britain', p. 36.
[16] Anon, *Motors and Motoring* (Robinson Printing Company, London, 1908), pp. 85–6.
[17] For a brief history of Coventry Climax, see Judith Gallagher, *The History of Coventry Clix Engines Ltd*, n.d., privately circulated, CRO, 1731/4.
[18] Lane, op. cit., p. 20.
[19] LBC, 314, 22 July 1905.
[20] M. Adeney, *Nuffield: a Biography* (Robert Hale, London, 1993), p. 46.
[21] Tripp, op. cit., p. 98.
[22] CRO, Acc/594, Daimler Directors Minutes, 18 September 1902.
[23] CRO, Acc/594, Daimler Company Repairs Committee Minutes, 21 May 1903, 19 June 1903.
[24] Foreman-Peck, 'Diversification and Growth', p. 188.
[25] LBC, 253, 7 December 1909.
[26] MBC, 149, 16 December 1908.
[27] RDM, 28 November 1910.
[28] LBC, 339, 5 November 1913.
[29] LBC, 325, 7 November 1907.
[30] LBC, 143, 14 August 1909.
[31] B. Beaven, 'Growth and Significance of the Coventry Car Component Industry, 1895–1914', *Business History*, 18 (1993), p. 115.
[32] LBC, 359, 30 December 1906.
[33] LBC, 17, 1 April 1912.
[34] LBC, 372, 25 January 1912.
[35] Saul, 'The Motor Industry in Britain', p. 23.
[36] *Motor*, 13 February 1906.
[37] *Motor*, 27 October 1908.
[38] CRO, Singer Company, Report to Debenture Holders, 12 March 1912.
[39] *Motor*, 5 April 1910.
[40] *Motor*, 2 August 1910.
[41] PRO, BT 31/7804/55841. Endurance was one of the first car companies in Coventry with works in Gosford Street. It folded in 1901 having manufactured one model using Benz designs. See, *Coventry Car Factories*, p. 1.
[42] PRO, BT 31/15146/33732.
[43] PRO, BT 31/7806/55841.
[44] PRO, BT 15146/33732.
[45] LBC, 234, 13 July 1906.
[46] University of Warwick, Modern Records Centre (MRC), 226/ST/1/1/1, Standard Directors Minutes (SDM), 22 September 1913.
[47] Morewood, op. cit., p. 10.

[48]   Harold Nockolds quoted by B. Beaven, 'Re-Constructing the Business Community: The Small Firm in the Coventry Motor Industry, 1896-1939', *Business Archives*, 72 (1996), p. 26.
[49]   Morewood, op. cit., pp. 99–100; Davy, op. cit., p. 18.
[50]   Saul, 'The Motor Industry in Britain', p. 31.
[51]   *Motor*, 8 October 1907.
[52]   R. Church, *Herbert Austin: The British Motor Car Industry to 1941* (Europa, London, 1979), p. 192.
[53]   PRO, BT 31/10236/76827.
[54]   A.E. Harrison, 'Joint Stock Company Flotation in the Cycle, Motor Vehicle and Related Industries, 1882–1914', *Business History*, vol. XXIII (1981), p. 188; LBC, 300, 8 November 1907.
[55]   LBC: 299, 25 November 1908; 327, 23 December 1908; 333, 24 December 1908.
[56]   LBC, 253, 7 December 1909.
[57]   CRO, 1060/1/1, Deasy Company Directors Minutes, 7 May 1914.
[58]   *Motor*, 7 May 1907.
[59]   LBC, 386, 13 January 1908.
[60]   Saul, 'The Motor Industry in Britain', p. 33.
[61]   MBC, 146, 9 April 1908.
[62]   LBC, 180, 6 September 1909.
[63]   LBC, 359, 24 June 1904.
[64]   MBC, 414, 19 September 1932.
[65]   LBC, 333, 24 December 1908.
[66]   MBC, 147, 22 April 1908.
[67]   MBC, 146, 15 April 1908.
[68]   MBC, 276, 28 February 1913.
[69]   LBC, 323, 19 October 1911.
[70]   Morewood, op. cit., p. 17.
[71]   Leppington, op. cit., p. 355.
[72]   PRO, Ed. 53/338, Board of Education, Area Record of Secondary Education in Coventry, July 1919, p. 6.
[73]   PRO, Ed. 114/953, Report of HMI on Coventry Municipal Technical Institute, 31 July 1911, p. 1.
[74]   CRO, 1060/1/1, Deasy Company Directors Minutes, 1 December 1906.
[75]   F. Carr, 'Engineering Workers and the Rise of Labour in Coventry', unpublished PhD thesis, University of Warwick, 1978, pp. 23–4.
[76]   Ibid., p. 24.
[77]   Amalgamated Society of Engineers, Coventry Branch Minutes, 9 March 1908; 20 March 1908.
[78]   Ibid., 10 June 1909.
[79]   Ibid., 31 January 1911.
[80]   Carr, op. cit., p. 26.
[81]   *Motor*, 13 November 1906.
[82]   Lewchuk, *American technology and the British vehicle industry*, pp. 126–7.
[83]   Foreman-Peck, 'Diversification and Growth', p. 188.
[84]   Lewchuk, *American technology and the British vehicle industry*, pp. 126–7.
[85]   For a discussion of these points, see R. Church, 'Markets and marketing in the British motor industry before 1914', *Journal of Transport History*, vol. 3 (1982).
[86]   C.F. Caunter, *The history and Development of Light Cars* (HMSO, London, 1957), p. 46.
[87]   B.E. Smith, *The Daimler Tradition* (Transport Bookman, London, 1972), p. 9.
[88]   Foreman-Peck, 'Diversification and Growth', p. 188.

[89] RDM, 24 February 1913.

Chapter 4

The Impact of War, 1914–1918

The most visible manifestation of Coventry's involvement in the First World War was a swift and marked acceleration of building activity as existing factories were extended and new ones built to accommodate the growth of military production. *The Times* noted at the beginning of 1916 that 'Men say with pardonable exaggeration that the Rudge-Whitworth works add a storey to their factories in a night in order to make room for expansion', adding that 'everywhere in the city it is the same'.[1] As one authority has noted, 'This rapid building programme clearly impressed contemporary commentators who often highlighted Coventry as a role model for wartime industrial reorganisation.'[2] Housing was also erected for the men and women who were recruited from elsewhere to supplement the local workforce. Between 1914 and 1918 the city's population rose from 119,000 to 133,000, but this disguised the true scale of demographic change, since in the first two years of war some 10,000 Coventrians enlisted for military service. The overwhelming majority of the early migrants were men but during 1916 women came to predominate, obtaining employment throughout broad sections of the engineering and munitions industries.[3]

Although much of the new labour, particularly in the early stages of the war, came from Coventry's immediate hinterland, many workers travelled from much further afield, including the Celtic fringes. This was said to have brought problems of cultural assimilation as a number of migrants experienced difficulty in adjusting to the ways of their new community. Local residents frequently held the new arrivals responsible for alleged outbreaks of dishonest or immoral behaviour. At the end of 1916 an official investigating committee found some substance in these claims, drawing attention to 'a serious increase of venereal disease and of loose and immoral conduct in recreation grounds'. This was attributed, at least in the case of the young women involved, to their removal from the discipline and comforts of home life, rather than to any more general decline in behavioural standards, and was said to reflect the most persistent social concern of wartime Coventry, namely an inadequate supply of suitable housing.[4] Many migrants found acceptable lodgings in the city, though others less fortunate could be involved in a lengthy commuter journey involving a round trip of perhaps 40 miles. At one point, for example, Daimler had some 1,300 employees commuting daily from the greater Coventry area. The army of factory commuters became so great that the crush at Foleshill station sometimes resulted in passengers fainting on the platform. Aided by government money, White and Poppe constructed hutted accommodation for their new recruits. By November 1916 the firm possessed thirty-two blocks of huts, each holding just over 100 young women who were under the care and supervision of a matron. But the early, rather spartan, buildings with their barrack-like appearance failed to appeal to most of the girls billeted in them and seem to have contributed to inmates' feelings of isolation and alienation. Under pressure from the Ministry of Munitions, the later buildings erected by White and Poppe and other Coventry firms were arranged in a more homely style, while the general conditions of residence, including diet, were also improved. Yet housing for specific groups, especially young married couples, remained a source of friction throughout the war and became a factor in the industrial unrest of 1917.

Coventry's industrial structure ensured that the city would be heavily involved in the manufacture of military equipment and by the end of 1915 most of the city's large engineering firms were on a full war footing and under government supervision as controlled establishments. As Alfred Herbert explained in 1919, 'the effect of the war on the engineering industry has been to render demand, enormously and continuously in excess of supply'.[5] The Coventry Ordnance Works, which was established in 1905 as a Cammell Laird – John Brown subsidiary, soon became one of Coventry's key suppliers of motor-vehicle components. Indeed, 'Such was the company's pre-war commitment to producing car components that at the outbreak of war, no orders for armaments had been placed with the firm for over five years and therefore only a small staff were conversant with the manufacture of field guns.'[6] However, with the onset of hostilities the works came under immediate pressure to expand its core business of land and naval armaments. In addition, the firm was encouraged to develop its aviation work which at the beginning of 1914 was still very much at the embryonic stage.[7] Reginald Bacon, the managing director at that time, later recalled that his life was spent taking telephone orders and planning ways to satisfy the escalating level of demand. The existing shops were soon 'overflowing with work' so that new ones had to be constructed and further machinery purchased from suppliers in Britain and the United States.[8] The Works' wartime output included 710 aircraft, 11 tanks, 92 anti-aircraft guns, nearly 400,000 cartridge cases and millions of fuses and detonators.[9] Income grew rapidly and the debts which had been accumulated before 1914 soon disappeared. When the Coventry Ordnance Works was sold in 1918 its new owners abandoned motor components, preferring instead to consolidate its work in heavy electrical engineering. Yet because of their eventual involvement with William Morris, the arrival in 1915 of the French machine-gun manufacturers Hotchkiss and Cie was of greater long-term significance to the development of Coventry's motor industry. When the parent works in France came under threat from the German advance, premises were acquired in Gosford Street which soon employed some 2,000 production workers and came to be regarded as a major centre of the country's war effort. The change of direction in the company's manufacturing profile occurred shortly after the war with the arrival of a large order from Morris for engines and gearboxes.[10]

Motor-vehicle manufacture was perhaps more profoundly influenced by the onset of war than any other sector of Coventry's engineering industry. Very few motorised vehicles crossed with the British expeditionary force, which relied largely upon horse-drawn transport, but the potentially wide application of the petrol-driven engine soon became apparent to the military authorities, with immediate and dramatic repercussions for several of Coventry's leading motor firms. Although the city's output of private cars declined sharply, this was compensated for by growing production of vehicles for field transport. Aero-engineering also expanded quickly, while the manufacture of munitions became the staple activity of a number of firms. The war was thus a catalyst which by modifying the scale, nature and complexity of Coventry's motor industry helped to fashion its later pattern of development.

Many of the small component firms making pistons, generators and other vehicle parts received a considerable boost from the expansion of wartime demand which was often reflected in substantial additions to plant and sometimes, as with Coventry Radiators and ML Magnetos, the adoption of public company status. However, all the component manufacturers were soon overshadowed by White and Poppe, whose phenomenal growth made it one of the largest engineering works in Coventry. Ironically, at the outbreak of war the firm's financial prospects appeared somewhat bleak since it was left holding engines valued at £15,000 which had been destined for the Morris Oxford.[11] Moreover, the production of new engine models required further large injections of working capital since the supply of Bosch magnetos, which had been obtained on three months' credit, had ceased, to be replaced by American equivalents purchased on cash terms.[12] Fortunes revived with the development of the partnership's aero-engine business and, more particularly, the reintroduction of large-scale munitions production. At the beginning of 1915 an order for 80,000 fuses a week from Armstrong Whitworth proved a significant turning point. This order necessitated the construction of additional premises which was financed by Whitworths and leased by White and Poppe on favourable terms with an option to purchase at the end of the war.[13] By 1918 the firm's engineering and shell-making activities were spread across the three major factories and employed a labour force of around 11,000 men and women. After the war White and Poppe concentrated solely on the manufacture of engines for commercial vehicles, perhaps hoping to benefit from the less seasonal nature of the trade compared with motor cars. In 1920 the firm was taken over by Dennis Brothers of Guildford, the consolidation of an established and successful business relationship.

The war also forced some of the smaller and more specialised car component firms out of business as they became overstretched by War Office orders or squeezed by competition from larger manufacturers. With the outbreak of war the firm of T.H. and T.F. Spencer was left with unwanted stocks of components for civilian vehicles. This created a cash flow problem which was compounded by the brothers' attempt to reorganise production, leading to financial collapse in 1915.[14] In the manufacture of electrical components Coventry Headlights Limited and United Motor Industries found themselves unable to compete with Lucas, while in the body-building sector a number of small concerns went under for similar reasons. Holley Brothers, an American-owned firm set up in Coventry specifically to manufacture carburettors for the War Office, found itself unable to attract normal commercial trade after 1918. This is a particularly interesting example of business failure since in 1919 the firm was acquired by T.G. John, formerly chief engineer at Siddeley-Deasy, who promptly used the assets to diversify into motor cars under the Alvis marque.[15]

The war inflated the general profile of Coventry's motor industry but the experience of individual firms varied markedly according to the willingness and ability of management to take advantage of the prevailing opportunities and, in the longer term, success in applying accumulated profits and knowledge to the radically different market conditions after 1918. Lea-Francis, for example, frittered wartime earnings in the design and production of a medium-sized car which proved virtually unsaleable.[16] By contrast, the Singer works was turned over almost entirely to government contracts, particularly for munitions, which brought substantial profits, a new share issue and the basis for further expansion in the post-war years.[17] Yet Rover's problems reveal how complex the history of a particular company could be and the consequent danger of generalising across the industry as a whole. Despite its domestic success, the Rover 12 was too light for military use, so the firm was forced to redirect its efforts towards the manufacture of mortars, gas shells, fuses and tank transmissions. In addition, subcontract work was undertaken for construction of the Maudslay 3-ton lorry and Sunbeam's 16 hp motor car, the latter being converted to ambulances and staff vehicles. This contract enabled Sunbeam to concentrate on building its successful aero-engines, but was crucially important for Rover since it allowed the firm to retain its association with motor-car production. Rover motorcycles were supplied for use by the army and found service particularly in France and the Middle east, though the main Coventry producer was Triumph which sold some 30,000 of its model 'H' machines to the War Office. Readjustment after 1918 was impeded by late payment on a number of government contracts, but more significant for Rover's business in the 1920s was the relatively limited opportunity which the company had received for technical innovation in motor-vehicle engineering or for an expansion of its physical capacity. Even without the war, however, it seems likely that a divided management would have found difficulty in responding successfully to the growth of competition from Austin, Morris, Singer and Ford.[18]

Daimler also turned to munitions work and at its peak the company had an output of around 2,000 shells a week. However, its most distinctive contribution to the war effort was in the construction of an exceptionally wide range of motorised vehicles and their components. Indeed, in terms of volume, Daimler became the principal supplier of chassis and parts to the British and Allied forces.[19] In the first year of the war Daimler supplied about 1,000 ambulances as well as staff cars and other vehicles. Some staff cars were converted to become mobile headquarters, with map tables and seats which doubled as bunk beds.[20] Increasingly, however, the firm was encouraged by government to concentrate upon the production of commercial vehicles, tank engines and aircraft. In total some 4,000 commercial vehicles were manufactured, including mobile wireless-telegraphy stations and a number of 3-ton lorries which were used as travelling workshops. These were equipped with a forge, a 6-inch lathe and a variety of small tools and were attached to convoys of lorries to enable repairs to be implemented with the minimum disruption. The workshops also serviced the Daimler sleeve-valve engine which was employed in the heavy tractors used for towing 15-inch howitzers, and later in tanks. So ubiquitous was the firm's contribution to the mobilisation of the British army that the Prince of Wales remarked: 'It seems to me that the Daimler people are running this war.'[21]

Daimler six-cylinder engines were placed in the first tanks, which were built by Foster and Co. of Lincoln, but when these were found to be of insufficient power the government turned to other engineering firms.[22] Daimler was also one of the first British companies to manufacture its own aero-engines, the prototype of which appeared less than two months after the outbreak of war. In addition, the company was given the role of co-ordinating construction of the BR2 aero-engine which had been developed by W.O. Bentley at Humber's Coventry works and which came to be used in the Sopwith Snipe.[23] Production was later extended to incorporate completed aircraft, and this involved the provision of additional workshop accommodation and the construction of an airfield at Radford. Near the close of the war some eighty Daimler aeroplanes left the Coventry works each month, making the firm one of the government's chief suppliers.[24]

Government contracts helped to rescue Daimler from the financial pressures of the immediate pre-war years, while its design work on tank and aircraft engines further strengthened the company's commitment to high-powered vehicles. Siddeley-Deasy also became heavily involved with the manufacture of aircraft and, unlike Daimler, continued to expand this part of its business after 1918, with John Siddeley becoming widely recognised during the 1920s as the most dominant figure in the British aircraft industry. The company's move into aero-engineering occurred at the beginning of the war when government contracts were offered on terms which Siddeley regarded as very favourable.[25] Within a short period the Coventry factory was in effect under the general control of the War Office's aircraft department, with public money and bank loans being used to help finance building extensions and purchases of additional machinery. In 1916, for example, accommodation was rented from Calcott Brothers and the Swift Motor Company for the construction of motor vehicles and airframes respectively. The manufacture of land vehicles continued, including lorries and field kitchens, and ambulances subcontracted from the Standard Motor Company, but it was aircraft production, engines and airframes, which brought the company its profits and enabled John Siddeley to develop his aviation interests after the war. By February 1917 Siddeley had decided upon his future course of action, for he informed the Board that 'it was our intention to remain in the aeronautical business',[26] a decision consolidated by the investment of some £90,000 in a new aircraft works. The company's net profit for 1913 amounted to £15,000 but by 1915 this had increased to almost £47,000 and by 1921 had reached over £652,000.[27] The key to the firm's success appears to have been the ability of management to maintain strong margins for as Siddeley noted in June 1915, 'our normal rate of profit amounts to an exceedingly handsome figure'.[28]

For most of the war Siddley Deasy's aero engineering work was based upon designs emanating from the Royal Aircraft Factory at Farnborough. However, a change of government policy in 1917 gave the manufacturers greater freedom to initiate their own projects and this led to the introduction of the famous Siddeley Puma, which was widely adopted in the 1920s by the infant European airlines. The Siskin fighter, which had been on the drawing board at the end of the war, was taken up by the Air Ministry in 1919 and was important in further consolidating the company's position in the aircraft industry.[29] The formation of a specialist design team also benefited the firm's motor-vehicle work and enabled it to be one of the first manufacturers after the war to introduce a new car. But John Siddeley's close personal involvement in the aviation side of the business inevitably diverted his attention away from motor vehicles, and was perhaps the main reason why Siddeley cars enjoyed only limited development in the interwar years.

Of the remaining Coventry motor companies, Standard was the one most critically influenced by the onset of war. Standard cars failed to attract government interest so that initially the company was largely concerned with the production of munitions. Shells were manufactured in vast quantities, and included among the military hardware produced by the firm were the first Stokes trench mortars.[30] Standard's contribution to the war effort increased substantially after it was awarded its first aircraft contract late in 1915, which brought it under government supervision as a controlled establishment. The first War Office order, which was for 50 tubular-framed BE 12s, left the factory in the spring of 1916. Before the Armistice the company manufactured some 1,600 aircraft, the best known being the Sopwith Pup. The first order for these highly manoeuvrable aeroplanes was placed by the Sopwith Aviation Company in May 1916 and eventually they were leaving the Standard works at the rate of twenty-four a week. Sadly, the very first Standard Pup became a German trophy when it was captured behind enemy lines near Bapaume on 4 January 1917. After the war a number of Standard Pups were used to help equip the

Royal Australian Airforce while another large batch was sold to the Japanese government.[31] Standard also shared in the manufacture of other aircraft and aero-components but, significantly, the company did not develop its own design facilities on the same scale as Siddeley-Deasy. This is important in explaining why Standard relinquished its aviation work after the war, though equally pertinent was Reginald Maudslay's own preference, apparently supported by his shareholders, to return to motor vehicle production at the earliest opportunity. In March 1917 Standard's directors decided to seek government authority to begin experimental work on cars in order to 'enable the Company to be in a position to resume their ordinary trade after hostilities have ceased'.[32] By July application had been made for patents relating to improvements in motor-car carburettors and electrical fittings, and a few months later Maudslay was able to reassure shareholders that a new vehicle model would shortly be ready for the market.

The war undoubtedly brought Standard many technical spin-offs. In addition, and of much greater long-term importance, it promoted an expansion of the company's physical assets which became central to its evolution as a mass producer of motor cars. In 1916 premises housing the skating rink in nearby Leamington Spa were purchased and later in the same year additional rented accommodation was acquired in the town. However, these and similar acquisitions were overshadowed by the purchase for aircraft construction of a 30-acre site at Canley from Lord Leigh in 1915. This was one of Maudslay's shrewdest business deals for not only was the property obtained on reasonable terms but, as he acknowledged at the time, it was almost certain to be a great benefit to the company once normal production was resumed.[33] The new factory was soon operational but as the company's business increased, further building extensions became necessary. This led to Maudslay's greatest property coup when in the summer of 1918 he negotiated the purchase of a further 110 acres of land adjacent to the main Canley works. These investments were facilitated by the profits which accrued from government business and by bank loans supported by debentures. Arrangements were also concluded which provided for advance payment in support of specific projects. For example, a contract for 150 BE 12 aircraft was only accepted in 1916 on condition that the money required for the associated additional workshop accommodation accompanied the order.[34] After the war the Canley site became the centre of Standard's motor-vehicle activities and was the envy of most other Coventry car manufacturers.

In responding to official exhortations for higher levels of output, Coventry's engineering firms often experienced difficulty in obtaining additional or replacement machinery and good-quality raw materials, but their most severe resource constraint was labour. The rush to join the services in the early months of war, which was sometimes strongly encouraged by management, left many firms short of experienced hands, so that it became increasingly difficult to satisfy the rising number of government orders. Some companies were so desperate by the summer of 1915 that they were even defying government regulations by advertising openly for new recruits in the local newspapers.[35] Moreover, the labour crisis in engineering was exacerbated by competition for workers from other sectors of industry. For example, Courtaulds found a ready market for all the artificial silk it could produce and in consequence remained one of Coventry's largest employers, though it is interesting to note that output was eventually restricted by labour and other resource problems.[36] Migrant workers eased the situation considerably but as late as November 1917 the Ministry of Munitions noted that the Coventry Ordnance Works 'had recently built two new shops for urgent Admiralty work, but no labour is to be had, and the shops stand empty'.[37] Although migration was high, it thus remained inadequate to meet the city's employment needs, a problem which Ministry officials attributed to a shortage of accommodation for married men and their families. In response to this, it was decided at the end of 1917 that Coventry's housing provision should qualify for special attention under the terms of the Defence of the Realm Act, an initiative which came too late to influence materially the output performance of the engineering industry.

New production techniques helped to expand output and the threefold increase in electricity consumption in Coventry during the war was partly accounted for by the growing application of machine tools in the engineering sector.[38] Employees also came under pressure to work diligently over long periods of time. The adult day shift at the Ordnance Works began at 6 a.m. and, punctuated by meal and rest breaks, continued until 8 p.m.[39] The dominant culture at Smith's Stamping Works was similarly one of continuous production, so that never 'was a hammer allowed to stand idle'.[40] Discipline within the factories could be applied with extreme vigour and was often supported by wartime legislation. Many workers accused of lethargy, lack of patriotism or worse were hauled before the munitions tribunals for punishment. The Amalgamated Society of Engineers suggested in 1915 that it should be allowed to handle cases of bad timekeeping among its members but this was rejected by the Engineering Employers' Association as impractical.[41] White and Poppe brought so many prosecutions of this and a similar kind that the firm's management even suggested that cases should be heard off the premises. A government enquiry into unrest reported in 1917 that long hours of work and severe nervous strain had exhausted many workers in the West Midlands, and the evidence of Coventry's workshops and factories no doubt contributed significantly to this assessment.[42]

The employment of women was one of the principal methods adopted by engineering firms in Coventry and elsewhere to alleviate their labour supply problems. Lower wage costs also brought financial benefits and this explains why male workers were sometimes dismissed when additional women were recruited. Some firms, including White and Poppe, Coventry Ordnance and Standard, used exceptionally large numbers of female operatives. Indeed, one of the main reasons why Standard gradually extended its activities in

Leamington Spa was the availability of a suitable pool of women workers.[43] Labour shortages even forced the chauvinistic Alfred Herbert to take on a substantial contingent of female employees and, although he argued that few women could ever become skilled mechanics, he did eventually acknowledge that they were well capable of performing tasks of a repetitive nature.[44]

The proportion of working women in Coventry, and their representation in the motor industry, increased sharply during the war period and although the range of jobs on which they were employed narrowed after 1918, they remained an important part of the city's engineering labour force. Some companies, such as Standard and Swift, used females on the shop floor for the first time, and a strong general trend developed of women taking up work formerly reserved for men. Shell-filling among other aspects of ammunition production was probably the largest single occupation for women, though in some factories they were employed in toolroom and engine departments. At Rover, for example, women stripped petrol engines and ground in the valves after the bench-test run, while at Siddeley-Deasy they replaced skilled men in engineering the pistons and cylinders to a close fit.[45] Large numbers of women were employed on aircraft construction, particularly trim-work on the wings and fuselage, though at Standard they were also engaged in other areas of airframe manufacture.

Trade union membership within Coventry's motor industry was significantly strengthened by the First World War. Recruitment to the Amalgamated Society of Engineers rose sharply, but the Workers' Union, which had established a branch in the city in 1906, experienced the most dramatic transformation with almost a threefold growth of membership between 1913 and 1919.[46] The expansion of the WU followed a number of bargaining successes in 1913, but was also the result of a sharp increase in the volume of semi-skilled machine work which accompanied the growth of wartime production.

Management attempts to dilute skilled jobs sometimes precipitated strong trade union opposition. The growing use of female labour was an early source of friction at Standard especially since, according to the National Union of Vehicle Builders, this could involve the dismissal of their own members.[47] In 1917 the NUVB threatened to initiate strike action if the company introduced more women into the woodworking aspects of airframe construction,[48] a challenge which appears to have curbed this particular example of de-skilling. At Daimler, the ASE managed to secure the exclusion of women from toolroom operations, while the company claimed that trade union opposition also prevented them from employing female labour in the aeroplane-erecting shop. Women represented about 15 per cent of Daimler's total labour force at the end of 1917, a figure which the Ministry of Munitions regarded as far too low.[49] What is uncertain, however, is how far this was the result of union pressure or simply a conservative management. In practice, considerable dilution occurred throughout the whole of Coventry's engineering industry, much of which provoked very little trouble. With respect to the motor trade, this was partly the result of the special circumstances of wartime production but also reflected the spirit of compromise which had emerged between the unions and employers in the pre-war period. The ASE in particular had developed a willingness to allow the spread of semi-skilled machine work in return for the higher earnings emanating from improved levels of output. Indeed, much of the trade union militancy surrounding dilution came from the WU whose leadership was anxious to ensure that the dilutees, many of whom were its members, received as near the full skilled rate as possible.[50]

The most serious labour agitation in Coventry during the war was concerned with workplace representation and the maintenance of living standards rather than the specific matter of skill erosion. These issues brought a series of strikes late in 1917 which seriously disrupted industrial production and caused dismay among officials at the Ministry of Munitions. Action by almost 700 toolroom workers brought chaos to the White and Poppe works in September which, while ostensibly concerned with the reinstatement of a sacked shop steward, was found by an investigating officer to mask 'a large number of collateral and miscellaneous grievances'. The same official noted that 'the air is very highly charged here and very little will cause a great blaze' and recommended the immediate establishment of a court of arbitration.[51] Another, more widespread, dispute brought work in the city to a halt during the weekend of 17–18 November and resulted in the loss of some 30,000 man hours. This was mainly caused by a serious local food shortage, but was also linked with other long-standing general grievances, especially inadequate and expensive housing.[52] A withdrawal of labour by engineering workers later in the same month was even more damaging because of its particular impact upon aircraft production. The central issue concerned the reluctance of a number of leading employers to recognise the legitimacy of shop-floor representation. The strike received the backing of the Coventry Engineering Joint Committee, a co-ordinating body involving all the skilled unions in the district. This support was largely dictated by the need felt by union officials to control the power of shop stewards by incorporating them within the movement's formal bureaucratic structure.[53] A compromise agreement was concluded with the employers in December which satisfied the CEJC and ended further talk of a general strike in Coventry. Significantly, the Ministry of Munitions, frustrated by the employers' intransigence, appointed a representative to attend the December negotiations, charged with preventing 'any conflict if at all possible'.[54] In effect, the agreement left workshop organisation in Coventry under the control of the official trade union organisation and was instrumental in isolating the more militant elements within the stewards' movement. Despite a number of limitations, the formula arrived at was an important initiative which led ultimately to the recognition of shop stewards within the negotiating framework evolved in the more significant agreements of 1919 and 1922. It became obvious in the interwar period, however, that many of Coventry's major employers were unhappy with the recognition of shop stewards as part of the industrial relations machinery.

Inter-union rivalry, resulting in particular from the spectacular rise of the WU, was exacerbated by the war and brought significant divisions within the movement as a whole. Yet increased membership, the strength and militancy of the WU and the development of shop-floor representation enhanced the ability of trade unions to influence the management of Coventry's engineering industry during the war years. Although many of these gains were not sustained in the very different economic and political climate which emerged after 1920, the war demonstrated the potential strength of organised labour and reinforced the city's reputation as an area prone to industrial unrest. This probably exerted some upward pressure on wage levels during the interwar years, but may also help to explain why in the same period most of the volume producers in the motor industry chose not to assemble their vehicles in Coventry.

Notes

[1]   *The Times*, 17 January 1916.
[2]   B.J. Beaven, 'The Growth and Significance of the Coventry Car Component Industry, 1895–1939', unpublished PhD thesis, De Montfort University, 1994, p. 81.
[3]   Imperial War Museum, Emp 45. 7, Advisory Committee on Women's War Employment, Report on Industrial Conditions in Coventry, November 1916, p. 3.
[4]   Ibid., pp. 2–3.
[5]   Committee on Women in Industry, Report, Cmd. 167 (1919), p. 54.
[6]   Beaven, 'The Growth and Significance of the Coventry Car Component Industry', p. 87.
[7]   C. Trebilcock, *The Vickers Brothers. Armaments and Enterprise* (Europa, London, 1977), p. 116.
[8]   R. Bacon, *From 1900 Onward*, (Hutchinson, London, 1940), p. 188.
[9]   Ibid., pp. 384–6.
[10]   Beaven, 'The Growth and Significance of the Coventry Car Component Industry', p. 85.
[11]   LBC, 96, 17 October 1914.
[12]   LBC, 124, 21 December 1914.
[13]   LBC, 192, 23 April 1915.
[14]   Beaven, 'The Growth and Significance of the Coventry Car Component Industry', p. 89.
[15]   Ibid., p. 86.
[16]   Price, op. cit., p. 32.
[17]   Atkinson, op. cit., p. 73.
[18]   G. Robson, *The Rover Story* (Stephens, Cambridge, 1981), p. 20; Foreman-Peck, 'Diversification and Growth', p. 120.
[19]   G.H. Frost, *Munitions of War* (BSA and Daimler, Birmingham and Coventry, n.d.), p. 127.
[20]   Brendon, op. cit., p. 176.
[21]   Ibid.
[22]   G.A.B. Dewar, *The Great Munitions Feat* (Constable, London, 1921), p. 168.
[23]   W.O. Bentley, op. cit., pp. 82–7.
[24]   PRO, MUN/5/214, 1962/3.
[25]   MBC, 276, 6 August 1914.
[26]   CRO, 1060/1/1, Deasy Company, Directors' Minutes, 7 February 1917.

27 MBC, 274, undated, details of balance sheets, 1911–21.
28 CRO, 1060/1/1, Deasy Company, Directors' Minutes, 1 June 1915.
29 Richardson, *Twentieth Century Coventry*, p. 129.
30 Davy, op. cit., p. 22.
31 R. Clinscales and B. Robertson, 'Flying Standards of World War One', *Air Pictorial*, June 1978, pp. 216–17.
32 MRC, MSS 226/ST/1/1/2/1, Standard Company, Directors' Minutes, 21 March 1917.
33 MRC,MSS 226/ST/1/1/2/1, Standard Company, Annual General Meeting, Report, 10 December 1915.
34 MRC, MSS 226/ST/1/1/2/1, Standard Company, Directors' Minutes, 28 June 1916.
35 Coventry and District Engineering Employers' Association (CDEEA), General Management Committee, Minutes, 8 June 1915.
36 D.C. Coleman, *Courtaulds. An Economic and Social History* (3 vols, Clarendon Press, Oxford, 1969), vol. 2, pp. 126–30.
37 PRO, MUN 2/28, 10 November 1917.
38 L. Hannah, *Electricity before Nationalisation* (Macmillan, London, 1979), p. 59.
39 *Coventry Evening Telegraph*, 7 June 1983.
40 Muir, op. cit., pp. 46–7.
41 CDEEA, Minutes, 11 October 1915.
42 Commission of Enquiry into Industrial Unrest, Report of the Commissioners for the West Midlands Area, Cmd. 8665 (1917), p. 9.
43 MRC, MSS 226/ST/1/1/2/1, Standard Company, Directors' Minutes, 11 July 1917.
44 'Committee on Women in Industry', p. 54.
45 PRO, MUN 2/28, 17 November 1917; 24 January 1917.
46 Carr, 'Engineering Workers', p. 76.
47 Amalgamated Society of Engineers, Coventry Branch Minutes, 16 August 1916.
48 PRO, MUN 2/28, 1 December 1917.
49 Ibid., 15 December 1917.
50 J. Hinton, *The First Shop Stewards' Movement* (Allen and Unwin, London, 1973), p. 220.
51 PRO, MUN 2/28, 29 September 1917.
52 Hinton, *The First Shop Stewards' Movement*, p. 223; Carr, 'Engineering Workers', pp. 64–74.
53 S. Tolliday, 'Trade Unions and Collective Bargaining in the Motor Industry, 1896–1970', paper presented to the Conference on the International Automobile Industry and its Workers: Past, present and future, Coventry (Lanchester) Polytechnic, June 1984.
54 PRO, MUN 2/28, 15 December 1917; Hinton, *The First Shop Stewards' Movement*, p. 225.

Chapter 5

Between the Wars: Mergers and Mass Production

Despite periodic setbacks which affected the economy a whole, the British motor industry made enormous gains during the interwar period and by the late 1930s was second only to the United States in the production and export of cars and commercial vehicles. This was achieved by expanding sales to both domestic and foreign markets. Shielded by tariff protection, the industry supplied 97 per cent of the home market by 1937, while falling car prices following the advent of mass-production techniques, together with the growth of consumer incomes, combined to bring motor-vehicle ownership within reach of a much wider public. Exports of cars and commercial vehicles also increased rapidly after the slump of the late 1920s and early 1930s, taking 14 per cent of the world market by 1937 which, though well behind the degree of penetration achieved by American manufacturers, was still greatly superior to that of the industry's European rivals.[1]

Expanded output was accompanied by major structural change. The immediate post-war boom attracted many new firms into the industry, a large number of which failed to survive the subsequent recessions and fierce price and other forms of competition. By 1939 only thirty-three car-producing firms remained in business compared with ninety-six in 1922, and of these just twenty were independent, with the remainder being under group control.[2] The principal amalgamations included Clement-Talbot and Darracq in the early 1920s, Morris and Wolseley in 1927 and the formation of the Hillman-Humber group in 1928. In addition, General Motors strengthened its position in the European car market through the acquisition of Vauxhall, also in 1928. By the end of the 1920s some 75 per cent of car production was dominated by Morris, Austin and Singer, but a decade later the market was controlled by the 'big six' which included Ford, Vauxhall, Rootes and Standard, Singer having fallen away as a volume manufacturer.

National trends were mirrored in Coventry, but the inability of a number of firms to realise their potential, coupled with the post-war growth of Morris and Austin in particular, meant that the city failed to realise its early promise as the dominant centre of large-scale motor-vehicle production. By 1939 Coventry's two largest car assemblers, Rootes and Standard, each accounted for 9–10 per cent of total output compared with over 26 per cent for Morris, the market leader. Rover, which on the eve of the First World War had been one of Britain's largest car firms, had effectively joined several other local companies as a specialist manufacturer, and was responsible for only 3.2 per cent of total output. The preponderance of relatively small-scale companies became central to the problems of Coventry's motor industry after 1945.

By 1931 there were eleven separate car-making firms in Coventry, though another forty had come and gone since 1918. Economic recovery from 1933 brought further entrants to the industry and by the end of the decade the number of manufacturers stood at eighteen, a total slightly below the immediate pre-First World War figure. Cars which enjoyed only a brief existence during this period included the Cooper, Warwick, Emms, Wigan-Barlow and Omega.[3] Calcott Brothers were taken over by Singer in 1926, but the collapse of Swift in 1931 represented perhaps the principal casualty among the Coventry car companies during the interwar years. However, several other important firms came close to bankruptcy, including Singer, Rover and Lea-Francis. The most successful of the new recruits were the specialist Alvis and Jaguar companies. Triumph, the cycle-manufacturing concern founded by Siegried Bettmann at the end of the nineteenth century, began car production in 1923 but experienced financial problems in the 1930s and was bought out by Standard in 1944. Earlier mergers involved the formation of Armstrong-Siddeley Motors in 1919, the absorption of Lanchester by Daimler in 1931 and the purchase of Riley by William Morris in 1938.

The number of car component firms in Coventry also fell, from around seventy-four in 1919 to sixty-four by 1936.[4] Overall, the components sector of the motor industry became increasingly dominated by a select group of large companies, including Pressed Steel, Dunlop, Pilkington, Triplex and Lucas. By 1935 bought-out components accounted for some 60 per cent of total car-production costs. In 1924–25 the Coventry firms of Rover, Standard, Humber and Armstrong-Siddeley were contracted to Lucas of Birmingham for the supply of electrical parts with a combined value of more than £271,000, but these orders were dwarfed by those of Morris which totalled over £840,000.[5] A number of major, if less dominant, component suppliers were located in Coventry. Carbodies, started by Bobby Jones, a former Daimler employee, became an important supplier of light-steel pressings in the 1930s, while Fisher and Ludlow in the same section of the industry opened a works at Tile Hill in 1938. Several companies founded before 1914 consolidated their position between the wars, including Coventry Climax, the Coventry Radiator Company and the British Piston Ring Company. In addition, Alfred Herbert remained important as a supplier of machine tools to the motor and other sectors of the engineering industry.

Several Coventry component manufacturers fell under the control of other business concerns, the best known of which was White and Poppe bought out by Dennis Brothers of Guildford at the end of 1919. The immediate reason for this was a disagreement between the partners concerning a proposal to diversify into car production. However, the adjustment to peacetime conditions confronted the firm with formidable problems, especially since William

Morris, one of its main pre-war customers, had transferred his business elsewhere. White and Poppe had been connected financially with Dennis for some time and this probably helped to smooth the negotiations for takeover and persuade Alfred White, in particular, to relinquish his interests in the firm he had helped to create. Thereafter, the firm specialised in the production of commercial vehicle engines and the operation was eventually transferred to the south east in 1935.

In 1923 William Morris formally acquired control of the coach-builders Hollick and Pratt, and the Coventry branch of the engine-makers Hotchkiss and Cie, both of which were already heavily committed to servicing the Cowley production lines. Interestingly, Lancelot Pratt was a close friend of Morris and in 1920 had provided him with a loan of £20,000 to help expand his Coventry works.[6] Although Morris rebuilt the Hollick and Pratt factory, which had been destroyed by fire in 1922, it became a centre for specialist coachwork while longer runs of standardised bodies were put elsewhere. Hotchkiss and Cie was the more significant purchase since as the Morris Engines branch it was of crucial importance to the group's total manufacturing programme. Shortly after Hotchkiss was taken over plans were agreed for an additional investment of £300,000 in order to double capacity at its Gosford Street premises. This, together with organisational changes, helped to make the plant a model of mass-production technology. Output of completed engines quadrupled in the two years after Morris gained control of the factory, reaching some 1,200 units per week. By the early 1930s production methods were said to equal best American practice, with machinery following in line according to the nature of the task rather than being grouped in particular areas of the factory. In 1929 Morris Engines opened a new works to the north of the city at Courthouse Green, which eventually became the focus of the firm's operations in Coventry and brought the closure of the old Hotchkiss plant in 1938.[7] William Morris's long association and affinity with Coventry was reflected in the role which he developed as a benefactor of the city's good causes.

Hollick and Pratt, and Hotchkiss and Cie, were acquired in order to guarantee the parent company a suitable supply of parts. However, an increasingly competitive market environment also explains why some Coventry component firms were amalgamated into larger organisations. One important example was Morris and Lister, the manufacturers of magnetos and other electrical equipment. The original partnership was dissolved in 1915, and the sale of the firm to Joseph Lucas in May 1930 was the result of financial instability caused by a lengthy period of severe price competition. The onset of war in 1914 increased the number of companies supplying magnetos so that during the 1920s prices and profits were badly depressed. By 1924 ML were selling some of their magnetos below cost but their attempt to persuade other firms to join them in a price maintenance scheme failed through lack of support. The company decided in the following year to trim overheads by halting research and 'in fact anything which involved immediate outlay for deferred results'.[8] Output was to be restricted to that which could be handled within existing resources. This was to be achieved by 'cutting out lines showing greatest loss, Magnetos with special features, least stable customers, etc.'[9] The company's problems were eased in 1929 with a large order for magnetos destined for the Austin 7, but heavy price competition from Lucas and Bosch later in the decade increased the firm's vulnerability to take takeover. Shortly after Lucas gained control of ML the Coventry works was closed as part of a rationalisation programme and magneto production was concentrated in Birmingham.[10]

Despite changes in the scale and organisation of the motor industry during the interwar years, the relationship between manufacturers and their component suppliers was similar to that already discussed for the pre-1914 period. The car-assemblers continued to benefit from credit provided by other firms. In 1935, for example, Coventry Motor Fittings was owed over £13,000 by Standard, which consumed almost all of its bank overdraft.[11] However, this facility was limited to the relatively short period of two months and assistance to other customers was very modest in scale, suggesting perhaps that a tightening up of trade credit had occurred since the earlier part of the century. The collapse of a motor company could still cause serious problems for its suppliers. Thus, Coventry Motor Panels lost some £1,300 when Swift went out of business in 1931, a significant embarrassment to a fairly small concern at a generally difficult time in the industry.[12] Similarly, the threat of heavy losses explains why Singer was saved from bankruptcy in 1936 by the action of its unsecured creditors in agreeing to a ten months' moratorium on debt payments. Apart from spreading development and production costs, important at a time when model changes were becoming increasingly frequent, discounts on large purchases and the deferment of orders during a slump in demand or disruptions to production were other ways in which car manufacturers secured financial advantages from the component firms. Thus, in ordering materials from White and Poppe in 1924 the Standard directors recorded in the company's minutes that 'should conditions warrant it, deliveries can be suspended at any time according to requirements'.[13]

As mass production increased, the relationship between the component firms and their customers was modified as orders became larger and the need for efficient systems of stock control more apparent. This led some component suppliers to locate close to their main customers. In the late 1930s, for example, Fisher and Ludlow built a new motor-body plant at Canley, close to the Standard works. This benefited both parties but in particular it enabled Standard, who co-operated in the design of the plant, to ensure a regular supply of quality products without the need for the company to invest its own resources. This type of arrangement, together with the financial benefits which accrued to the assemblers, helps to explain why most British motor companies came increasingly to rely upon bought-out components during the interwar period and why backward integration was less common than might have been expected. Although many car manufacturers experienced problems with the quality of bought-out components, this appears to have been a less significant issue than before the First World War, was probably due to improved production methods and to the high standards insisted upon by the companies in a period of growing competition which involved quality as well as price. Reliability, comfort and finish were important considerations for all the motor manufacturers, but particularly the specialist producers. Percy Martin, the managing director of Daimler, noted in 1924 that 'We find every day that there is much greater interest being taken in the springing and perfect riding of the car than almost any other feature.'[14]   Towards the end of the 1930s Jaguar found itself subject to long delays in the supply of some components, which had a major adverse impact upon delivery dates. More serious, however, in view of the high-quality image of the firm's products, was the purchase of large quantities of defective body panels which had to be contracted out again in order to be brought to the required finish. Jaguar not only changed to another manufacturer but also claimed heavy damages from its original supplier.[15]

Throughout the interwar years the supply of non-specialist cars generally exceeded demand, which pushed some manufacturers into frequent model changes in order to capture more of their rivals' trade and also to create new outlets for their vehicles. It became clear in the 1920s that the expandable market for car sales lay in the area of low-powered, relatively inexpensive vehicles which were also economical to run. This trend, which was reinforced by the onset of depression in 1929, continued into the 1930s and was generated by the market perceptions of the manufacturers as well as the autonomous preferences of customers. Between 1924 and 1938 the average price of new cars fell by almost 50 per cent. Morris initiated this trend when in 1921 he reduced the price of the Cowley and Oxford by 35 per cent and 22 per cent respectively compared with the figures for 1920. Other manufacturers followed and in addition several new models under 10 hp were introduced, including in 1922 the highly successful Austin 7. A perceptive appreciation of the relationship between car prices and sales explains why Morris changed his marketing strategy, but price competition was also facilitated by more efficient techniques of manufacture and by falling costs of components and raw materials. The rapid expansion of car output during the 1930s, involving the growing use of mass-production methods, saw the rise to prominence of the 'big six' and thus the consolidation of the major groups which were to dominate the industry after 1945.

Of the major Coventry firms, Calcott Brothers and Swift suffered the ultimate penalty for failing to respond quickly enough to the changing conditions of the 1920s. The Calcott light car had been one of the pioneers in its class before 1914, though it was relatively expensive compared with the equivalent versions produced by Singer and Standard.   New models were introduced in the early 1920s but these were high-powered cars which proved expensive to develop and enjoyed only a limited clientele. In practice, however, the company would have had difficulty in expanding into the volume production of cheap motor vehicles since its premises were extremely cramped and cash flow had been insufficient to generate the large resources needed for expansion. William Calcott, the company's chairman, died in 1924 and this, together with a net loss of over £26,000 in 1925, created the situation for a takeover by Singer in 1926. At the time of its demise Calcotts had produced a total of some 2,500 cars.[16]

Swift was the oldest and most prestigious of the Coventry motor firms to enter liquidation during the interwar period. Although the 1,100 cc Swift Ten brought the company considerable success in the Edwardian years, it was no match for the new models of the post-war era, being expensive to purchase and operate and respected chiefly for its durability rather than performance.[17] The company lacked positive leadership and a constructive approach to forward planning. Costs were kept high by the retention of antiquated production methods and a failure to rationalise, reflected in the manufacture of several completely separate engine types. It was not until 1930 that a serious attempt was made to invade the lower end of the market with the 8 hp Cadet, but this came too late to save the company from bankruptcy in the following year. No dividends were paid on ordinary shares after 1919 as turnover dropped to uneconomic levels, while several years of exceptionally heavy losses in the 1920s drained the company of its capital and inhibited the investment which might have recovered its fortunes. Foreclosure on debts owed to Swift's suppliers brought in the receiver and precipitated the firm's final collapse.[18]

R.J. Overy claims that of the eighty-nine car firms which existed in 1920 no more than a handful were of real significance, with Singer and Rover being the only Coventry manufacturers represented in his list.[19] Yet the subsequent performance of these two companies was a disappointment, although for a time Singer appeared to be establishing itself as one of the dominant forces in the industry. The 10 hp Singer introduced in 1912 was the first and one of the most successful light cars of the pre-war period. Its successor, the Senior was another popular model which helped to sustain the company during the 1920s, while the launch of the Junior in September 1926 took Singer into the 'baby'-car market in direct opposition to the Austin 7. Although well behind Morris and Austin in terms of market penetration, by 1929 Singer was Britain's third-largest car manufacturer with an output of around 27,000 vehicles. A dramatic reversal of fortune occurred in the following decade as the firm lurched on the edge of bankruptcy before it was rescued by the combined efforts of its creditors, bankers and major shareholders and reconstructed as Singer Motors in 1936. Despite the injection of fresh capital, the new company failed to climb back into the 'big six', partly because it diversified into the quality market which was already well catered for.

Singer emerged from the First World War in relatively robust condition. It had a popular light car, a sound financial base and a progressive and experienced senior management. The key element in the company's subsequent decline was the financial burden imposed by the purchase from BSA of a large factory on the Coventry Road, Birmingham, intended for the mass production of the Junior. W.E. Bullock, Singer's managing director, who had first-hand knowledge of American factory organisation, was anxious by the late 1920s to consolidate the company's role as a volume car producer, but despite the earlier purchase of Coventry Premier and Calcotts, the firm was handicapped by a shortage of factory accommodation. This explains the acquisition of the new works which, was not only a financial albatross, but with its 34 acres of floor space distributed between six storeys, was not even particularly well suited to the large-scale manufacture of motor vehicles. This was a case of ambition overcoming sound business judgement. The additional overheads proved too great at a time when the industry was entering recession and when competition in the small-car market was being intensified by the advent of the Morris Minor. New models, including light commercial vehicles, were introduced in a desperate attempt to stimulate sales, but this policy proved expensive and sometimes highly unprofitable. In 1931 Singer's larger cars were said to be a particular drag on the company's financial resources.[20] Economies were made, but turnover remained too depressed to prevent a net loss of over £200,000 in 1935 and the onset of the crisis which led eventually to reconstruction.[21]

Growing output, based on the popularity of Owen Clegg's 12 hp four-cylinder light car, appeared to leave Rover on the eve of the First World War poised for future success. Readjustment was swift after 1918 but sales, production and profits dipped in 1923, with the company's subsequent financial position remaining extremely precarious until a limited and slow recovery was achieved in the mid-1930s. With the exception of 1939, no dividends were paid to shareholders from 1923 until 1936. On several occasions during this period Rover was saved from collapse only by the willingness of its bankers to extend substantial overdraft facilities. Early in 1927 the Midland Bank's head office noted in connection with the company's overdraft that 'It must be distinctly understood that £250,000 is to be the extreme limit',[22] reflecting impatience with Rover's mounting financial problems. Nevertheless, support continued to be provided, and when in 1929 the Midland expressed reservation on the matter of a loan of £30,000 to purchase the New Meteor Works in Helen Street, Coventry, the account was quickly taken over by Lloyds. Although Rover's debts were cleared by 1935, profit margins remained low on a range of vehicles developed for the luxury end of the middle-class market. Unlike Singer, Rover failed to achieve even transitory success in the volume production of cars.

In 1922 Rover car sales totalled 6,466 vehicles but by the end of 1928 were down by 40 per cent on this figure. Much of the capital borrowed by the company during the 1920s was used to hold stock rather than promote further development. At the beginning of 1926, for example, Rover held finished cars to the value of some £300,000.[23] Even by 1939 the firm produced only just over 11,000 cars, or approximately one-fifth that of Standard, Coventry's leading producer in volume terms. Although the 8 hp twin-cyclinder air-cooled Rover proved very popular in the immediate post-war period, its market position was increasingly undermined from 1923 by the Austin 7. By that time, too, the 12 hp model was becoming outdated and uncompetitive, so that sales declined as Morris cars in particular became a serious challenge in this sector of the market. Peter Poppe was recruited as consulting engineer from Dennis Brothers to help design a replacement for the Rover 12 but his engine for the new 14/45 proved noisy, underpowered and high in fuel consumption so that deliveries were stopped in 1925, just a few months after the car's official launch. The loss of income which resulted from this deal was a major factor in the company's heavy deficit for that year. A modified version of the car, incorporating a larger engine, was introduced in 1926 but it too failed to attract the motoring public.

Poor-quality management appears to have been responsible for the company's weak performance after 1922. The decision to discontinue the ageing Rover 12 came relatively late, while its replacement was introduced prematurely, before the vehicle had been adequately tested and its faults corrected. Although the Rover 8 sold well in its early years, it was technically inferior to the Austin 7 and its bodywork was of less attractive appearance. It was superseded in 1924 by the water-cooled four-cylinder Nine which evolved into the successful 10/25, and remained in production until 1933. Yet Rover failed to compete on equal terms in the small-car market, reflecting an inability to arrange production in the most cost-effective manner. Thus, output at the Tyseley works in Birmingham, which was purchased in 1919 for manufacturing the Rover 8, was poorly organised, limiting the degree of price competition which the company could engage in.[24]

Following Harry Smith's retirement through ill-health in 1922, Rover experienced a lengthy period of indifferent and unsettled management which brought staff changes and boardroom disputes. J.K. Starley, who became managing director in 1923, was gradually shorn of his authority and in 1928, while on a business trip to Australia, his employment with the company was formally terminated.[25] In the following year Peter Poppe was dismissed from his post as works manager after a clash with one of the firm's directors. Smith, Starley and Poppe shared responsibility for some of Rover's deficiencies in the 1920s, but intervention by board members in the running of the company renders it difficult to apportion blame in any more than a general sense. Lack of experience among Rover's directors also contributed to some of the problems of this period. W.D. Sudbury, who became chairman in 1928, probably by virtue of his large holding in the firm, was a Yorkshire-based food importer with little knowledge of the motor industry. The same criticism applied to Colonel Frank Searle, who assumed responsibility for the company's management in May 1928. Searle enjoyed some success in restoring Rover's ailing fortunes, but in 1931 his failure to maintain adequate financial control and his policy of rapid expansion took the firm into the heaviest deficit in its history. The significance of these managerial problems was exacerbated by the general economic recession. Rover lacked firm and informed decison-making at a time when it was most needed.

Recovery began under the guidance of H.E. Graham and Spencer Wilks. Graham, a chartered accountant, was appointed financial director in 1932 and quickly introduced a tight and effective method of cost control. He also negotiated extended credit terms with two of Rover's major suppliers and a higher overdraft limit from Lloyds Bank. Together, these manoeuvres were decisive in saving the company from liquidation. Spencer Wilks was originally hired to replace Peter Poppe and served as works manager before his elevation to managing director in January 1933. Wilks had the benefit of substantial experience in the motor industry, including a period as joint managing director of Hillman, and his insistence upon careful regulation of output, coupled with the introduction of a revised range of quality cars, gradually placed the company on a much improved financial basis.[26]

With the decline of Singer, Rootes and Standard became Coventry's major volume car-producers during the 1930s. The Rootes group had its origins in the commercial side of the industry, William Rootes senior having built up one of the largest sales outlets in the south of England from his base at Maidstone in Kent. His two sons, William and Reginald, extended the business after the First World War by acquiring the agencies of George Heath in Birmingham and Tom Garner in Manchester. The brothers complemented each other well, William having been an apprentice with Singer, but with a particular flair for marketing, while Reginald was an accountant with employment experience in the civil service. Their achievements in the 1920s were also based upon an association with successful motor manufacturers, including Herbert Austin, though that particular sales contract was lost following Rootes's acquisition of Hillman and Humber with the potential conflict of interest which this involved.[27] William Rootes bought into the equity of the Standard Motor Company in 1920, but the brothers' first real incursion into the manufacturing side of the industry was in 1925 when they gained control of the old-established London coach-building partnership of Thrupp and Maberly. After an unsuccessful attempt to take over Clyno and to buy a controlling interest in Standard, William and Reginald did manage to purchase the smaller Hillman operation in 1928, which enjoyed a favourable reputation even though by that time it had a poor range of cars.[28] In the following year Humber, which had experienced financial problems for some time, began to be assimilated into the expanding Rootes empire. Although the company attacked the small-car market in the 1920s, its output, which peaked at just 4,000 units in 1929, was never large enough to compete effectively with Morris, Austin or Singer. Outdated production methods also pushed up

Humber's costs and prices to unacceptable levels.[29] Rootes's interests were expanded further in the next decade through the acquisition of a number of other motor and related firms, including Sunbeam and Clement-Talbot, both of which had a successful history in motor sport.

The Rootes Group became well established during the 1930s as one of Britain's leading motor manufacturers. This owed much to the business talent of William Rootes, whose foresight in taking over ailing firms enabled the total enterprise to be assembled relatively cheaply. However, development capital was made available and by 1931 the Hillman and Humber works had been reorganised and new machinery installed to facilitate an increase in output.[30] A rather authoritarian style of management was developed in the 1930s, reflected in the tough approach which was frequently adopted during labour disputes. The working environment was closely regulated to aid labour productivity and in 1934 time-study experts were introduced at both the Hillman and Humber plants.[31] At first there was little attempt to rationalise product development, with Humber being allowed considerable autonomy under its chairman, Colonel Cole, who remained with the firm until 1943. Gradually, however, Humber became identified with high-quality cars, while Hillman concentrated upon family saloons for the popular market. In practice, the group's prosperity relied heavily upon the success of one model, the Hillman Minx, which filled an important gap in the 10 h.p. market when it was introduced in 1931. The Minx quickly became the price leader for its class and by the late 1930s was still managing to outsell its growing band of rivals. As the firm's historian notes, 'It ensured Rootes a secure place among Britain's big six motor manufacturers and became the greatest commercial success of all their models.'[32]

After the Armistice of 1918, Standard, like many other motor companies, found considerable difficulty in adjusting to peacetime conditions. An overdraft of £130,000, largely the result of late payment on wartime Government contracts, left the company with a liquidity problem which impeded the development and production of new vehicles for the post-war era. Shortages of components and the completion of military orders further delayed a return to normal production so that during 1919 the company manufactured a total of only 350 cars.[33] Despite Standard's success in the construction of airframes and aero-engines, Maudslay was determined to return to motor-vehicle work and in March 1917 the company began to plan its post-war strategy. Some of the results of this followed a year later with numerous applications for patents under the Standard name. Yet according to Maudslay, the Armistice 'had come with unexpected suddenness' so that as an interim measure the company was forced to reintroduce the pre-war Model S and a variant incorporating a more powerful engine.[34] It was not until July 1921 that Standard announced its first new model of the post-war years, the SLO 11.6 hp tourer. This was a four-seater family car which sold well, partly because of the particular effectiveness of the Maudslay-designed weather-proof hood and side-screens.

Standard was responsible for almost 5 per cent of total car production in 1929. This was achieved by concentrating upon a range of well-tried and reasonably popular models, allied to a cautious financial policy directed towards reinvestment rather than the payment of large dividends. Substantial capital went into buildings and machinery so that by the end of 1924 the Canley works had a floor space of some 10 acres, representing an increase in accommodation of more than 100 per cent in two years. Yet Standard's failure to yield a dividend in the five years up to 1931, and the heavy losses sustained in 1927–28, were caused by weaknesses within the company as well as by the general recession in the industry following the onset of the slump. In 1927 the company once again flirted unsuccessfully with the market for large cars when it introduced its first post-war six-cylinder model, while in the following year sales of the early version of the Standard Nine were also disappointing, principally, claimed Maudslay, because of its 'stumpy appearance'.[35] A revised version of the Nine was launched in September 1928 and soon began to sell in significant numbers. The company's main problem towards the end of this decade was the financial embarrassment which resulted from its overcommitment to a large Australian order, the withdrawal of which in 1927 was said to have been responsible for a 25 per cent reduction in turnover compared with the previous year.[36] Without the timely assistance of Barclays Bank it seems almost certain that Standard would have been absorbed within the developing Rootes empire. This major error of judgement was based on the assumption that growth in overseas markets would have revived the firm's prospects in a period of rising domestic competition. However, the very low profit margin which had been accepted on the Australian contract hints strongly of desperation rather than a considered appreciation of alternative outlets.

Standard's overdraft stood at £160,000 in 1930, but two years later this had been transformed into a credit balance of over £200,000, pointing to a sharp change of fortune in the company's trading activities. Record sales of 2,400 cars were reported in September 1933, taking the firm's share of the market for that year to around 9 per cent, where it hovered for most of the remainder of the decade. This improvement was partly the result of a growth in foreign sales. By 1932 the company traded in 33 countries and enjoyed an extensive overseas network for sales, spares and service. Yet the real impetus for recovery was the domestic success of the revised Standard Nines, over 9,000 of which were manufactured in the two-year period covering 1929–30.[37] In the twelve months up to the end of 1931 Standard's share of total car output among the 'big six' more than doubled, projecting the company into the realms of the mass producers.

Standard's escalating car output in the 1930s coincided with John Black's involvement with the company. Demobilised after the First World War with the rank of captain, Black was recruited by William Hillman for his administrative and organisational skills and rose eventually to become the company's joint managing director with Spencer Wilks. When the Rootes brothers gained control of Hillman, Black moved to Standard where he became Maudslay's personal assistant. Although he invested some of his own capital in Standard, Black's appointment was principally designed to strengthen the management team and help rescue the company from its financial crisis. After a period as general manager, Black was elevated to joint managing director in September 1933, with 'responsibility for the executive management of the company'.[38] He became sole managing director after Maudslay's death at the end of 1934.

Black was reported to have been an inveterate organiser, his interests ranging from the restructuring of the company's system of manufacture to planning, with military precision, arrangements for the works outing. By the close of 1931 the whole of the assembly shops at Canley had been reorganised and mechanised to facilitate mass production, with ten complete cars leaving the assembly line every working hour. In October 1932 it was reported that sales were 80 per cent up on the previous year and that profits had almost trebled, suggesting that more efficient manufacturing systems had yielded a significant increase in productivity. Throughout the 1930s Standard's management appears to have placed continuing emphasis upon the organisation of production, including appropriate investment in machinery and factory accommodation and it was this which enabled the company's output to soar from around 8,000 vehicles in 1931 to almost 55,000 in 1939, while over the same period the workforce hardly fluctuated at all.

Another aspect of Standard's recovery plan was the introduction of a system of bonus payments on a team output basis designed to stimulate greater personal effort among the workforce.[39] Despite Black's autocratic style of management, labour disputes at Standard were kept to a minimum during the 1930s and the firm was even notable for the high degree of unionisation among its women sewing machinists. Like other motor manufacturers, Standard's management could act arbitrarily and unfairly, but the general impression is one of industrial paternalism which worked reasonably well and was possible because of the company's increasingly healthy financial status. Both of these features of the firm's development are reflected in the wish of the directors expressed in 1937 that holidays with pay should be introduced, since 'something in the way of distribution or part of the profits to the work-people was required'.[40]

Standard's chairman said of Black in 1938 that 'To his enthusiasm, his untiring energy, his far-sighted grasp of the motor industry and his loyalty to the company ... I attribute very largely the position in which the company stands today, not only in the motor industry but in the country as a whole.'[41] Black's shrewd business mind and his strong personality are central to an explanation of Standard's growth during the 1930s, but the engineering design team also deserve recognition for producing a range of cars which satisfied popular taste, including the famous Flying Standards introduced in 1936. In addition, Maudslay's purchase of the Canley site in 1916 proved extremely good business for it facilitated both the concentration of production and its expansion as demand for the company's products increased.

One of the most striking and persistent characteristics of Coventry's motor-car industry during the interwar period was its large number of specialist manufacturers. Pre-war firms such as Riley, Lea-Francis, Daimley and Siddeley-Deasy were joined after 1918 by two other famous marques, Alvis and Jaguar, while Rover and Triumph, both of which at one time appeared likely to invade the mass market, eventually settled for the production of relatively expensive quality vehicles. Availability of skilled labour and access to component suppliers were probably the key factors in accounting for the city's exceptionally large contingent of specialist motor firms. Bought-out components spread research, development and production costs which could be particularly important for small companies with limited resources. When William Lyons first arrived in Coventry, he purchased Standard chassis and engines for his Swallow cars in very small batches according to his own cash-flow situation. Some small firms even operated a semi-barter arrangement, exchanging one or two finished vehicles for components. Even so, most of the specialist manufacturers experienced frequent and often severe liquidity crises. Triumph, Lea-Francis and Alvis all came perilously close to collapse in the 1930s and Riley was saved from bankruptcy only by the personal and last-minute intervention of William Morris. Outmoded production systems, vulnerability to sudden fluctuations in demand and the expense of maintaining a racing team were particular concerns which threatened the economic stability of the specialist car firms.

Although Rover, Armstrong-Siddeley and other firms developed a reputation for good-quality saloon cars, some of Coventry's best-known specialist producers were particularly famous for their sports, touring and racing models, including Lea-Francis, Riley and especially Alvis. Alvis was founded in 1919 by T.G. John, formerly works manager at Siddeley-Deasy. John's manufacturing policy aimed at that sector of the motoring public concerned with style and performance and as managing director he firmly resisted pressure to enter the mass market, informing shareholders in 1934 that 'we have never left our straight and narrow path'.[42] With the design team of G.T. Smith-Clarke and W.M. Dunn, both of whom had previously worked for Daimler, Alvis made a range of cars in the 1920s and 1930s which were well received for their good looks and quality engineering. Yet by 1935 sales, at about 1,000 cars a year, were beginning to flag and in response to what was perceived as 'changing conditions in the Motor Car Industry' the company diversified into aero-engines and armoured vehicles.[43] However, this initiative proved only partially successful since the company failed to attract significant government orders for aero engines, partly because of what was felt to be its 'sparsely equipped, old fashioned factory'.[44] Alvis may have been successful in keeping down costs during the interwar period but to some extent, at least, this was at the expense of investment in modern plant and equipment.

With hindsight, the most significant development in the specialist car market in the 1930s was the rise of Jaguar, which had its origins in the Blackpool-based Swallow Sidecar Company founded by William Lyons and William Walmsley in 1922. Lyons appears to have been the main force in the partnership, with a gift for motor-bodywork design and strong entrepreneurial qualities. In 1927 he concluded an agreement which allowed Swallow bodies to be fitted to the Austin 7, an imaginative combination of style and technical achievement which quickly proved a commercial success. Chassis eventually arrived at Blackpool station at the rate of fifty to sixty a week where they were tied together and towed to the factory in batches of six. The increase in turnover initiated a search for larger premises and in 1928 Coventry was selected as a suitable base for expansion, partly because of the availability of suitable leasehold accommodation, but also because, as Lyons later recalled, 'we would have a better chance of work people and materials'.[45] Swallow coach-built bodies were attached to chassis and engines manufactured by a number of motor companies, including Fiat, Swift and Standard, the latter becoming the firm's sole supplier from 1932, a position it retained until after the Second World War. The first car displaying the company's own SS badge appeared in 1932 and was based on the Standard Sixteen. In the circumstances of the period, a different and more distinctive trade name seemed desirable. The result was the introduction of the Jaguar marque in 1935, though the SS brand letters did not finally disappear until 1945.

SS and Jaguar cars sold well during the 1930s, with demand often far in advance of supply so that some customers were obliged to wait many months for delivery. Shortly before the onset of the Second World War the company employed a workforce of 1,400 and had a weekly output of around 200 cars, a comparatively large operation for a firm of that type. Unlike most other specialist motor manufactures, the company remained in profit throughout the 1930s, though efficiency was almost certainly seriously depressed by the cramped conditions in which the vehicles were assembled. Credit for Jaguar's success in the period belongs to William Lyons for his belief in the marketability of cars which were stylish in design, performed reliably and well, and yet were within the price range of a significant body of motoring enthusiasts. Apart from their 'rakish look', the cars competed well on price with the popular SS 100, for example, costing much less than its German rivals.[46] But Lyons also benefited enormously from the willingness of Standard to supply chassis and engines of the appropriate type and quality for the SS and Jaguar models, and in this he was particularly indebted to John Black's personal interest in high-performance cars.

Daimler's reputation for craftsmanship, and the company's particular significance within the history of the industry as a whole, elevated it to a special position as one of Coventry's premier motor manufacturers during the interwar period. Yet competition was severe and Rolls-Royce, Bentley and other prestige marques consumed a large share of what was a rather limited market. All the quality-car firms experienced financial hardship in the late 1920s, but Daimler's plight seems to have been particularly serious. Sales fell sharply in 1927–28, taking the balance sheet into deficit, and even greater losses were recorded in the following year. No dividends were paid between 1929 and 1936 and it was not until near the end of the 1930s that signs appeared of a genuine recovery in the company's prospects.

Among the reasons for Daimler's predicament was the retention of the sleeve-valve engine well beyond its useful life. Despite F.W. Lanchester's work on it during his nineteen years as consulting engineer to the company, the Knight engine was never completely perfected, suffering in particular from excessive smoke emission.[47] Daimler's production methods in the 1920s fell behind those adopted by some of its major competitors and an extravagant range of vehicle models also exerted upward pressure on costs. In 1931 the company's bankers noted of Daimler's dwindling car sales that 'there is no doubt price has something to do with this as well as performance'.[48] These problems partly reflected the company's failure during the 1920s to invest sufficiently in modern capital equipment. The report of a special internal inquiry into the company's financial position indicated in 1929 'the necessity for the installation of up-to-date machine toll equipment', and regretted that during the last ten years only the relatively small sum of £70,000 had been invested in this way.[49] In addition, the practice of using Stratton-Instone as the sole distributor for Daimler cars was attacked on the grounds that the commission rate of 20–25 per cent was unduly high. This arrangement probably resulted from Ernest Instone's personal links with Daimler, for at one time he had been the company's secretary and later its general manager. Under pressure from BSA, the parent company, a wider range of distribution outlets was sought in 1932 as part of the firm's recovery strategy.[50]

Daimler's initial response to the crisis of the late 1920s was to introduce whatever economies were immediately possible and to realise some of the firm's liquid assets. Its holding in Singer was run down and in 1931 the company's own hire business was sold off to help reduce its bank overdraft. Savings were made in staffing, including the dismissal of Frederick Lanchester in 1929. The bodywork department was closed in the same year, though this was not particularly cost effective in the short run since it left Daimler with unusable coachwork valued at around £40,000. Daimler's problems became so severe that in the spring of 1931 motor-car production virtually ceased, and for a short period the firm was kept in business by its commercial vehicle and aero-engine work. The main initiative designed to stimulate recovery involved the purchase in January 1931 of the Lanchester Motor Company of Birmingham, one of its rivals in the luxury market but a firm with which it had maintained close contacts over many years. Soon after its sale the Lanchester company's stock and most of its plant was transferred to Coventry and the premises which had been vacated were occupied by another subsidiary of BSA. This takeover enabled Daimler to manufacture a range of smaller cars without the danger of undermining its own reputation in the prestige market, since the new models would carry the Lanchester marque. It also provided the opportunity to introduce the poppet-valve engine developed by the company's general manager, Lawrence Pomeroy, without the likely adverse publicity which would have surrounded the demise of the Silent Knight engine. Although the Lanchester cars of the 1930s were said to be sluggish downmarket versions of their Daimler counterparts, they did help to pilot the company through one of the most difficult times in its history and, according to Percy Martin, rescue it from the verge of total collapse in the exceptionally grim period of 1931–32.[51]

This survey of the Coventry motor industry between the wars has indicated a number of factors which influenced the pace and shape of change. One particularly material and recurring theme has concerned the external environment, especially policies of price and design adopted by major competitors located elsewhere in the country, such as Morris and Austin. By contrast, the remainder of this chapter focuses upon three essentially domestic, but key elements, namely management, finance and labour.

Generalisations on the nature and importance of management are fraught with danger. In this instance the limitations of the data has rendered it impossible to assess performance across a range of companies in precise quantitative terms, using such criteria as productivity and rates of return. Moreover, decision-making was frequently highly pragmatic in character and not readily amenable to neat forms of classification. The Coventry motor manufacturers were often pushed into certain lines of action through practical necessity rather than choice, with forward planning normally limited to short periods and projected initiatives easily reversed by falling sales and financial crises. The special relationship between motor suppliers and their agents was a further complication. Perceptions of market trends and the appropriate product response could bring together sales and manufacturing interests within the industry to a point where the lines of responsibility for particular decisions became blurred and difficult to follow. The sleek body styles adopted by Lea-Francis, Alvis and Jaguar in the 1930s reflected the influence of London-based motor distributors as well as Coventry design specialists, and illustrate the point that management was a concept without clear boundaries.

The outstanding feature of the management of Coventry's motor industry during this period was the powerful influence exercised by a small number of company chairmen and managing directors. Although attention may gravitate naturally towards such men as Maudslay, Lyons and the Rootes brothers, and in the process obscure the contribution of other individuals, a clear difference of management style may be identified, for example, between Rover in the 1920s, where responsibility for decision-making was widely diffused, and the majority of companies where a more personalised approach was apparent. In some cases, like Jaguar, this was based upon financial control of the company, while in others ability and sheer force of personality produced managers of great personal stature. John Black was probably the most striking example in the

1930s of an autocratic-type manager whose personal authority permeated his company's activities. Alick Dick recalled that when he joined Standard in 1933 his impression of management 'was one of great dominance by the managing director (Black). His word was all powerful and he was feared.'[52] Yet Black, like many of his contemporaries, had a strong sense of paternalism which, combined with his business success, brought him respect among his work-force and in the industry as a whole.

This strongly hierarchical management structure helps to explain the different stages of company development. The commercial experience of the Rootes brothers was important in the construction of their motor empire, based as it was, in the first instance, upon the takeover and development of existing operations rather than the establishment of new ones. Similarly, the imagination of William Lyons in the art of motor-body design led to the creation of what was essentially an assembly firm, utilising the technology and production facilities of other manufacturers. Reginald Maudslay was also primarily a designer, concerned particularly with the comfort of his vehicles, including all-weather protection.[53] Many Standard models were widely praised for their quality of finish and range of accessories but this was partly the result of Maudslay's personal inclinations rather than a planned attempt at non-price competition. By contrast, John Black was a skilful organiser and it was this talent which contributed greatly to the rise of Standard as a volume car-producer in the 1930s. The attempt by Singer to break into the mass market in the late 1920s and the diversification of Alvis into military equipment in 1935 were other turning points which appear to be directly attributable to the power of individual managing directors.

The professional longevity of some of Coventry's leading personalities in the motor industry created its own problems. Although Reginald Maudslay had a flair for business, his commercial judgement could be surprisingly obtuse, as his somewhat blinkered pursuit of foreign orders in the late 1920s indicates. However, Maudslay did have the foresight to recruit Black to help strengthen his management personnel, though at the time he was under some pressure from shareholders to reverse a run of bad results. John Siddeley's management style also combined elements of autocracy and paternalism but, in addition, he remained for many years the engineering inspiration behind the Armstrong-Siddeley motor business.[54] Although Siddeley toyed briefly with a light car, his general development programme was firmly directed towards powerful and expensive limousines. Siddeley's cars gained a special reputation for craftsmanship, but their limited market orientation inevitably served to restrict the firm's growth potential. The long influence of Percy Martin and Edward Manville, respectively managing director and chairman at Daimler for almost thirty years, may well have placed similar constraints upon the company's development. Reports of poor management were circulating at Daimler by the early 1930s and it does seem likely that some of the problems of that period, such as underinvestment, late diversification into small vehicles and excessive loyalty to the sleeve-valve engine were symptoms of entrepreneurial fatigue. One of the criticisms directed at entrepreneurship in the motor industry during the interwar period concerns a supposed reluctance to adopt Fordist methods in order to achieve high levels of mass production.[55] Instead, manufacturers adopted a strategy of frequent model changes rather than low-priced standardised vehicles in order to retain or expand their customer base. The practice of using bought-out components rather than fully integrated processes of manufacture on the American model is said to be symptomatic of this form of supply-side conservatism. In practice, however, the market for cars in Britain was essentially middle class, and one which favoured variations in model type for reasons of taste and status.

Price was an important factor in competition, especially for the volume producers, though the Armstrong-Siddeley board minutes reveal that even manufacturers of cars directed at the upper end of the market could be highly sensitive to this aspect of the marketing process. Despite significant price reductions, model changes remained the central feature of many car firms' competitive strategy during the 1930s. The Hillman Minx, for example, launched in 1931, was given a facelift in 1934 and completely rebodied the following year. During the same period the car was produced in several different versions catering for the touring, sports and saloon markets. This was niche marketing of a high order, though the nature of its impact on the firm's balance sheet remains debateable.[56] In practice, most manufacturers introduced frequent technical and styling modifications, as well as changes to their range of accessories. By 1938 the 'big six' car manufacturers were between them responsible for forty different engine types, many of them produced in relatively small batches.

Attention to the demands of its niche market was particularly important to the specialist motor manufacturers. Armstrong-Siddeleys, for example, were said to be suitable cars for the gentry, along with Bentleys, Lanchesters and Rolls-Royces. Significantly, in 1928 the firm introduced a 12 hp six-cylinder model designed to appeal to 'the daughters of gentlemen'.[57] This image may help to explain why Armstrong-Siddeleys reputedly enjoyed considerable popularity among colonial officials and expatriates. Niche marketing of this type was aided by appropriately constructed advertising campaigns, the development of a network of carefully selected and supported motor agents and repair depots, and success in motor sport.

Alvis was another Coventry-based firm which used motor sport as part of its marketing strategy. During the 1920s Alvis was one of only three British firms – the others were Bentley and Sunbeam – which regularly took part in the major track and road events, enjoying considerable success.[58] Apart from the glamour associated with motor racing, the sport enjoyed considerable publicity value if it could be demonstrated that the vehicles were able to withstand punishing driving conditions. Failure, however, could have the reverse effect, as Singer discovered following an unsatisfactory performance at the Ards TT race of 1935. As Atkinson notes, 'The much publicised series of crashes did more than lose Singer the race, it also lost the public's faith in Singer to produce sports cars.'[59]

Most Coventry motor companies continued to function between the wars at relatively low levels of capitalisation. It was not until the mid-1930s that the Standard board made plans for increasing the firm's capital to £500,000, a figure less than that achieved by Austin nearly twenty years earlier. The smaller manufacturers operated on the slimmest of budgets. When SS cars went public in 1935 the capital issue amounted to only £100,000 in preference shares and £35,000 in ordinaries.[60] This financial conservatism probably emanated from considerations of company control and an acute awareness of the dangers of overexpansion. The problems experienced by Singer following the purchase of its Birmingham plant in 1929 were a sharp reminder of the consequences of excessive investment in a period of economic uncertainty. The marked increase in Standard's capital in the late 1930s was a natural concomitant of the company's growth but it also reflected the changing pattern of management following the founder's death in 1934, as well as the arrival of a more favourable business climate generally.

Investment in factory space and replacement or additional machinery was inhibited by the slender resources of the majority of firms in the Coventry motor industry and, in some instances, perhaps, by their unwillingness to sacrifice dividends for capital development. This limited both physical production capacity and the incorporation of new technology into the manufacturing process, particularly since for much of the interwar period cash flow was by itself insufficient to finance major capital projects. Yet the extent to which progress was impeded by low capitalisation varied between different firms. Standard was particularly fortunate in benefiting from a large site with room for considerable factory growth. In addition, in 1933 the company sold some of its land at Canley for residential development which served the dual purpose of facilitating further capital investment and providing housing for potential employees at a time of growing labour shortage.[61] Standard's success after 1933 became self-generating since its long production runs – this stage represented some 15 per cent to 20 per cent of average manufacturing costs[62] – and profitability increasingly made it possible to expand the works and buy and install expensive new machinery, though it soon became evident that to secure the company's position as a volume producer required substantial assistance from the capital market.

Building- and assurance-society finance was a new and important source of support in the 1920s and beyond when, for example, Bobby Jones of Carbodies and William Lyons of Swallow each received large advances from the Coventry Permanent Economic Building Society.[63] The acquisition of Humber, Hillman and Commer by the Rootes brothers was facilitated by assistance from the Prudential Assurance Society, which also helped with the purchase in 1935 of Clement Talbot and Sunbeam.[64] Of more general significance, however, was bank credit which continued to be provided for both working capital and investment projects. Riley Motors acquired the independent Riley Engine Company in 1931 with a bank loan of almost £39,000,[65] while in the following year William Lyons secured £8,000 on overdraft from Lloyds to purchase a factory adjoining his own works.[66] In return for providing assistance the banks sometimes expected to be brought into a company's business affairs. When Standard obtained a loan from Barclays in 1920 it was on condition that E.J. Corbett, the Coventry branch manager, became a member of the board. Although this arrangement carried the threat of unwelcome intervention in Standard's policy-making, the cordial relationship which developed was probably a factor in the way Barclays helped to rescue the company from its financial crisis at the end of the 1920s.[67] Many car firms, including some of the major producers, were largely carried through the slump by the willingness of their bankers to grant emergency loan facilities. Personal factors may in part explain this, though the fear of losing assets tied up in an ailing company was perhaps of more general significance. The critical aspect of bank support in this period, as Foreman-Peck has argued in connection with Rover, is that it helped to maintain the unique structure of the Coventry motor industry, characterised as it was by a large number of relatively small and inefficient firms.[68] The process of rationalisation which market forces demanded was impeded, as on earlier occasions, by the decisive intervention of the banking sector.

By 1939 the motor-car industry dominated Coventry's employment structure, absorbing about 38 per cent of the city's total labour force of just over 100,000 workers. Throughout the interwar period migration supplemented the city's natural population growth, while large numbers of workers commuted daily from Birmingham and other neighbouring areas. However, the minutes of the Coventry and District Engineering Employers' Association reveal that periodic labour shortages occurred in the 1920s and that these became increasingly common and more severe after 1933 as the car industry recovered from depression and the rearmament boom gathered pace later in the decade. Although difficulty was experienced with all grades of labour at various times, the recruitment of skilled workers was often a very serious problem. For example, the craft nature of motor body-building put traditional coach-building skills at a premium in the early 1920s, while a decade later the spread of mass production systems gave toolroom workers a special marketability.

In addition to subcontracting, employers adopted a variety of strategies to alleviate their labour supply problems. Dilution was a popular remedy, especially in coach-building departments where by 1924 determined efforts were being made by employers to introduce second-grade labour.[69] This policy achieved considerable success, especially in the trim-shops where boy and female labour soon came to be used fairly extensively. By the mid-1920s the motor companies were beginning to employ married women on this work since the supply of single girls was said to have become virtually exhausted. However, it was the growing adoption of mass-produced steel bodies in the 1930s which finally proved the solution to the broader question of skill in the coach-building side of the industry. Indeed, the application of large-scale manufacturing techniques involving sub-division of work and repetitive tasks was an aspect of dilution which came to affect the character of the labour force throughout much of the industry.

In addition to utilising the local employment exchange, many companies maintained their own labour offices to help with recruitment and sometimes also advertised quite widely to attract specialist grades of workers. Another tactic adopted by some firms in the mid-1930s was to bring youths into Coventry from regions of high unemployment under the Government's juvenile transference programme.[70] Armstrong-Siddeley, which participated in this arrangement, also formulated a scheme under which boys of particular engineering promise were taken off production work and trained as tool-setters with enhanced rates of pay to compensate for any consequent loss of bonus earnings.[71] In addition, in 1935 the firm purchased a substantial house in Kenilworth as living quarters for its apprentices. Several motor firms gave active support to a graduate course of training developed by Coventry Technical College in conjunction with the Engineering Employers' Association. By 1939 the college was almost unique in technical education in catering for more than 1,000 part-time day engineering students.[72]

Poaching was the most common short-term expedient used by employers to strengthen their labour force. This practice was found even before the First World War but it became more pronounced in the 1920s and rose to a new peak after 1935. Daimler became notorious in the early 1920s for its manipulation of the premium bonus system to attract experienced coach-builders. Hillman and Standard engaged in similar practices and on one occasion the specialist body firm, Hollick and Pratt, threatened in reprisal 'to take as many workpeople from the Standard shops as possible'.[73] By 1936 the engineering sector of Coventry's labour market appears to have degenerated into a virtual free-for-all. Several leading motor firms were said to be offering excessively high rates to pattern-makers, while one enterprising works official had gained access to the technical college records and was circulating the most successful students with offers of employment. Finally, at the end of the year it was reported that Rootes had recruited so many employees from the drawing office of one company that the jig and tool department had practically been brought to a standstill. As war approached and rearmament began in earnest the situation deteriorated even further and at the beginning of 1939 the Employers' Association was bombarded with complaints of workers being openly enticed from one firm to another.

Trade unionism made relatively little progress in the motor industry during the interwar years. The organisation of Coventry's unskilled car workers was frustrated by the virtual annihilation of the Workers' Union during the post-war recession which weakened the larger firms and sent several of the smaller ones into bankruptcy. Similar problems affected the craft-based Amalgamated Engineering Union, though these were compounded by defeat in the 1922 lock-out. The National Union of Vehicle Builders was also in retreat for much of the 1920s as employers sought to enforce dilution and adopt new systems of manufacture. Despite some gains in the 1930s, trade unionism remained in its infancy in the Coventry motor industry until the Second World War, with organisation largely restricted to the toolrooms and craft shops. It seems likely, therefore, that the more specialist firms employing a comparatively high proportion of skilled labour were proportionately more influenced by trade union pressure than the mass producers. Perhaps this explains why the closure of the body shop was seen by Daimler's management as such an important part of its economy programme in 1929.

Despite the restricted nature of trade union development, tightness in the labour market enabled many Coventry car workers to enjoy exceptionally high levels of remuneration. Indeed, by 1937 the city's engineering workers in general were said to be the best paid in the country.[74] Not only did competition for labour push up basic and bonus rates of pay, but it also provided the opportunity for overtime working, which the trade unions complained was often excessive. Upward pressure on wages affected costs of production, prices and profit levels. In 1934 Coventry Motor Panels found it impossible to recruit a full complement of skilled manpower, with the result that overtime payments became so large that they actually forced the firm into the red. The company's labour position remained difficult for the rest of the decade and in 1938 the chairman reported that 'we were compelled to advertise continually through several months and finally had to pay increased rates of wages to induce toolmakers to take up employment with us'.[75] According to Andrews and Brunner, William Morris deliberately restricted his firm's motor-bodywork operation in Coventry to special projects requiring particular skills because of the high cost of local labour.[76] Although it is impossible to guess how far this was symptomatic of a more widespread problem, it seems clear that the close proximity of so many car firms in one city fashioned a unique employment market which, because of its affect on wages, placed certain limits upon the motor manufacturers' competitiveness. It was also possible for shortfalls of manpower to impede the application of new technology and to place physical restrictions upon output levels. Again, it is impossible to estimate the general significance of such constraints, though it is worth quoting Singer's management to illustrate the nature of the problem. The company's annual report noted in the spring of 1938 that a shortage of toolmakers had affected the introduction of two new models, leading to 'serious interruption of the expected flow of production, with decreased output and consequent higher costs of production'.[77]

Productivity was also influenced by labour agreements relating to the organisation of manufacture. One of the most interesting examples of this, even though it was never put into practice, was the attempt by Rover in 1930–31 to introduce the Bedaux time and action work system among its female trim operatives. This system was widely associated with the sweated trades and was resisted by the women who, with the support of some members of the National Union of Vehicle Builders, stopped work for some four weeks. Spencer Wilks eventually reached an agreement with Ernest Bevin of the Transport and General Workers' Union which allowed the introduction of Bedaux in return for a higher guaranteed wage, together with bonus payments once output reached a specified target. This arrangement, which was concluded without reference to Rover's workforce and without the support of the Coventry and District Employers' Association, was an attempt to raise production to the point where the company could challenge for entry to the mass market.[78] However, a change of sales strategy in favour of more expensive vehicles meant that the system was never given an opportunity to turn Rover into a high-wage, high-output manufacturing concern. What remains unclear is how far Bedaux deterred other Coventry motor firms from introducing schemes of scientific management.

Industrial disputes principally concerned attempts by employers to shed labour, alter piecework rates and introduce dilution through the use of boy and female operatives. There appears to have been relatively little organised opposition to the introduction of new production methods. Although strikes were fairly common, they were normally short-lived and limited to particular factories or sections of factories. This is explained partly by the high wage nature of car production in Coventry, but also by labour weaknesses derived from the trade depressions of the period and the continuing problem of seasonal unemployment. Moreover, the CDEEA frequently adopted a noticeably conciliatory stance towards the trade unions, while labour officials were probably discouraged from more militant action by their own organisational weaknesses. Yet employers were forced to make important concessions, particularly in periods of industrial expansion. The successful action of the electricians at Humber, whose strike in 1936 totally disorganised the factory, reflected the wider ability of key groups of workers to influence the policies of management.[79] The limited progress of organised trade unionism did not mean that the workforce as a whole was powerless and the course of industrial relations was certainly an important element in shaping the characteristics of Coventry's motor industry between the wars.

Coventry firms contributed fully to both the strengths and weaknesses of the British motor industry during the interwar period. Standard and Morris, the latter in the manufacture of engines, demonstrated what could be achieved by the application of mass-production techniques, while some of the specialist concerns, such as Jaguar and Alvis, were important in developing the industry's reputation for quality and style. At the same time management weaknesses were reflected in many examples of poor model design and production strategies, underinvestment, low productivity and poorly developed systems of human-resource management. With the benefit of relatively favourable market conditions and supported by the largesse of the financial institutions, an organisational structure and management style proliferated which in the longer term detracted from the strength of the industry as a whole. It has been argued, however, that the major achievement of the industry during the interwar period was that 'the motor vehicle had permeated British society'.[80] The assumptions behind this relationship may be debatable, but at least it can be claimed with certainty that the Coventry manufacturers played a highly significant role in the spread of the motoring habit.

Notes

[1]   A.E. Musson, *The Growth of British Industry* (Holmes and Meier, New York, 1978), p. 346.

[2]   G. Maxcy and A. Silberston, *The Motor Industry* (Allen and Unwin, London, 1959), pp. 14–15.

[3]   Richardson, *Twentieth Century Coventry*, p. 45. The Cooper and the Warwick were produced, over a short period, by Cooper of Lythalls Lane, Holbrooks.

[4]   Beaven, 'The Growth and Significance of the Coventry Car Component Industry', p. 267.

[5]   H. Nockolds, *Lucas: the First Hundred Years* (2 vols, David and Charles, Newton Abbot, 1976), vol. 1, p. 179.

[6]   Atkinson, op. cit., p. 71.

[7]   Richardson, *British Motor Industry*, pp. 102–3.

[8]   Lucas Works Birmingham, ML Magneto Syndicate Ltd, Directors' Minutes, 9 March 1923. We are grateful to Messrs Lucas for allowing us access to these records. The ML material is now located at the Coventry Record Office, Acc 1040.

[9]   Ibid.

[10]   *Lucas Reflections*, vol. 3, no. 6 (1931), p. 5.

[11]   MBC, 390, 18 October 1935.

[12]   MBC, 453, 20 January 1932.

[13]   MRC, MSS 226/ST/1/1/5, Standard Company, Directors' Minutes, 7 October 1924.

[14]   CRO, Acc 594, 144, P. Martin to J. Hamilton Barneley, 10 December 1924.

[15]   Jaguar Works Coventry (JWC), SS Cars Ltd, Directors' Minutes, 30 August 1938. We are grateful to the company for allowing us access to these records.

[16]   CRO, Calcott Balance Sheet and Report, 31 August 1925; Richardson, *The Motor Industry*, p. 99.

[17]   C. Clutton and J. Stanford, *The Vintage Motor-Car* (Batsford, London, 1954), p. 141.

[18]   CRO, Swift and Co, Summary of the Statement of Affairs Hearing in the High Court, 7 October 1931; Morewood, op. cit., pp. 17–19.

[19]   R.J. Overy, *William Morris, Viscount Nuffield* (Europa, London, 1976), p. 16.

[20]   CRO, Singer Balance Sheet and Report, 31 July 1931.

[21]   Ibid., 31 December 1935; *The Times*, 21 October 1936.

[22]   MBC, 97, 19 January 1927.

[23]   MBC, 94, 28 November 1925.

[24]   J. Foreman-Peck, 'Exit, Voice and Loyalty as Responses to Decline: The Rover Company in the Inter-war Years', *Business History*, vol. XXIII (1981), p. 195.

25 Ibid., p. 194.
26 Ibid., pp. 201–2; Robson, op. cit., p. 35.
27 Church, *Herbert Austin*, p. 92.
28 J. Bullock, *The Rootes Brothers. The Story of a Motoring Empire* (Stephens, Yeovil, 1993), p. 61.
29 A. Holme, 'Some Aspects of the British Motor Manufacturing Industry During the Years 1919–1930', unpublished MA thesis, University of Sheffield, 1964, p. 260.
30 CRO, Humber Balance Sheet and Report, 31 July 1930.
31 CDEEA, Minutes, 28 May 1934.
32 Bullock, op. cit., p. 61.
33 *Midland Daily Telegraph*, 3 July 1920.
34 MRC, MSS 226/ST/1/1/3/1, Standard Company, Annual General Meeting, Report, 20 December 1918.
35 Ibid., 18 December 1928.
36 Ibid., 29 December 1927.
37 Davy, op. cit., p. 30.
38 MRC, MSS 226/ST/1/1/6, Standard Company, Directors' Minutes, 29 August 1933.
39 Anon, *The Story of the Vanguard* (Standard Motor Company, Coventry, n.d.), p. 44.
40 CDEEA, Minutes, 19 April 1937.
41 MRC, MSS, 226/ST/1/3/1, Standard Company, Annual General Meeting, Report, 1 November 1938.
42 CRO, 985,985/1/2, Alvis Annual General Meeting, Report, 28 May 1934.
43 CRO, Acc 985, 98/1/2, Alvis Company, Directors' Minutes, 14 June 1935.
44 RAF Museum, Hendon, B963, unpublished autobiography of Major George Bulman, pp. 297–8.
45 Coventry University, Audio History of the Coventry Motor Industry, interview with Sir William Lyons, 1983.
46 S. Morewood, 'Classic and Desirable: The Mystique of the British Sports Car' in Thoms, Holden and Claydon, op. cit., p. 141.
47 A. Bird and F. Hutton, *Lanchester Motor Cars* (Cassell, London, 1965), p. 132.
48 MBC, 440, 7 March 1931.
49 JWC, BSA, Reports on Accounts and Balance Sheets of all Subsidiary Companies, Daimler, 9 July 1929.
50 JWC, Daimler Company, Directors' Minutes, 27 May 1932.
51 MBC, 506, 5 May 1932.
52 Coventry University, Audio History of the Coventry Motor Industry, interview with Alick Dick, 1983.
53 *Standard Car Review*, vol. 4, no. 8 (1935), pp. 345–6.
54 Armstrong-Siddeley Motors, *Evening and the Morning*, p. 55.
55 For a useful summary of the Fordist interpretation and its critics see R. Church, *The Rise and Decline of the British Motor Industry* (Macmillan, London, 1994), pp. 20–26.
56 Bullock, op. cit., pp. 65–6.
57 N. Baldwin, 'Siddeley After Armstrong', *Classic and Sports Car*, August 1983, p. 57.
58 K. Day, *Alvis. The Story of the Red Triangle* (Haynes, Yeovil, 1989), p. 113.
59 Atkinson, op. cit., p. 171
60 A. Whyte, *Jaguar. The History of a Great British Car* (the company, Coventry, 1980), p. 87.
61 MRC, MSS 226/ST/2/1/22/2, Standard Company, Annual General Meeting, Report, 25 October 1933.
62 Church, *The Rise and Decline*, p. 61.
63 Our thanks to Dr Martin Davis for this information.

64   Bullock, op. cit., p. 69.
65   *The Times*, 30 December 1933.
66   JWC, Swallow Coachbuilding Company, Directors' Minutes, 26 December 1932.
67   Richardson, *Twentieth Century Coventry*, p. 63.
68   Foreman-Peck, Exit Voice and Loyalty', p. 204.
69   CDEEA, Minutes, 18 February 1924; R.C. Whiting, *The View from Cowley; The Impact of Industrialisation upon Oxford, 1918–39* (Clarendon Press, Oxford, 1983), p. 48.
70   CDEEA, Minutes, 20 April 1936.
71   Ibid., 19 November 1934.
72   Coventry Technical College, *Report of the Principal for the Year 1938–39*, p. 11.
73   CDEEA, Minutes, 23 April 1923.
74   Ibid., 20 June 1938.
75   Motor Panels Ltd, Chairman's Report, 31 May 1938. We are grateful to the company for allowing us access to these records.
76   P.W.S. Andrews and E. Brunner, *The Life of Lord Nuffield* (Blackwell, Oxford, 1959), p. 127.
77   CRO, Singer Balance Sheet and Report, 31 March 1938.
78   S. Tolliday, 'Militancy and Organisation: Women Workers and Trade Unions in the Motor Trades in the 1930s', *Oral History Journal*, Autumn (1983), pp. 46–7.
79   Amalgamated Union of Engineering Workers, Coventry Branch Minutes, 6 October 1936.
80   J. Foreman-Peck, S. Bowden and A. McKinlay, *The British Motor Industry* (Manchester University Press, Manchester, 1995), p. 65.

Chapter 6

The Motor Manufacturers and the Second World War

In the mid-1930s the prospect of war concentrated the government's mind on rearmament and it very quickly became clear that if Britain were to be involved in prolonged hostilities, Coventry's industrial experience and expertise would be crucial to the country's military effort, particularly in terms of the manufacture, assembly and repair of transport vehicles, airframes, engines of all types and machine tools.

By February 1936 Stanley Baldwin's Cabinet was committed to a major programme of development for the Royal Air Force which involved the construction of some 8,000 front-line aircraft, including new fighters and bombers which were then in their early stages of design and development.[1] This initiative was intended to help Britain strike a parity with Germany in the air. Both government and industry recognised that such an ambitious project demanded new sources of production and the recruitment and training of additional labour on a very extensive scale. This was imperative since on the eve of rearmament Britain's aircraft industry was relatively small in scale, poorly organised and technically backward. In April 1936 Lord Swinton, the Secretary of State for Air, called a meeting to discuss how Britain's motor manufacturers might assist in expanding output in the aircraft industry. This was attended by seven of the country's most prominent personalities in the motor-vehicle sector, including Lord Austin, John Black, William Rootes, Spencer Wilks and Sir Geoffrey Burton of Daimler. During the course of this meeting the start was announced of what later became known as the 'shadow factory' scheme. A co-ordinating committee was established under the chairmanship of Herbert Austin to manage production of aero-engines designed by the Bristol Aeroplane Company. This scheme proved a success, in that the shadow factories soon became the principal suppliers of Bristol aero-engines. The leading Coventry and other Midlands-based motor manufacturers accepted the invitation to use their fast-growing experience in modern production methods to expand their operations into aero-engine production becoming, in the process, the principal supplier of Bristol aero-engines.[2]

The new factories were government financed and equipped, while the motor manufacturers were paid a fee for their services as managing agents. For example, in 1940 Standard received £4,000 a month in respect of its No. 2 Aero Engine Factory.[3] Aircraft production facilities were to be separate from existing motor operations and, although subject to government audit, were free

from Whitehall interference in their daily management.[4] Under the early
scheme it was envisaged that the co-operating firms would concentrate on
making and repairing Bristol Pegasus and Mercury aircraft engines for the
lightweight Blenheim bomber, and during 1936–37 four factories were built in
and around Coventry for this purpose. Standard erected their No. 1 Shadow
Factory in the firm's grounds at Canley and in addition constructed a separate
shop for producing the Claudel Hobson aircraft-engine carburettor. Similarly,
Daimler opened its first shadow plant close to the parent works in Capmartin
Road. To begin with, the Rootes Group built two shadow factories. The first
was in Alderman's Lane adjacent to the existing Humber and Hillman plants
and by 1937 the new premises provided some 105,000 square feet of additional
factory space and had also been equipped with 344 new machine tools.
Rootes's initial order, which was for 200 Bristol engines, was received by
February 1937 and, despite problems in recruiting certain grades of skilled
labour, production was soon in full swing.[5]

    By the outbreak of war, aircraft production from the shadow factories
was rising but remained well below the level needed to meet the needs of the
Royal Air Force. This was largely the result of defence strategy rather than the
manufacturers' inability to meet their production targets. Rearmament could
have proceeded at a brisker pace had the Air Force chiefs been willing to
sanction new purchases, but these would have been for older, increasingly
obsolescent, models whose military value was declining, and so they chose to
wait before placing orders until new aircraft such as the Spitfire, Hurricane and
Whitley bomber had passed beyond the prototype stage.

    The Pegasus and Mercury engines, though adequate for the Blenheim,
were lacking in thrust and power for the heavier Stirling and Lancaster
bombers. Rather than disrupt existing production it was decided to erect
additional shadow factories for the manufacture of the more powerful Hercules

Table 6.1
**Production and labour employed in Rootes' No. 1 Aero Engine Factory
1937–39**

Year	Mercury engine	Pegasus engine	Spares	Males employed	Females employed
1937	11	0	4	811	9
1938	3,491	0	119	1,517	18
1939	14,666	912	889	1,780	24

Source: Museum of British Road Transport, Coventry. Calculated from Rootes
at War Mss, Rootes Securities No. 1 Aero Engine Shadow Factory Report, 31
September 1939 – 31 January 1941.

engine, when it became available in 1939.[6] This time the firms were to join in a joint production effort, with Standard and Daimler on one side and Rootes and Rover on the other. Within the team each company made either the whole or part of the relevant engine so that in the event of one being out of commission the other could continue production to ensure that at least some output of supplies and spares was maintained. To facilitate this increase in production Daimler and Standard both added substantially to their existing plant. The new Standard works in Banner Lane became the company's No. 2 Aero Engine Shadow Factory and was the largest of its type in Coventry. Lack of space prohibited similar expansion by Rootes at Stoke Aldermoor and so there was little alternative but to choose a greenfield location. A suitable 60 acre site was found at Ryton on Dunsmore on the Banbury–Oxford Road, some four miles from the city centre. Within fifteen months nine new buildings and a sewerage plant had been constructed by MacAlpines, a truly remarkable pace of building which included the installation of specialist facilities for both electric power and water supplies. Production began as soon as was physically possible and between December 1940 and November 1941 the new factory produced 1,010 crankcases, 1,116 crankshafts, 972 blowers and 787 rear covers for the Hercules engine. By the early part of 1943 all twelve of Coventry's shadow factories were functioning and in the following year their combined output reached 800 aero-engines a month.[7]

Coventry's role in the shadow factory scheme was only part of its response to the war effort. Indeed, the city became a hive of engineering activity as almost all of its industries turned their attention to the making of war materials, which in turn had a far-reaching impact upon its economic structure, wage levels and pattern of labour relations during the post-war decades. Although economic performance is hard to assess in the non-competitive nature of wartime production, Coventry's motor, aircraft and metal industries were certainly of critical importance in sustaining the country's military operation. Almost 50 per cent of total aircraft output emanated from Vickers, Hawker and Armstrong-Siddeley, the latter of which had a very significant presence in Coventry with its three sites at Parkside, Whitley and Baginton. The company's Whitley bomber had been selected for use by the Royal Air Force in 1936. At that time the work-force numbered 3,000 but by 1939 this had more than doubled, while in the same period a total of 121 aircraft had been assembled. The Whitley proved highly successful and by the time its production ceased in 1941 some 1,824 aircraft had left the Coventry plant. Attention then switched to the Lancaster and Stirling bombers, of which 550 and 106 respectively were built during 1943 and 1944, with a labour force which increased to more than 10,000. The firm also manufactured a large number of Cheetah engines for the Avro Hanson and Oxford trainers. The scale and technical sophistication of Armstrong-Siddeley's contribution to the war effort was an outstanding achievement. As one senior government official remarked, 'There is no doubt that Armstrong Siddeley's have got together a competent and ingenious team.'[8]

Managing two shadow factories in addition to the Canley plant enabled Standard to diversify its manufacturing programme. By 1939 the company was already producing 100 De Haviland Gypsy Moth aircraft and 400 constant-speed De Haviland air screw devices a month and had secured a contract to supply 300 Oxford trainer aeroplanes for the Royal Air Force. With the onset of war, Standard's entire capacity was redirected towards the manufacture of military equipment, though a limited number of cars continued to be produced until the beginning of 1940. The company's work-rate in the early months of war was frenetic. A consignment of 150 Standard Tens was quickly supplied to the Air Ministry for use as staff cars, while the 12 hp and 14 hp chassis were converted for use as utility and pick-up vans in 1 ton and 12 hundredweight form. In 1940 the Beaverette light armoured car was launched and came to be issued mainly to the Home Guard. In its original form it weighed 2 tons and its armour was of the 'ironclad' variety. Several versions of this were made in the course of the war and the final one, the Mark IV, of which 1,935 were delivered, was like a small mobile pill-box mounted with twin machine guns. Standard became widely recognised as one of Britain's most important and efficient manufacturers of war materials, reflected in John Black's knighthood in 1946.[9]

Table 6.2
Selected wartime output of Standard Motors

2,800	Armoured cars
10,000	Light armoured vans
5,000	Standard Gwynne fire pumps
20,000	Bristol Hercules engines
54,000	Aircraft carburettors
417,000	Cylinders for Bristol Mercury and Pegasus engines
63,000	Constant speed units for aero-engines
250,000	Bomb release clip
3,000	Beaufighter fuselages
1,066	De Haviland Mosquito fighter bombers
300	Oxford trainers

Source: Davy, *The Standard Car*, pp. 40–41.

Output of SS cars approached 200 a week in 1939, but once the company turned to war production this side of the business was necessarily run down. It was originally anticipated that part of the engine contract for the new Manchester bomber would go to the firm, but when this failed to materialise Lyons was forced to search elsewhere for work. Consequently, Jaguar became official repairers under licence for Whitley bombers and as subcontractors made spare parts for the Stirling, Spitfire, Lancaster and Mosquito aircraft. Considerable expansion of facilities was necessary and a new factory was acquired at Swallow Road which the Air Ministry equipped with the most advanced machinery available. It was here, under contract to Armstrong-Siddeley, that much of the work on the Cheetah radial aero-engine was conducted.[10]

Despite its growing interest from 1935 in the manufacture of military equipment, Alvis was slow to become fully involved in the rearmament programme. This was partly explained by T.G. John's decision to establish a plant for producing Gnome-Rhone aero-engines under licence. The French parent company had a sound reputation and enjoyed good trading and industrial links in the United Kingdom but was not willing to permit Alvis to manufacture its more advanced designs, and so the Coventry firm found itself saddled with engines that were heading for obsolescence and was therefore excluded from the shadow factory scheme. There was also suspicion within government that the company was not fully in control of its own affairs.[11] Undaunted, John went ahead and with his manager, Smith-Clarke, built a more modern aero-engine plant which was to prove invaluable when war eventually broke out. The firm became connected with Rolls-Royce as a subcontractor in maintaining, servicing and repairing Kestrel and Merlin engines as well as making spare parts for a variety of other models. In addition, Alvis manufactured a huge number of bomb trolleys, components for undercarriages and motor-vehicle pick-ups, wireless vans and trailers. Nevertheless, relations between the company and the Ministry deteriorated so badly during the late 1930s – telephone conversations were monitored – that Alvis's very considerable physical and human resources were almost certainly seriously underutilised throughout the wartime period.[12]

As soon as war was declared Rootes's Humber and Hillman plants were put at the government's disposal. Although relatively little is known about Humber's wartime activities, some production records have survived for Hillman. Here, work soon began on the manufacture of six-cylinder utility vehicles for the army and the Royal Air Force, gearboxes for tanks and Pegasus and Mercury aero-engines. An agreement was also reached with Guy Motors of Wolverhampton for the joint production of armoured cars, which began in 1940. The first of these vehicles proved disappointing, largely because it had been hastily designed, but after a number of modifications some success was achieved with later models. As the war progressed Hillman continued to extend its output by developing a series of pick-ups, staff saloons and tourers, scout cars and four-wheel-drive ambulances.

So pressing was the need to accelerate industrial production that almost all of the smaller motor firms and their component suppliers soon found themselves heavily engaged in the manufacture of various types of military equipment. Singer and Triumph, both of which had been excluded from the shadow factory scheme, became involved in repairing aero-engines, though the latter's contribution to this was greatly disrupted by extensive bomb damage to its Clay Lane–Briton Road factory in November 1941. Another old-established firm, Coventry Climax, built 25,000 trailer pumps for the National Fire Service as well as a wide selection of generators and landing lights for airfields. Dunlop Rim and Wheel produced tyres, barrage balloons, anti-gas clothing and underwater swimming suits. Beyond the motor industry, the city's three largest machine-tool companies, Herbert, Wickman and Coventry Gauge and Tool all had to expand their production schedules. Between September 1939 and November 1944 Herbert delivered some 65,000 machine tools. Similarly, Wickman, whose output stood at only 300 units in 1935, raised this to over 3,000 by 1940, while Gauge and Tool supplied over 75 per cent of all the gauges required for weapons systems during the war, as well as a significant number of machine tools.[13]

Table 6.3
Output of motor vehicles from Rootes's Hillman works 1939–45

Utility Truck Mark I	501
Utility Truck Mark IA	750
Utility Truck Mark II	507
Utility Truck Mark IIA	6,352
Utility Truck Mark IIB	11,426
Utility Truck Mark IV	500
Hillman Chassis Red X	22
10 hp convertibles	1,530
Minx Sallons De Luxe	6,364
Lauder vans	693
Minx touring saloons	117
Civilian Minx	4,598
ExportMinx	4,489
Commer vans	50

Source: MBRTC Rootes at War Mss. Hillman, Report 1/6/1945 – 31/8/45

It had long been suspected that Coventry would be vulnerable to attack by enemy bombers and during 1940 and 1941 the city was subjected to forty air raids. The most serious of these occurred during the night of 14–15 November 1940 when 554 people were killed and 865 seriously injured. Two-thirds of the medieval city was either destroyed or heavily damaged, and about 12 per cent of its housing stock was also lost. Similarly, gas, water, electricity and transport services were severely disrupted, though surprisingly few industrial plants were badly harmed.[14] For example, the main Standard works sustained three direct hits by incendiaries, but damage was confined to paintwork and windows with only the canteen being in any way seriously affected.[15] Less fortunate was the Daimler factory at Radford which suffered severe bomb damage, while at Alvis the car plant was almost completely destroyed. By contrast, the company's nearby aero-engine factory, which was the real target, suffered little damage. Rootes' Hillman-Humber complex received twenty-six direct hits, but was quickly back in action with a full night shift being resumed within six weeks.[16]

As a consequence of this and other bombing in the Midlands, the government began to revise its production strategy and embarked upon a systematic policy of factory dispersal to what were regarded as safer areas. Rootes, for instance, moved a significant proportion of its six-cylinder engine production to Tipton, part of its service work to Holmes Chapel and some of its repair work on aero-engines to Pontefract. By 1945 the combined total of aero-engines repaired, overhauled and delivered to the Royal Air Force by the Humber and Pontefract aero-divisions exceeded 10,600 units. Other factories were opened at Stoke and Bridgenorth. Alvis's work was even more widely dispersed, involving some twenty factories scattered between nearby Hinckley, Ansty and Mountsorrel, and Ealing and Maidenhead to the south.[17] Apart from creating or adapting physical resources, it was also necessary to move some skilled labour to the reception areas for training purposes. Naturally, the workforce in Coventry was concerned that the men transferred should not suffer financially and, indeed, reluctance to move often sprang from fear of losing the high earnings and reasonable working conditions generally enjoyed in the city. The strength of feeling on this issue was reflected at Alvis in March 1943 when the whole of the car and aero-divisions were brought to a halt as workers refused to join the morning shift because the Manpower Board was known to be in the process of selecting employees for transfer to the Mountsorrel plant. In this case the shop stewards interceded, urging a return to work so that negotiations could take place, and a satisfactory agreement concluded.[18] In general, the dispersal policy was successful, for not only did it create much needed industrial capacity elsewhere but it gave respite to the intense pressure on some of Coventry's own economic and social resources.

The expansion of Coventry's motor and aircraft industries between the wars was accompanied by an upsurge in population growth, particularly from the late 1920s. In 1937 the city's population stood at 204,000 after it rose sharply, peaking in October 1940 at just over 250,000, an increase which was largely due to immigration as fresh supplies of labour sought employment in Coventry's burgeoning war industries. However, the call-up and emigration from the city following the severe air raids of 1940–41 meant that by March 1941 the number of residents registered with the Ministry of Food had fallen to 188,000, and did not reach 200,000 again until April 1942. Yet the fall in the working population was not quite so precipitate since many former residents continued in the same place of work but commuted into the city from outlying towns and villages. This increased the number of daily travellers and placed additional pressure on the already overstretched bus and train services. The rate of growth of immigrant labour in the early days of war was swifter than that of the overall population expansion. The peak year for immigration was 1940, a time when management in the city estimated that 5,000 additional operatives were required each month if production targets were to be met. Female immigration did not peak until 1941 and the absolute increase in the number of women workers was lower than that for men, though their percentage rise was much superior.[19]

By 1935 approximately 35 per cent of Coventry's occupied population were employed in the motor and aircraft industries. This proportion fell slightly in 1939, but with the onset of war the downward trend was quickly reversed and by 1941 motors and aircraft accounted for over 60 per cent of the city's labour force. Closely connected with, and often difficult to separate from, these two sectors was general engineering which included machine tools and motor and aircraft components. This category also enjoyed a very rapid and high proportionate rise in employment, increasing from a total of 5,540 operatives in 1935 to over 20,000 by 1941, again illustrating the engineering industry's increasingly dominant role in the local economy. With few exceptions, Coventry's other metal-related industries remained either static or showed no appreciable growth in employment and indeed the numbers working in drop-forging, electric-cable manufacture and ironfounding actually declined.

The overall picture which emerged was one of exaggerated specialisation. The city's growth industries expanded at a faster rate than elsewhere in the region, while those in decline fell more sharply. Within the service sector, however, building and catering increased, stimulated by new factory construction and the need to provide food and essential facilities for the

Table 6.4
Insured persons employed in Coventry (by sex) 1939–41

	Males		Females	
	Over 18 yrs	Under 18 Yrs	Over 18 yrs	Under 18 yrs
July 1939	74,200	8,600	18,308	6,200
July 1940	87,500	7,900	25,700	6,900
July 1941	91,400	7,800	30,000	6,400

Source: Shenfield and Florence, 'Labour for the War Industries', p. 34.

Table 6.5
Percentage change in workers insured, July 1941 compared with July 1939
(1939 = 100)

	Midlands region	Coventry
Motors and aircraft	142	154
General engineering	214	228
Ironfounding	70	22.5
Electrical engineering	118	128
Electric cables, etc.	107	80
Rayon (artificial silk, etc.)	60	47
Hotels and restaurants	87	106
Distributive trades	80	62
Building, public works	77.5	–

Source: Shenfield and Florence, 'Labour for the War Economy', p. 39.

growing workforce. By contrast, the distributive trades fell even more rapidly than the temporary drop in the population after the blitz appeared to warrant, though the reason for this remains unclear. Coventry's occupational profile in 1941 continued virtually unchanged until 1945, leaving the city to face the post-war years supported by a very narrow industrial base. It was becoming almost a staple town, as others had in the previous century, but with a different product mix, and although this brought prosperity in the short term, it was to have dire long-term consequences.[20]

As rearmament progressed in the 1930s there was still no great sense of urgency within Coventry's engineering factories, mainly because it was perceived as essentially a peacetime project and had been designed as such.[21] This complacency was rudely shattered by the outbreak of war, as adjustments to manufacturing programmes brought most firms a period of extreme confusion. For example, Rootes found that they had to cancel the launch of the new Hillman Minx, while vehicles which had been earmarked for distribution to retailers for the 1939–40 season were immediately impressed by the Army and the Royal Air Force, thus throwing their relationship with the dealers into disarray.[22] The company was also instructed to give priority to the Metropolitan and other police forces over the supply of new cars since in the prevailing uncertainty there was no telling when capacity would be available to satisfy future needs.[23] More seriously, at Rootes's No. 1 Aero Engine Plant production schedules had to be revised downward because of shortages of both labour and raw materials. Indeed, delays in the supply of raw materials and components remained a persistent and frustrating problem, not only for Rootes, but for many other manufacturers, and was sometimes a serious impediment to the maintenance of high levels of output. Thus, similar complaints were voiced at Standard's Canley plant, though here the main problem was an acute shortage of factory accommodation which resulted in work on the Oxford trainers and Gypsy Moths being carried out in whatever free space happened to be available.[24]

The overall impression is that government orders came fast and furious in 1939–40 with firms being expected to respond almost immediately. However, even if adequate physical capacity and supplies had been readily available, an all-out war effort would have been seriously constrained by labour shortages, despite the presence in 1940 of almost 1 million unemployed. Shortages of skilled manpower, in particular, caused great alarm in the early months of the war to members of the Coventry and District Engineering Employers Association. John Black wrote to Air Chief Marshall Sir Wilfred Freeman expressing his great concern at the situation. He claimed that the labour problem was exacerbated by inadequate housing provision and argued that unless the necessary dwellings, roads and services were provided quickly, Standard's inability to recruit to its required manning levels would dangerously retard the company's production schedules. In fact, because of the large number of highly-skilled men who volunteered for war service, Coventry's labour market actually tightened. In 1939, much to the employers' consternation, the Navy embarked upon a recruitment drive in the city which proved particularly successful in attracting men from Morris Motors. The CDEEA viewed this development with considerable apprehension and instructions were issued to all its members that while workers should not be prevented from volunteering for the forces neither should they be given any encouragement.[25]

Competition for skilled labour, especially apprentice-trained toolmakers and fitters, had been rife in the aircraft factories since 1936, when it was first brought to the attention of the Air Ministry, but at that time little could be done about it. During the opening months of the war such shortages intensified. Nationally, firms advertised in the press to recruit workers and Coventry companies were no exception. In May 1939 complaints were received by the CDEEA that the turnover of skilled operatives was extremely high as workers moved between different firms almost at will in search of higher earnings. Morris Motors appear to have suffered badly from this, as did Alvis, which prompted Major Smith-Clarke to appeal to all employers for 'solidarity and a uniform approach'. With a predicted shortfall of nearly 7,000 such suggestions fell upon deaf ears and within four weeks Smith-Clarke himself had introduced a new premium bonus to help prevent labour from drifting away. He argued, though, that this provision was purely defensive and was not intended as a recruiting ploy. How many of his fellow employers believed him is a moot point. More openly, the self-confident John Black informed the CDEEA that

Standard would determine its own labour policy and if the association objected then the 'connection between it and the firm would be severed'.[26] In May 1940 a proposal for a voluntary moratorium on labour poaching was put forward by an anxious CDEEA executive, but members rejected it on the grounds that it would not be binding on non-federated firms. However, some semblance of order was introduced in June with the passing of the Restriction on Engagement (Engineering) Order, forcing employers to recruit through either the labour exchanges or trade unions, and in the following year this was strengthened by the Essential Works (General Provision) Order which placed further constraints on labour mobility. Although both measures lessened the degree of poaching which occurred, employees were still relatively free to move between firms provided they remained within the same industry and performed broadly similar functions.[27]

There were a number of potential solutions to the manpower problem, including attracting labour from other areas, using short training programmes to upgrade semi-skilled men to skilled work, de-skilling specific jobs, increased mechanisation, and the employment of women and youths on tasks traditionally reserved for men. All of these had major implications for work practices, wage rates and labour relations to say nothing of the difficulties of training and retraining as tasks and jobs changed with the advent of new technology and methods of production. In their investigation of workers' geographical origins, Shenfield and Florence examined Coventry's labour-exchange registration books for 1941 on a sample basis of one-sixth. These books contain the name of the exchange where the insured was first registered and so it was possible to construct a limited picture of the movement of labour into Coventry's motor and other war industries. Shenfield and Florence divided the books into 'Coventry' and 'Foreign', the latter including Birmingham but not the rest of Warwickshire since it was assumed that these registrations concerned daily commuters. Their results show that even before the war the proportion of 'foreigners' was very high. Indeed, roughly 25 per cent of the city's migrant workers present in 1939 had arrived in the twelve months before July. However, although the number of male arrivals declined during the period 1940–41, they were compensated for by a rapid increase in women migrants. Table 6.6 is interesting because it points to the rising proportion of females and boys drawn in from the surrounding areas. The figures suggest that many of these migrants were secondary wage earners in the family and, living in rural districts and towns, had little alternative but to travel and seek work wherever it could be found. In this case Coventry beckoned willingly.

Apart from Greater London, the major suppliers of immigrant labour to Coventry in the 1930s were the depressed areas of Lancashire, Tyneside, Clydeside, Cardiff and Newport. Over the three years 1939–41, however, there was a distinct change in this pattern of recruitment with the geographical balance gravitating in favour of Greater London, East Anglia, Leicestershire

Table 6.6
Warwickshire books as a percentage of all Coventry Labour Exchange
registrations in 1941

Men over 21	4.25
Youths 18 –21	25
Boys under 18	16.5
Women over 21	25
Women 18 –21	34

Source: Shenfield and Florence, Labour for the War Industries', p. 42.

and Northamptonshire, even though in absolute terms Lancashire, Clydeside and the Cardiff–Newport axis continued to predominate numerically. By 1941 migration from the Hinckley area of Leicestershire accounted for 4.2 per cent of all 'foreign' registered males and for 16 per cent of similar females, while those for Greater London stood at 10.7 and 14.4 respectively. Thus, the migrant intake in this period probably included a large proportion of workers without experience in factory, mine or workshop. The exception to this, of course, were the women who had previously been employed in the Leicestershire hosiery and boot and shoe industries. Such a change in labour sourcing was only to be expected once employment picked up in the depressed areas as their own indigenous industries became more involved in war production. Thus the factories received labour, but of a kind that required swift training and integration into the work process in order to maximise its utility.[28]

Wartime production involved the maintenance of very high output targets. Manufacturers attempted to realise these through capital investment and the efficient use of labour and materials. Rootes Securities, the separate body which governed all of the company's shadow factories, attempted to ensure that every operation that could feasibly be automated in their No. 2 Aero Engine Factory was so adapted by 1940.[29] Similarly, the number of machine tools in use by Rootes's No. 1 Aero Division rose rapidly from 344 in December 1937 to 606 in 1939 and then to 1,035 by December 1941.[30] New equipment involving very heavy expenditure was also installed at the Alvis, Daimler, Standard and Jaguar plants. This trend can be illustrated by the particular example of Standard.

Despite the increased pace of mechanisation, a very large volume of work still had to be effected by hand, particularly in the airframe and aero-engine factories. Early production of aircraft was carried out in a traditional manner with craftsmen working on individual parts at their own benches and employing a high degree of manual precision. The war called for the same

Table 6.7
Expenditure by May 1942 on the four shadow factories controlled by
Standard Motors (£)

No. 1 Engine Factory	7,469,596
No. 2 Engine Factory	9,043,057
No. 3 Carburettor Factory	2,876,517
No. 4 Carburettor Factory	15,520
Total	19,404,690

Source: MRC, Mss 226/ST/1/1/9, Standard Directors' Minutes, 31 May 1942.

levels of quality, but demanded a faster pace of work and a higher output than was possible using craft methods, and so production by jig and tool became the norm. This was especially true in the shadow factories, which had been designed to achieve the highest possible standards and output schedules and where no significant experimental or developmental work was allowed to hinder normal production runs.

Though at first muted, by 1940 demand for dilution of labour gradually became more vocal. Yet compared with the First World War, progress by both management and unions was extremely slow. The unions feared the possible adverse impact of dilution on wages and employment practices, presumably because even during rearmament some unemployed skilled men did have difficulty in finding work. There were also considerations at national level that the government would use dilution as a basis for wage control at a time of rising prices and profits. Management, too, had reservations, mainly because it was felt that attempts at de-skilling could easily provoke labour disputes, and because of the special circumstances of the time it was imperative that peaceful relations be maintained. Concern was also expressed that the price demanded by the unions for their co-operation would be excessive wage increases for the remaining craftsmen at a time when employers were becoming more aware of the need to restrain costs. Moreover, many employers still fondly hoped that a combination of technical advance and a higher intake of youths would lessen both the need and the demand for skilled manpower.

Dilution in manufacturing industry, particularly in engineering, had been under discussion since 1938 and, despite their natural reservations, the unions were prepared to agree to it in principle provided that there were acceptable guarantees of a speedy return to established practices once the emergency had passed. In 1939 agreement was reached between the Amalgamated Engineering Union and the engineering employers on broad aspects of dilution, including the use of semi-skilled assistants on machines formerly operated by skilled men

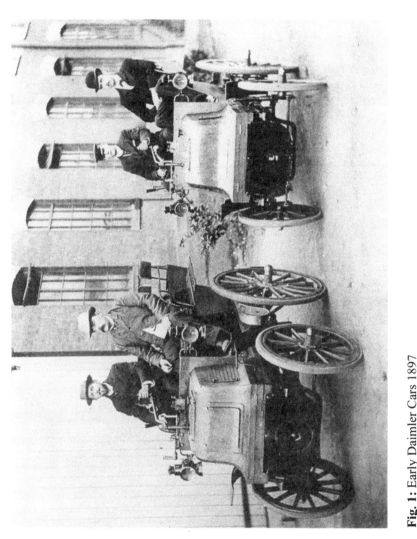

Fig. 1: Early Daimler Cars 1897
Source: Coventry Museum of British Road Transport, Coventry.

Fig. 2: Daimler Factory *c*. 1900
Source: Coventry Museum of British Road Transport, Coventry.

Fig. 3: Daimler Factory *c*. 1913
Source: Coventry Museum of British Road Transport, Coventry.

Fig. 4: Swift Factory and Cars, n.d.
Source: Coventry Museum of British Road Transport, Coventry.

Fig. 5: Calcott Factory, Gosford Street, 1921
Source: Coventry Museum of British Road Transport, Coventry.

Fig. 6: Alvis Factory *c.* 1930
Source: Coventry Museum of British Road Transport, Coventry.

Fig. 7: Alvis Repair Shop, c.1930
Source: Coventry Museum of British Road Transport, Coventry.

Fig. 8: Rootes No.1 Aero Engine Shadow Factory
Source: Coventry Museum of British Road Transport, Coventry.

Fig. 9: Singer Machine Shop, 1956
Source: Coventry Museum of British Road Transport, Coventry.

alone. These arrangements were implemented in 1940 and by and large covered the whole of the engineering industry, though significantly they did not refer to the highly sensitive issue of female labour. The degree of dilution achieved nationally was very considerable, even though it cannot be quantified on the basis of individual firms or regions. It seems likely from the available evidence, however, that Coventry's experience was similar to that of the rest of the country, and if anything dilution probably occurred more rapidly than elsewhere. This may have been facilitated by arrangements for payment of the skilled rate, which in Coventry was based upon the nature of the job itself rather than to the training or experience which it was perceived to require. Coventry's skilled engineering workers were not necessarily apprentice-trained and performed tasks which elsewhere might have been regarded as no more than semi-skilled. In the North East, by contrast, only full apprentice-trained operatives qualified for the full skilled rate and in Glasgow a worker had to perform a particular task for several years before becoming eligible for even the semi-skilled wage. In Coventry the skilled rate was paid irrespective of the time on the job.[31]

To facilitate dilution some of those employees being upgraded or retrained were sent on day-release crash courses to Coventry Technical College, or were given in-house instruction. Even then, complaints were voiced that the college's programme concentrated too heavily on theory and neglected the more practical aspects of training.[32] Once started, dilution progressed quite rapidly. In 1940 Humber began to use semi-skilled men to strip aero-engines and although this attracted protest from the AEU a compromise was soon reached which provided for the supervision of three semi or unskilled men by a single skilled operative. Labour of this type was also introduced into the engine-reconditioning department at Alvis. Occasional disputes did arise, and one of these was at Armstrong Whitworth when in 1943 the coppersmiths demanded full responsibility for all the pipework on Lancaster bombers. The company would not agree to this and the ensuing debate centred upon whether the pipes were actually 'fixed' or merely 'assembled'. The firm was able to demonstrate that although at A.V. Roe's Manchester factories coppersmiths made the pipes, their installation was the work of semi-skilled men, which was also the case at Vickers Armstrong's Weybridge plant. In the light of these precedents the coppersmiths had little alternative but to accept that both apprentices and dilutees could perform the task when supervised by a fully-trained operative. An additional qualification was that the full skilled rate should only apply to the 'alternative assistants' after they had become fully proficient and that in the event of redundancies they would be the first to go.[33] Although both Coventry's management and unions showed a high degree of flexibility towards dilution, the award of skilled rates was often the subject of protracted negotiations and was by no means automatic. For example, in 1941 two men employed in the toolroom at Coventry Gauge and Tool were refused the normal skilled rate because management and unions agreed that the tasks involved did not justify an upgrading of status.[34] Employers were sometimes accused of giving preferential treatment to dilutees at the expense of craftsmen. The coppersmiths at Alvis took strike action in November 1941, claiming that the company had kept some of them on waiting cards while the dilutees were fully occupied. In reply, the management argued that since no work had been available for these particular skilled operatives there had been little alternative but to stand them down. This explanation helped to defuse the situation and the 'smiths returned to work the next day'.[35]

Perhaps the ultimate in dilution was the introduction of women to the shop floor and even, in some cases, to the toolroom. Billy Stokes, a senior AEU official, declared in 1940 that 'the tool room is that last place where women can be employed ... The tool room is a place for only the highly skilled and should be reserved for male labour.' Yet even as he spoke, women were being introduced on toolroom operations previously done by apprentices.[36] As we have already seen, women were employed in the motor industry before 1939, but it was the pressure of war which significantly increased their participation in the car and aircraft factories and allowed them to upgrade their existing skills and acquire new ones, as well as carry out responsibilities formerly denied them. Under the various agreements between the government, employer associations and the unions, women could perform men's work provided a strict register was kept. The accord with the AEU specifically required women to serve a thirty-two week probationary period during which they would be paid on an increasing percentage scale before receiving the full male rate, providing equal tasks were performed. However, if after training any male assistance or additional supervision was still required then only a proportion of the male rate was awarded, which itself often became the subject of negotiation. All these agreements contained clauses to the effect that when women were used in factories without a previous tradition of female employment and continued to perform what was generally regarded as women's work, payment was to be in accordance with the Women's Wages Schedule, or at the rate for boys and youths, whichever gave the higher return.[37] The influx of women into industry for Britain as a whole was substantial and rapid, with motors and aircraft quickly outstripping other sectors of employment. In 1939 women comprised 18 per cent of the workforce in the engineering and related industries and by the end of 1943 this had increased to around 39 per cent. Unfortunately, no overall data exists to indicate the varying degrees of skill which these women had on joining or leaving employment. However, in 1940, 75 per cent of women in the engineering industry were employed in either skilled or semi-skilled occupations and by 1944 this had climbed to 85 per cent of the total. Perhaps only a tiny proportion of these could be described as apprentice-trained but, equally, a large number necessarily acquired a certain degree of skill and in the case of Coventry and the Midlands generally this would probably have been of sufficient standard for the local classification of skill to apply. Finally, as Inman argues, only a few

THE SECOND WORLD WAR

women engineering workers would have acquired enough experience to achieve highly-skilled status.[38]

Standard and Rootes were two of the first Coventry companies to welcome women recruits in the early days of war and to put them through a formal scheme of training. By May 1941 Standard employed over 700 females in its No. 2 Aero Engine Factory, most of whom worked on the Hercules engine, while at the same time approximately seventy-five women a week graduated from the firm's training school.[39] Similarly, between June and December 1941 Rootes trained 102 women machine operators, 61 inspectors and 15 fitters.[40] However, the company developed a reputation at the beginning of the war for a certain reluctance to pay the agreed rates. For example, it was reported in 1940 that women machine operators, working with male assistants and 'making a success of it', were not being paid the union rate. It was also discovered in the same year that women who had completed an eight-week probationary period were being underpaid, despite earlier assurances by the company that this would be remedied. When accused by the unions of reneging upon negotiatiated agreements, Rootes's management retorted that in future the company would operate its own labour scheme which, it was claimed, would save time and money. At the same works conference the AEU pointed out that Rootes's female grinders and machine operators received less than their full entitlement and reminded the company that only a few days earlier women on the night shift had withdrawn their labour, partly at this but also because the firm had unilaterally reduced their bonuses by up to 62 per cent. Not surprisingly, the meeting broke up in some disarray.[41]

Much of the debate on women's wages and conditions revolved around the interpretation of the Relaxations Agreement, and sometimes involved casuistry of an extremely high order. Thus, when female inspectors at Standard complained in 1941 that they were not being paid the full rate for the job, the company replied that since the women were merely involved in a visual inspection of aircraft plates their work differed significantly from that of their male colleagues who were expected to conduct a more thorough examination. Similar attempts to devalue the status of skilled work performance by women were fairly widespread in Coventry's engineering factories.[42] One result of this was that some firms experienced particular difficulty in recruiting suitable female workers. On one occasion Jack Jones, District Secretary of the Transport Workers' Union, warned Rootes in blunt terms that unless the company adopted a more enlightened labour policy it was unlikely to attract sufficient women operatives of appropriate calibre to satisfy its requirements. The firm appears to have been quite unconcerned by this and continued for some time to operate discriminatory wage scales for the same tasks in its No. 1 and No. 2 Aero Engine factories. By comparison, when it was pointed out to Jaguar's management in 1944 that two female polishers were being paid less than the agreed rate, the firm responded immediately, even awarding back pay.[43] Breaking down specialist jobs into their constituent elements was another popular device for remunerating women at less than the male equivalent wage, the usual justification being that this involved an important measure of de-skilling.[44]

Not all union officials and members were as scrupulous as Jones in their interpretation of the various national labour agreements. For example, in 1941 the Sheet Metal Workers claimed exclusivity in the body assembly shop at Carbodies. Unlike the AEU and the Transport Workers, this was a small and very old union much of whose members' work involved the use of hand and bench tools. Moreover, their work was a dying craft which, under pressure of war, was being replaced by both the power press and automatic tools, which in turn offered great scope for dilution, including the use of women workers. Using new techniques it was possible to dilute easily and to accelerate output, but in general the Sheet Metal Workers in Coventry and the Midlands as a whole opposed this as representing a threat to their interests. However, the management at Carbodies stood firm, arguing that dilution was steadily becoming common practice throughout the industry in general, in the face of which the union was forced to negotiate the best deal it could obtain.[45]

Central to the debate on female wage levels was the term 'work commonly done by women', which was often invoked by both sides of industry when opposing payment of full male rates to women. One typical example of this occurred at Morris Engines in 1944 when two female water-pump assemblers demanded to be placed on the same pay scale as men. This was a potentially awkward case since equal pay for this particular task had already been granted at nearby Coventry Climax. However, the management proved quite unsympathetic and rejected the claim on the basis of historical precedent, noting that women had been performing this type of work at the company and receiving the female rate since 1937.[46] Almost a year later, union attempts to replace women welders at Armstrong-Siddeley Motors with men returning from the forces floundered because the company was able to demonstrate that female labour had commonly been used in this way long before the outbreak of war.[47] Similarly, when Morris Motors was challenged on its right to employ women in the male preserve of cushion-making, the firm produced two female employees who had been performing this task since 1937.[48] Although such disputes abounded, there were occasions when particular consideration was shown towards women workers, especially in the case of 'dirty work'. Probably the best example of this occurred at Rootes's physical laboratory where many girls worked amid such noxious and dangerous chemicals that a rota system was devised for their own safety and comfort.[49]

Prior to the outbreak of war, hours of work were determined by voluntary agreement or by statutory Act of the Board of Trade and, in the case of women and youths, by the various Factory Acts. Upward pressure on output in the early days of hostilities ensured that normal working hours, including overtime, were frequently exceeded. The lesson of the First World War, that beyond a certain point work often brought fatigue, sickness and, in the end, reduced production was either ignored or conveniently forgotten. Yet conditions varied so much between industries and firms, the latter even in the same sectors, that at first it proved difficult to lay down hard and fast rules to regulate hours of work and general conditions of employment. The usual working week in the motor and engineering industries in 1939 was 47 hours, with monthly overtime limited to 30 hours, giving a maximum of 54.5 hours per week. Women and youths were precluded from night work under the factory legislation, except where this was essential to maintain continuous output, while their total working week was restricted to 48 hours. A number of Coventry firms soon exceeded the regulatory norms and, for example, complaints were voiced that at Armstrong-Siddeley and Rootes the working week rose well above 60 hours. The Engineering Employers' Association noted with concern in 1940 that fitters and turners both averaged 59–60 hours a week.[50] Yet it is perhaps understandable that the manufacturers should attempt to push their workers to the limit since they were themselves operating under government instructions to raise output as quickly as possible, with the pressure becoming particularly intense after Dunkirk.

Some attempt was made by government to secure a degree of control over working hours. Under the General Emergency Order of 1940, which covered shipbuilding and engineering, women and youths were allowed to work up to 60 hours, with youths under sixteen limited to 48 hours, but the need for high levels of production caused these provisions to be more honoured in the breach than the observance. In particular, women in the aircraft industry continued to exceed the agreed limits, and so in 1943 their hours and those for youths were revised downwards to a maximum of 55. It was increasingly recognised that excessively long working hours were injurious to health and could prove counter-productive simply because many operatives, particularly women, suffered the cumulative effects of strain caused by repeated twelve-hour shifts. This led inevitably to a high incidence of absenteeism, especially among women with young families to care for. A flexible approach to hours of employment was essential in order to allow time for both relaxation and domestic chores and in this respect most Coventry employers had a rather poor reputation, which helps to explain why absenteeism among the city's female industrial workers was sometimes double the national average. By 1943 it was obvious that such a furious pace of work could not persist and from then onwards formal working hours were gradually reduced so that by the end of the war the average working week for men had fallen to 48 hours, 43.8 for women, 45 for youths and boys, and to 42.6 for girls.[51]

Very long working hours was only one cause of absenteeism, especially in the early years of the war. Shenfield and Florence attempted to measure absentee rates in Coventry factories and to compare these with equivalent plants in the Black Country. As table 6.8 indicates, Coventry's absentee rates were higher in almost every sector than those for the Black Country. From this

Table 6.8
Rates of absence June to November 1943: Coventry and the Black Country compared

	Men	Women
Black Country		
Factory: Screws	6.4	13.7
Aircraft	6.9	11.9
Machine tools	4.7	8.8
Tubes	6.2	10.1
Chemicals	6.1	12.1
Coventry		
Factory: Aircraft (parent)	6.3	12.6
Aircraft (shadow)	7.9	16.8
Aircraft (shadow)	9.8	19.6
Aircraft (parent)	7.9	16.8
Aircraft (shadow)	13.9	20.7
Aircraft (shadow)	7.7	13.7
Aircraft (old factory)	8.6	15.0
Motor engines	6.6	13.9
Telephone equipment	6.3	16.8
Machine tools (day shift)	8.3	16.5
Machine tools (night shift)	6.3	12.6

Source: Shenfield and Florence, 'Economies and Diseconomies of Concentration', p. 87.

research came three additional reasons for absenteeism: high earnings, poor housing and transport, and community patterns of behaviour. When comparing wages between three typical factories, two in Coventry and one in Wolverhampton, all involved in aircraft production, Shenfield and Florence were able to show that earnings in both Coventry plants had risen faster than those in the Black Country. This led to the conclusion that the reality of higher incomes made losses from absenteeism much more bearable once a certain plateau of weekly earnings had been achieved. The Birmingham study also asserted that the siting of the shadow factories on Coventry's periphery was an important element in explaining absentee rates since employees could face a lengthy and often uncomfortable journey to work. Finally, it was argued that absenteeism was often caused by migrants' disillusionment with their new environment, caused particularly by inadequate housing accommodation, which brought a withdrawal of commitment from the workplace.

Table 6.9
Estimates of earnings per week: two firms in Coventry, one in Wolverhampton.

	July 1940	March 1943
Factory B 2 (New Coventry)		
Toolroom men	c. £12	£12–£14
Skilled production men	c. £12–£16	£12–£16
Semi-skilled production men	c. £8–£14	£10–£15
Factory B 1 (Old Coventry)		
Toolroom men	£8	£9–£12
Skilled production men	£8–£10	£8–£12
Semi-skilled production men	£6–£9	£7–£11
Factory W (New Wolverhampton)		
Toolroom men	£7–£8	£8
Skilled production men	£6–£8	£7.50–£8
Semi-skilled production men	£6–£7	£6–£6.50

Source: Shenfield and Florence, 'Economies and Diseconomies of Concentration', p. 89.

As we noted earlier, Coventry's wages in the 1930s were among the highest in Britain and this pattern continued throughout the war years. Even during the rearmament period the government became increasingly aware of the potential inflationary consequences of excessive wage-drift in a war economy. The problem had been examined as early as 1927 when the Ministry of Labour proposed that wartime wage rates should be restricted to their peacetime levels and should subsequently be adjusted by a Central Administration Tribunal. It was also suggested that prices and profits should be brought under state control and in 1929 such a policy was accepted by the Committee on Imperial Defence.[52] Within a short time the Ministry of Labour had modified its position. It was now argued that control over profits would be very difficult to achieve and that in the event of failure, relations with the unions would be seriously impaired, as had occurred during the First World War.

This warning helped to ensure that wages were left alone as the price for industrial peace during the rearmament period. Both time and piece-rate systems applied in the Midlands generally, though in Coventry the latter predominated and was supplemented by a variety of additional rewards, such as merit bonuses. Indeed, even during rearmament the gap between Coventry and national wage rates widened. The close relationship between the aircraft and motor industries in the Midlands encouraged high earnings in both, with each competing vigorously for labour, and giving Coventry a reputation for the highest possible earnings. Soon after the outbreak of war the Ministry of Labour expressed its concern about excessive labour costs when its enquiries revealed that during 1939 and 1940 wages rates in the engineering industry in the Midlands had increased between 30 and 50 per cent and in aircraft manufacture by as much as 100 per cent. The Ministry was caught in an awkward dilemma. It had left the management of the shadow factories to private industry and, because of the similar and often identical nature of the work, could not enforce wage restraint without doing the same in the parent factories. More significantly, perhaps, in the early days of war there appeared to be little difficulty in finding the money to meet the escalating wage bill, mainly because of the favourable levels of productivity in Coventry's factories. Indeed, Standard, which enjoyed a reputation in 1941 as a 'high payer', was singled out by a government report for praise, being described as 'an object lesson to the rest of the country'.[53] As Mrs Inman concludes, there is no evidence to suggest that production costs in Coventry were greater than in other parts of the country, rather the reverse.[54]

The Coventry Tool Room Agreement of 1941 is fundamental to an appreciation of the pattern of wage movements in the city. Moreover, it was an accord which was to have major implications for the motor and engineering industries as a whole until its unilateral termination by the CDEEA in the early 1970s. Amid the scramble for improved wage rates during the opening months of the war it became apparent that semi-skilled workers and dilutees were able to push their pay above that of apprentice-trained toolroom craftsmen. Some trained fitters and turners consequently sought jobs as production workers or alternatively moved between firms in search of more favourable wage levels and employment opportunities. In 1939 the CDEEA expressed its fears about this development, with Major Smith-Clarke stating openly that toolroom wages were too low in comparison with those earned by less skilled employees.[55] Management's concern was shared by senior trade union officials in the city and against this background the Coventry Tool Room Agreement was drawn up in 1941, thanks largely to the personal efforts of Jack Jones. Framed against the background of legislation introduced in the previous year concerning national engineering wage levels, this agreement stated that fitters, turners and machinists in toolrooms should be paid at a rate calculated monthly which should not be less than the 'the average hourly rate paid to production workers in nine selected factories'.[56] There is little doubt that this mechanism substantially benefited apprentice-skilled men and that, since other groups used toolmakers' earnings as a negotiating guide, it contributed also to a general upward drift of wages in the city.

A major factor which probably encouraged laxity over wage controls and industrial costs in the early days of war was the system by which government contracts were awarded on a cost-plus basis. The wage rate for specific jobs was the outcome of mutual agreement between workers and rate-fixers. When firms were handling only a small number of orders of a similar nature, experienced rate-fixers were able to use their judgement and price the job keenly. This situation was changed markedly by the war. Jobs changed or were modified with great rapidity and with the expansion of the workforce many new rate-fixers with little or no experience were appointed, which led to considerable overpricing, either of the sum agreed or the time allotted.[57] It was not long, however, before firms tried to impose tighter control over wage costs, especially after fixed-price contracts were introduced. Within the revised system the price received per batch of aircraft engines or airframes, for example, was reduced as the production line lengthened. In 1940 Standard received £7,413 for each of the first forty Oxford trainers manufactured, but thereafter the price was gradually reduced so that for units 351 to 508 the company was paid £4,425 per aircraft. This was sufficient to concentrate John Black's mind on the necessity of achieving cost reductions.[58] The most obvious method of wage control lay in reducing bonus rates, but the workforce saw no good reason why wages should fall simply because the price received by the firm for a particular job had been reduced or because the specification of an aircraft, tank, armoured car or engine had been modified. The main problem was that the rate for each task lasted only as long as the job itself, and so any change led automatically to new mutually-agreed rates being negotiated with the rate-fixers. As part of the general attempt by CDEEA members to reduce all bonus rates in excess of 100 per cent, Standard tried in 1942 to cut its bonus payments of 175 per cent in the Bristol engine shop by up to 60 per cent, a move dismissed contemptuously by the operatives. Although this dispute did not reach sufficient momentum to provoke strike action, it did drag on for three months, at the end of which a reduction of 25 per cent was agreed. A year later Standard secured an agreement with workers in the Bristol engine shop to reduce bonus rates by 10 per cent, but only after giving a guarantee that there would be no further interference with wages for a period of two years. The men had accepted this offer after a ballot in which 87 per cent had voted in favour.[59] Not all such agreements were achieved so easily. By contrast, at a local works conference convened to discuss ways of reducing costs, the AEU accused Rootes of attempting to depress wage levels in order to put them on a par with those found in other areas. During the course of a heated and acrimonious debate Billy Stokes made it perfectly clear that 'we, as representatives of the workers, are not going to have Birmingham or any other district conditions forced upon us'.[60] Similarly, when in 1943 Rover attempted to introduce time study in order to determine prices and wages more accurately, the unions blankly refused to co-operate, arguing that the use of stopwatches had never been agreed in Coventry and was not part of the city's custom and practice. The company had little alternative but to give way, as Dunlop Rim and Wheel had done on the same issue.[61]

A further complicating factor, especially at Standard, was the 'gang system'. Here it was not simply a matter of fixing rates for individuals, but for a group of up to a hundred people, a task which was made even more difficult by the introduction of women as gang members. There was a genuine fear that if women received lower rates for the job then the bonus earnings for the whole gang would drop. In negotiating the total bonus for the gang, and taking into account the varying degrees of differentials that existed between the varying grades of workers, great care had to be exercised, not only on wage rates, but on the numbers to be involved on a particular task and how long the job should take. This was extremely time-consuming, but was essential to ensure that the task was awarded the correct price. One example of this negotiating complexity occurred at Standard in 1941 and was concerned with bonus payment and manning level reductions on a group known as 'Seymour's Gang'. This gang had been working on a batch of educational engines and once the initial training period had been completed its productivity rose sharply, dragging wages up from 2s 9d an hour to 5s, which was far above the going rate. The management wanted to reduce the rate to 3s 6d an hour and argued that the total bonus should be reduced from £69 to £32 based upon an output of six aircraft a week and a manning level of twenty rather than twenty-six. This the gang refused, suggesting an alternative reduction to £46 and to twenty-one men, even though the local AEU officials had described Standard's offer as generous. In the end the firm's offer prevailed, but only after some tough bargaining.[62] Although initial concern had been expressed at women gangs, this tended to disappear once they had proved their worth and, indeed, gang leaders soon accepted responsibility for their interests, if only because the female members contributed significantly to the groups' total output and earnings. Thus, union officials and gang leaders at Standard went out of their way in 1944 to persuade women who had threatened strike action over piecework bonus rates to remain at their benches and negotiate a settlement.[63]

Under wartime regulations, and the interrelated nature of production between the motor and aircraft plants, labour could be transferred from one factory to another within the same controlling firm. When this occurred in Coventry, care was taken by the unions to ensure that no loss of earnings was suffered and that any increased transport costs should not leave the operative out of pocket. For example, when in 1941 vital toolroom workers were transferred from Alfred Herbert to Rootes, particular arrangements were devised to ensure that existing wage levels were maintained. On the matter of transport, the CDEEA noted at about this time that its members were being forced to provide buses to convey their employees to and from work. Jack Jones also attempted to secure an agreement with Standard under which Canley workers transferred to the company's new engine-testing centre at Ansty should receive travelling time, but in the event he could only manage to obtain free transport for his members.[64]

The rapid growth of the city's workforce led to new opportunities for expansion and development by the trade unions. Following the national pattern, the attitude of labour leaders such as Jack Jones, Billy Stokes and others was essentially one of co-operation with the employers, though the latter were at first suspicious of union intentions. Lack of space precludes a detailed analysis of the growth of the union movement in the city, but both the transport and engineering unions were able to increase their membership substantially, though by exactly how much is unknown. As Jack Jones commented, the new labour entering the factories was ripe for recruitment. There is also little doubt that the industrial role of union leaders at national level during the war encouraged new initiatives at regional and district levels, but in Coventry, as elsewhere, there was a degree of employer opposition. When in 1942 it was suggested that Joint Production Committees should be formed, the CDEEA opposed its members being forced to participate on a compulsory basis, but in the end the employers were obliged to comply. A mere four months later the reports filtering back to the association indicated that early meetings of these committees had proved both helpful and constructive, and gradually opposition to them diminished.[65]

One outstanding feature of this period was the vigorous growth of the shop stewards' movement. The role of the stewards and of union politics in Coventry factories has been analysed elsewhere and it suffices at this point to say that the number of recognised shop stewards in engineering firms rose sharply, reaching a peak figure of 441 in 1943. The records of both the AEU and the CDEEA convey the general impression of a high level of trade union responsibility in labour relations, especially concerning strike decisions: though it must be emphasised that the first concern of union officials was the interests of their members. Wartime labour stoppages in Coventry tended to be of short duration and usually every effort was made by the various union officials to minimise production losses. Sometimes such efforts were successful, sometimes not. A large number of men in the fitting and machine shops at Rootes's Ryton factory came out on strike in October 1941 because they were 'being asked to work at unfavourable piece rates until procedures were exhausted'. The district secretary listened to their 'numerous expressions of discontent' but after a 'frank discussion' with his members advised them to return to work the following morning and allow negotiations to proceed.[66] Similar advice was given to some sixty toolroom workers at SS cars when they struck following the dismissal of ten men whom the company considered to be unsuitable for employment, and within days the dispute was settled amicably. Some nine months later the local district committee specifically forbade strike action at Standard after the sacking of four men until the formal appeals procedure had been exhausted.[67] Even when unofficial strikes occurred it was often union officials or recognised shop stewards who were instrumental in achieving a peaceful solution.[68]

Despite their willingness to co-operate with the employers there were inevitably occasions when labour officials had no other course but to stand firmly behind the membership and support industrial action in defence of union rights and against victimisation and breaches of agreements by the employers. For example, contrary to existing arrangements in November 1944 Humber introduced semi-skilled men into its service department, maintaining that it now disagreed with the AEU's contention that only skilled men should service aero-engines. The skilled operatives stopped work and received full union backing.[69] Victimisation of labour did occur from time to time, but was not common practice. When it happened the employers usually took the line that they were merely freeing themselves of troublemakers, and most dismissals of this type appear to have taken place in 1939 and 1940. Nevertheless, it seems likely that in some cases old scores were being settled between management and individuals. Indeed, throughout 1940 much of the time of AEU officials was devoted to cases of alleged victimisation. In January the unions became involved at Standard when a convenor in the aero-engine shop was sacked, while in March it handled the affair of nine trade union activists who had lost their jobs at SS cars. A short time later two stewards were dismissed by the Alvis management, and at Coventry Gauge and Tool a man was sacked for allegedly holding 'Communist beliefs'. In the light of these events and the ousting of a third convenor, Horace Wilcocks at Standard, the Coventry District Committee of the AEU had little alternative but to respond in a positive fashion. At that time the trade union movement was beginning to gain a foothold in Standard's various plants, something the company was anxious to reverse. As late as January 1940 John Black and his management team had refused to recognise the AEU's presence in the company's factories. Matters came to a climax in September when Wilcocks reported that the firm was dictating when and where union meetings could be held. Wilcocks attempted to negotiate with the management on this issue but failed, and shortly was dismissed for conducting a meeting at what was described as an inconvenient time. Despite appeals from district officials to stay at their benches pending negotiations, some 250 men walked out. With little sign of the company being prepared to shift its position the district committee made the strike official on 27 September, declaring that stewards and convenors should be entitled to carry out union duties at their place of work. Almost spontaneously, support came from workers at Armstrong Whitworth and it seems certain that the possibility of the strike spreading to other firms across the city was instrumental in persuading Standard's management to accede to the union's demands, including the reinstatement of Wilcocks.[70]

By the spring of 1944 both the employers and labour were beginning to consider the problems of adjustment once the war was over. Many Coventry manufacturers were unsure of their ability to convert their premises back to peacetime production, while maintaining high levels of output and pay during a period when the market was expected to be highly competitive once government contracts were reduced in scale. Similarly, workers had no wish to return to the seasonal nature of employment common to a number of industries before 1939, and were also anxious to keep the substantially improved level of earnings which the war had brought. With these issues in mind John Black informed his friend, Hugh Dalton, in 1944 that a return to normal motor-vehicle production could only be achieved if the government could ensure a steady supply of steel, light alloys, forging and castings. Black emphasised that the motor industry would be vital to economic and industrial reconstruction and stressed that the authorities should do everything in their power to assist its progress once peace returned, including the prevention of labour dislocation. Dalton readily agreed with all of this.[71] Perhaps the main source of concern for trade union officials was how far the essentially co-operative labour relations enjoyed during the war would survive in the longer term. By the beginning of 1945 there were already indications of a more authoritarian management style with attempts to deflate wages and talk of redundancy. Many workers viewed the closure of the Nuffield Mechanisation plant in Gosford Street as a portent of things to come. Soon after the war ended, and just when shop stewards were demanding that existing wage levels should be maintained, the management announced that since the works was no longer central to the Morris operation it was to be shut down.[72] The unions tried to ensure that in the event of redundancies dilutees, women and youths were dismissed first so that scarce jobs could be reserved for skilled men, but in general such requests appear to have gone unheeded. The particular example of Rootes illustrates the extent of the problem which confronted the trade unions. In May 1945 the Ryton plant employed a total workforce of 3,123 men and women but by the end of the year this had shrunk to a mere 98 as the firm laid off all but essential workers to facilitate the factory's conversion to motor-car production.[73]

The unions' fears over redundancies and a possible return to the working and labour conditions of the previous decade were crystallised by events at Humber in 1945, where the works manager had for some months adopted an unusually abrasive attitude towards the workforce. Complaints were made against him at a works conference, ranging from his refusal to allow payment of a subsistence allowance to transferred workers to padlocking the tea urns. Labour relations eventually deteriorated so badly that nearly 5,000 workers came out on strike for nine days, refusing to go back during this period despite the effort to effect a return by both the trade unions and the employers' organisation. When work eventually resumed the atmosphere within the plant was more that of a truce than industrial peace. Mistrust and friction continued into 1946 when the firm tried to reduce wages in the old Humber factory, which had long suffered a reputation for low productivity, poor pay and a high level of discontent. The cause of the trouble was an attempt to break locally-agreed wage rates, coupled with the installation of new and highly efficient equipment which, it was feared, would inevitably lead to redundancies. The workers responded by adopting a go-slow, reducing output to one car per week. Retaliation was swift and involved the dismissal of 500 men. This action precipitated an extremely acrimonious strike which lasted for four weeks before an agreement was negotiated which included the reinstatement of the sacked men. This effectively demonstrated that there could not be a direct return to the style of labour relations which prevailed in the interwar period, and was an important lesson for the whole of Coventry's engineering industry. It was widely recognised that co-operation between both sides of industry was fundamental to an orderly return to peacetime production and industrial prosperity.[74]

The Second World War brought considerable change to the various stakeholders in Coventry's motor-vehicle industry. Under the pressure of government orders and regulations, management focused increasingly upon the technical, organisational and financial aspects of volume production, while labour benefited from favourable employment opportunities and greater collective strength and authority. The creation of new factory space, particularly associated with the shadow aircraft firms, modified Coventry's physical landscape and extended its manufacturing possibilities. However, the artificial conditions of war also helped to ossify parts of the city's economic structure. Firms such as Singer, Lea-Francis and Rover, which might well have collapsed without the benefit of a controlled market-place, limped into the post-war era to add to the problems of reconstruction.

Notes

[1]   Richardson, *Twentieth Century Coventry*, p. 65.
[2]   S. Ritchie, *Industry and Air Power. The Expansion of British Aircraft Production 1935–4* (Frank Cass, London, 1997), ch. 4.
[3]   MRC, Mss 226/ST/1/1/9, Standard Motor Company, Directors' Minutes, 17 January 1940.
[4]   A. Shenfield and P. Florence, 'The Economies and Diseconomies of Industrial Concentration: The Wartime Experience of Coventry', *Review of Economic Studies* (1943–45), pp. 79–84.
[5]   Richardson, *Twentieth Century Coventry*, pp. 65–8.
[6]   Ibid.
[7]   Ibid. MRC, Mss 226/ST/1/1/9, Standard Motor Company, Minutes of Directors' Meetings, 17 January 1950; MBRTC, Rootes at War Mss, No. 2 Engine Shadow Factory, 3 September 1931 – 31 December 1941.
[8]   PRO, AVIA, 15/320. CRD to DSR, 25 June 1942.

[9] Davy, *The Standard Car*, p. 50.

[10] Whyte, *Jaguar*, pp. 111–17.

[11] PRO, AIR, 19/6, John to Swinton, 7 November 1936.

[12] PRO, AIR, 19/6, John to Kingsley Wood, 27 December 1938.

[13] Richardson, *Twentieth Century Coventry*, pp. 70–72.

[14] For a discussion of the economic impact of the raids, see D. Thoms, *War Industry and Society. The Midlands 1939–45* (Routledge, London, 1989), ch. 5; see also, Lancaster and Mason (eds), *Life and Labour*, ch. 11.

[15] MRC, Mss 226/ST/1/1/9, Standard Motor Company, Minutes of Directors' Meetings, 7 November 1941.

[16] MBRTC, Rootes at War Mss, Humber, 30 September 1941 – 31 December 1941; Day, *Alvis*, pp. 86–7.

[17] Ibid., MBRTC, Rootes at War Mss, Humber Aero Engine Factory, 1 December 1939 – 28 February 1945.

[18] Amalgamated Union of Engineering Workers, Minutes of the Coventry District Committee (MDC) 23 March 1943.

[19] A. Shenfield and P. Florence, 'Labour for the War Industries: The Experience of Coventry', *Review of Economic Studies* (1943–45), pp. 32–3.

[20] Ibid.

[21] Ibid.

[22] MBRTC, Rootes at War Mss, No. 2 Aero Engine Factory, 31 September 1939 – 31 December 1939.

[23] Ibid., Hillman-Humber, 31 September 1939, 30 September 1940 – 31 December 1940.

[24] MRC, Mss 226/ST/1/1/9, Standard Motor Company, Minutes of Directors' Meetings, 9 April 1940.

[25] Ibid., 11 January 1940; AEU (MDC) 9 January 1939.

[26] MRC, Mss 226/1/1/9, Standard Motor Company, Minutes of Directors' Meetings, 8 May 1939; CDEEA, Minutes, 5 June 1939.

[27] P. Inman, *Labour in the Munitions Industries* (HMSO, London, 1957), p. 25; S. Pollard, *The Development of the British Economy 1914–80* (Arnold, London, 1983), p. 198.

[28] Shenfield and Florence, 'Labour for the War Industries', p. 40.

[29] R. Croucher, *Engineers at War* (Merlin Press, London, 1982), p. 76.

[30] MBRTC, Rootes at War Mss, No. 2 Aero Engine Factory, 21 September 1941 – 31 December 1941.

[31] Inman, *Labour in the Munitions Industries*, pp. 33–4, 79. A. Friedman, *Industry and Labour* (Macmillan, London, 1977), p. 204.

[32] CDEEA, Minutes, 16 February 1942.

[33] MBRTC, Rootes at War Mss, No. 2 Aero Engine Factory, 30 September 1939 – 31 December 1939; MRC, Mss 66/1/160, Coventry and District Engineering Employers Association (CDEEA) Records, 6 January 1943.

[34] Ibid., Mss 66/1/126, 25 May 1942.

[35] AEU (MDC), 25 November 1941.

[36] MRC, Mss 66/1/2, CDEEA Records, 30 July 1940.

[37] Inman, *Labour in the Munitions Industries*, p. 59.

[38] Ibid.

[39] MBRTC, Rootes at War Mss, No. 2 Aero Engine Factory, 21 September 1939 – 31 December 1939.

[40] MRC, Mss 226/ST/1/1/9, Standard Motor Company, Minutes of Directors' Meetings, 12 May 1941.

[41] MRC, Mss 66/1/1 CDEEA Records, 15 August 1940.

[42] Ibid., Mss 66/1/1 CDEEA Records, 28 February 1940.

[43]   Ibid., Mss 66/1/5, CDEEA Records, 9 July 1941, Mss 66/2/255, CDEEA Records, 8 February 1944.
[44]   Ibid., Mss 66/1/94, CDEEA Records, 10 March 1942.
[45]   Ibid., Mss 66/1/157, CDEEA Records, 2 November 1941.
[46]   Ibid., Mss 66/2/59, CDEEA Records, 20 April 1944.
[47]   Ibid., Mss 66/2/228, CDEEA Records, 22 November 1945.
[48]   Ibid., Mss 66/2/297, CDEEA Records, 6 August 1946.
[49]   Ibid., Mss 66/2/145, CDEEA Records, 24 February 1941.
[50]   Inman, *Labour in the Munitions Industries*, p. 289; CDEEA Minutes, 8 December 1940; MRC, Mss 66/1/256, CDEEA Records, 2 November 1943; Croucher, *Engineers at War*, p. 260.
[51]   Inman, *Labour in the Munitions Industries*, p. 356.
[52]   Ibid.
[53]   MRC, Mss 225/ST/1/1/9, Standard Motor Company, Minutes of Directors' Meetings, 12 May 1941.
[54]   Inman, *Labour in the Munitions Industries*, p. 356.
[55]   CDEEA, Minutes, 5 June 1939.
[56]   Richardson, *Twentieth Century Coventry*, pp. 111–12; K.G.C. Knowles and D. Robinson, 'Wage Movements in Coventry', *Bulletin of Oxford University Institute of Economics and Statistics*, vol. 51 (February 1969), p. 1; W. Brown, 'Pieceworking in Coventry', *Scottish Journal of Political Economy*, vol. 18 (February 1971), pp. 2–3.
[57]   Inman, *Labour in the Munitions Industries*, pp. 321–2.
[58]   MRC, Mss 226/ST/1/1/9, Standard Motor Company, Minutes of Directors' Meetings, 5 December 1941, 22 May 1942.
[59]   AEU, (MDC), 31 March 1942, 14 April 1942, 16 June 1942, 7 July 1942, 14 July 1942, 11 May 1943, 18 May 1943.
[60]   MRC, Mss 66/1/3, CDEEA Records, 15 August 1940.
[61]   Ibid., Mss 66/1/207, CDEEA Records, 4 June 1943, Mss 66/1/193, CDEEA Records, 30 April 1943.
[62]   Ibid., Mss 66/1/137, CDEEA Records, 17 July 1941; AEU (MDC) 24 January 1944.
[63]   Ibid., 7 March 1944.
[64]   MRC, Mss 66/1/36, CDEEA Records, 12 October 1940, Mss 66/1/54, CDEEA Records, 15 October 1941.
[65]   CDEEA, Minutes, 16 February 1942, 15 June 1942.
[66]   AEU (MDC), 21 October 1941.
[67]   Ibid., 30 December 1941.
[68]   Ibid., 30 December 1941, 6 January 1942, 23 September 1942.
[69]   Ibid., 11 January 1944, 14 November 1944.
[70]   Croucher, *Engineers at War*, pp. 95–7; AEU (MDC), 29 September 1940.
[71]   MRC, Mss 226/ST/1/1/9, Standard Motor Compnay, Minutes of Directors' Meetings, 20 October 1944.
[72]   Richardson, *Twentieth Century Coventry*, p. 122.
[73]   MBRTC, Rootes at War Mss, Humber 30 September 1945 – 31 December 1945.
[74]   Richardson, *Twentieth Century Coventry*, p. 113; Croucher, *Engineers at War*, p. 343; AUE (MDC), 11 March 1946; Shenfield and Florence, 'Economies and Diseconomies of Concentration', pp. 87–97.

Chapter 7

Growth, Stagnation and Merger, 1945–68

The post-war years down to the mid-1960s were a period of very considerable success for the British motor industry as output expanded, jobs multiplied and new markets were cultivated. Moreover, the expansionist influence of American companies was felt through the activities of Ford and Vauxhall, and eventually Chrysler after it linked itself with the near bankrupt Rootes Group. Government economic policy was also of central importance to the motor industry's post-war experience. Companies were pressed into developing new manufacturing capacity in areas of high unemployment, such as Scotland and Merseyside, far removed from the industry's traditional heartland in the Midlands and the South East, while sharp changes in fiscal and monetary policies served to create an uneven pattern of domestic consumer demand. Coventry was widely depicted during these two decades as the epitome of the motor 'boom town'. Its car factories attracted labour from all over the country and at one time accounted for almost 35 per cent of the city's total employment.[1] However, before discussing the motor industry's significance within the local economy, it is necessary to emphasise that Coventry was and remains a centre of final assembly for vehicles directed at the volume passenger market, and that this principally involved Rootes and Standard. It was this end of the trade that gave the city its particular image and the components used were in the main bought out from suppliers in the Birmingham and Wolverhampton areas. Indeed, of the leading British component suppliers, only Dunlop had a plant of any real size in Coventry and even its activities involved aircraft and aerospace rather than cars. Thus, most of Coventry's motor-vehicle output was directed towards the final, fashion-conscious and essentially volatile end of the trade, which helps to explain why the local industry was particularly vulnerable to periodic booms and slumps.[2]

As we have already noted, the Second World War caused Coventry's economic structure to narrow in an exaggerated manner with an over-reliance upon motor vehicles, aircraft, electrical and mechanical engineering. This trend continued throughout the ensuing fifteen years and significantly in 1959 *The Times* pointed to the city's lack of industrial diversity compared with the West Midlands region as a whole and warned in particular of the serious risks involved in excessive dependency upon motor-vehicle manufacture.[3] Yet the metal-based industries had been central to Coventry's post-war recovery and so successful were they that in 1950 the *Financial Times* reported that at least a dozen government ministries were trying to limit Coventry's growth and expansion.[4] The redundancies and unemployment anticipated by both sides of industry towards the end of the war never materialised and from 1946 many firms remained chronically short of labour. In that year the CDEEA reported a shortfall of 17,000 check workers in the city and asked the government for special assistance to meet housing needs to help attract the necessary labour.[5] But by 1950 the situation had changed little. In that year one national newspaper carried an article entitled "'Blitz Town' becomes 'Boom Town'". This acknowledged that the physical devastation of war remained apparent, the commercial area appearing much as it was immediately after the blitz with people being forced to take refuge in temporary accommodation. A near shanty-town of derelict railway coaches had grown up near the city centre while wartime army camps and hostels were occupied by squatters. Despite these privations, it was noted that Coventry was a city of opportunity with many well-paid manual job vacancies remaining unfilled. Over the next two weeks 17,000 letters of application arrived at the Coventry Employment Exchange, while hundreds of men came in person to seek work. This was not the depression which had been forecast but a manifestation of full employment.[6]

Coventry's favourable employment prospects and relatively high wage levels help to explain the city's population growth from a total of 232,000 in 1946 to 258,000 in 1951 and 335,230 by 1971. Indeed, from the end of the war until the mid-1950s Coventry's population increase averaged the remarkably high figure of 3,000 per annum, much of which was accounted for by young migrants from Wales, Ireland, Scotland and the north-east of England who came either to seek employment for the first time or to join relatives and friends already settled in the area. Prime-aged males represented the most significant group of migrants. In 1951 the city housed 14,400 males aged between fifteen and twenty-four. A decade later there were 21,600 in the age group twenty-five to thirty-five, an increase of 50 per cent over the period, while the corresponding figure for England and Wales as a whole was only 3 per cent.[7] Parallel to crude population increase was concomitant expansion in the numbers employed. These rose from 122,248 in 1951 to 161,960 in 1961, an increase of 24.5 per cent. Breaking these figures down into industrial groups indicates just how substantial a role the metal industries, including motor vehicles, played in Coventry's economy. Further disaggregation of the employment returns indicates that in 1952 the motor-vehicle industry employed 63,135 operatives and that this subsequently rose to a peak of 74,626 in 1966 before falling away to 70,171 in 1970. Over a period of twenty years, therefore, some 35 to 40 per cent of all employment in the city was located in this sector, a degree of concentration not repeated anywhere else in Britain, and which was to have profound consequences in the 1970s and 1980s.[8]

At the end of the war Coventry's motor and aircraft manufacturers quickly looked to the future, but their plans could only be realised within the framework of the Labour government's own policies for reconstruction. Rather belatedly, the motor industry came to be regarded as an important way of earning the dollar imports that were essential to the general process of economic recovery through bridging the dollar gap. Before 1939 the United Kingdom car industry concentrated its main sales effort at home, but the post-war market was quite different with world demand at a level which was unprecedented. Despite their vast resources, American firms could not even satisfy domestic consumption, while in Europe the French, German and Italian industries lay in disarray as a consequence of war damage.[9] Almost as soon as the war ended, Coventry's manufacturers turned their attention to getting back into automobile production as their core business, but it transpired that this was not an easy linear progression, with several keeping their foot in more than one camp, and so the return to cars was not carried out at uniform pace. Alvis, for example, was by no means convinced that a return to vehicle production was in its best long-term interests. In 1945 Rootes announced their decision to return to car production as quickly as possible and Jaguar, as SS cars formally became known, adopted a similar policy. Conversely, Standard made it known that for the time being the company would continue to manufacture aero-engines and airframes.[10] However, a rapid expansion of industrial output required an increase in production facilities and several Coventry firms were quick to take advantage of the shadow factories they had operated during the war, leasing them from the government and converting them for motor-vehicle manufacture. Rootes retained their Ryton factory, while Standard leased both the Banner Lane and Fletchampstead Highway plants. Not to be outdone by Sir John Black, in the late 1940s and early 1950s William Lyons acquired the whole of the Brown's Lane complex to facilitate Jaguar's rising output. Finally, in addition to shadow factory accommodation, some 707,355 square feet of new production space was approved in Coventry between 1945 and 1948, further proof of the growing dynamism of the local economy.[11]

In 1946 car production stood at only two-thirds of its pre-war output and as table 7.1 indicates, recovery was slow with 1937 production levels not being achieved until 1949. The share of total output retained by Rootes and Standard remained remarkably steady and conformed to the pattern that had been established in the 1930s. Because of the endemic balance-of-payments difficulties of the immediate post-war period the Ministry of Supply informed Britain's motor manufacturers that at least 50 per cent of production should be for export. Although the Ministry did not invoke nationalisation nor Draconian powers to control the industry as a whole, it was able to enforce its will through its ability to influence the distribution of scarce raw materials. Home sales were deliberately restricted, leading to long queues of customers and a thriving trade in second-hand cars, as new production was earmarked for foreign markets. In 1947 export quotas stood at 50 per cent of an output of approximately 267,000 units and were then revised upwards to 66 per cent of the 1948 output of 334,815 vehicles. Such figures were hard to attain due to repeated raw-material shortages and bottlenecks to say nothing of working mainly in old premises with near-obsolete equipment, conditions which were not helped by the 1947 fuel crisis. Eventually, too, the pressure of domestic demand forced the government to moderate the proportion of vehicles allocated for export to around two-thirds of total output.

The government appeared to believe that favourable export conditions would continue for several years, but this optimism was not shared by the motor manufacturers, most of whom fully appreciated that overseas sales would become more difficult once their former rivals recovered from the war. Equally, they had misgivings about the impact of the export drive upon the industry's long-term development. Without new models to offer, Coventry's car firms, like others, had to manufacture vehicles which had been designed in the 1930s. Standard had its range of Eights, Nines and Tens, while Rootes relied upon its Humber and Minx models. These vehicles had largely been intended for British roads, weather and driving conditions and, though good in their own right, were not necessarily suitable for foreign markets. Their main advantage was that, unlike their chief European and American rivals, they cars were available, even though they sometimes offered less value for money. Yet, when new models appeared they did not always meet with immediate success. Soon after the war ended the Standard board authorised the introduction of new cars under the Triumph marque, the Roadster and the Renown. Both were poorly designed with development being rushed and neither sold particularly well and, even allowing for minor design changes, their combined output did not exceed 20,000 vehicles between 1946 and 1954, when they were phased out of production.

Exports of British-made cars were continually hampered by shortages of raw materials, which retarded production and, by obliging firms to operate below capacity, forced down productivity levels. Sir John Black reported in 1946 that Standard's output was seriously impeded by inadequate supplies of steel and castings. He, therefore, approached the government with a scheme which would allow the company either to establish its own foundry to lease one. Black was ultimately permitted to invest £125,000 in re-equipping two factories in West Bromwich owned by Dartmouth Castings, with the intention that Standard would be the sole customer. Similarly, production at Canley almost ground to a halt in May 1948 because of a serious fuel shortage.[12] Virtually identical problems surfaced at Jaguar. Lyons complained frequently that deficiencies on the supply side held back exports and that because of this, competitors abroad were threatening to recapture their old markets. He also dwelt at length upon the question of industrial costs.[13] By 1950 Jaguar and other British firms were already being squeezed by their lower-priced rivals. Coventry wage levels were the highest in the motor industry, but the impact of the export drive was probably of greater significance in raising production costs since it slowed down rationalisation in the industry as a whole and also delayed much-needed investment.[14]

On the vexed issue of rationalisation, the government expressed its considerable anxiety in 1946 at the large number of different models leaving Britain's car factories and was even prompted to suggest the creation of a volume-produced, standardised car.[15] Although there was much to be said in favour of this idea, in retrospect it is hard to envisage such a scheme working in Coventry, let alone nationally. It would have required time to plan and introduce and would have involved ruthless rationalisation as well as great deal of co-operation. Equally, it is difficult to see how Rootes and Standard could have achieved this in the short or even medium term given the pressure they were under to proceed with the task of producing and exporting. Black certainly favoured bringing order to the production line, but he interpreted the government's suggestion in terms of a family of cars for all sectors of the market, and to him this probably meant a family of the Standard variety and not one that involved other manufacturers.[16] The buoyant nature of the car market in the post-war era, coupled with government unwillingness to enforce a scheme of rationalisation, combined to place the structure of the industry in virtual suspended animation. This enabled weaker firms, such as Singer and Lea Francis, to survive a little longer and hence delay the rationalisation that was so essential to the industry's long-term future if further economies of scale were to be achieved.

The range of models available and the large number of markets in which penetration was attempted tended to weaken overseas car sales. Distributors often carried insufficient stocks to satisfy demand, while shortages of spares contributed to a rather poor after-sales facility. These factors meant that some British cars developed an adverse commercial reputation which probably deterred many customers from indulging in further purchases.[17] The experience of Standard illustrates the general nature of the problem. In 1946 the firm created agencies in twenty-four countries and subsequently established subsidiary companies in South Africa, Canada, India and Australia.[18] With Standard's output for the first five years after the war hovering between 20,000 and 50,000 vehicles a year, the spread of markets was probably too great for more than a few to

Table 7.1

Total UK car production and estimated share produced by the 'big six' and others 1946–52

Year	Total Output	Austin Nuffield	Rootes	Standard	Vauxhall	Ford	Others
1946	269,612	43.4	10.7	11.6	9.0	14.4	11.0
1947	287,000	39.3	10.5	12.9	10.6	14.8	12.0
1948	334,815	40.2	10.3	11.2	11.8	18.8	7.7
1949	412,290	39.4	13.3	11.1	11.0	18.7	7.5
1950	522,515	39.4	13.5	11.1	9.0	19.2	7.8
1951	475,919	40.3	12.3	12.6	7.4	18.9	8.4
1952	448,000	39.4	12.0	10.6	8.1	21.1	7.0

Source: Maxcy and Silbertson, *The Motor Industry*, p. 117.

be developed intensively.[19] By contrast, Jaguar concentrated on manufacturing primarily for the American market and, to a much lesser extent, for continental Europe. Having established a distinct sales target, both in terms of geography and product, a solid foothold was quickly gained in the United States, using both New York and Los Angeles as main distribution outlets. By 1950 production totalled nearly 8,000 cars with approximately 80 per cent going abroad, the greater proportion crossing the Atlantic rather than the English Channel, with only a few retailing in the home market.[20]

New investment by the car manufacturers in machine tools and other equipment was restricted by government regulations relating to capital imports and expenditure. Coventry's principal motor firms were well aware of the financial problems which development initiatives, including factory modernisation, involved.[21] For example, after Standard had concluded a deal in 1945 to manufacture the Ferguson tractor at its own Banner Lane plant, government permission had to be obtained to acquire the dollars which were needed to purchase the Continental engines used to power the vehicle before the company's own production models became available. Similarly, in the absence of suitable British-made equipment, Standard was forced to obtain additional dollars to purchase specialist American machine tools. Fortunately, both Hugh Dalton at the Treasury and Stafford Cripps, president of the Board of Trade, proved particularly helpful in securing the necessary currency.[22] Some £230,000 was spent at Jaguar between 1946 and 1952 on factory extensions, plant and equipment, but overall this figure was probably below the firm's actual needs during that period. This was matched by similar expenditure at Rootes, but such levels of investment were too small and piecemeal to give Coventry's

Table 7.2
Pre-tax profits /(loss) in the UK motor industry 1945–51, £m

Year	Austin	Morris	Standard	Rootes	Vauxhall	Ford
1945	0.9	1.9	0.3	1.5	2.1	1.4
1946	1.0	3.0	0.3	(0.4)	1.5	3.2
1947	1.8	2.6	0.3	0.6	2.0	3.9
1948	1.1	1.5	0.9	1.2	2.0	5.5
1949	1.6	2.6	1.2	1.1	2.7	5.5
1950	5.2	2.1	1.3	2.0	2.7	9.7
1951	7.2	8.7	2.3	3.4	2.7	9.8

Source: Dunnett, *The Decline of the British Motor Industry*, p. 39.

volume producers a capacity approaching that of Ford, Nuffield or Austin.[23]

Investment patterns were influenced by profitability. Despite operating in a sellers' market, none of Britain's car producers made anything like adequate profits until 1951, by which time Rootes and Standard were beginning to fall significantly behind the 'big three' in terms of market share.

A number of factors explain such modest profit levels. Rootes and Standard had the particular problem that relatively low output forced up unit costs and so squeezed the margin between income and expenditure. Yet behind the crude production figures a variety of political and economic considerations affected profitability throughout the industry as a whole. Dunnett makes the point that the motor firms had to avoid the appearance of profiteering since this could have encouraged government to impose tighter financial controls or even introduce nationalisation. Moreover, it was important that customers' goodwill be retained, since a sudden increase in competitiveness from rivals could place additional strain upon brand loyalty. There was also concern that foreign governments would accuse British manufacturers of dumping and take retaliatory action, particularly if the gap between domestic and export car prices appeared too wide. In fact, overseas prices were generally maintained at a lower level than those at home in order to help stimulate volume sales and profits. The growing competitiveness of European firms by the late 1940s made this type of price discrimination essential for British car manufacturers desperately trying to retain their grip on foreign markets. In the United States some British cars were even sold at less than cost price.[24]

Hopes were high in 1950 of a return to more normal trading patterns, but these were quickly dashed by the onset of the Korean crisis which brought a close monitoring of economic activity and the introduction of strict controls over the supply of raw materials. As a result, car output fell sharply, further delaying the post-war recovery process.[25] Several motor firms again became involved in armaments production. Standard was willing to accept the government's invitation to participate in the Avon Jet programme, but was also anxious to increase output of both cars and tractors, and this brought the first evidence of Whitehall intervention to restrict the natural growth of a Coventry firm. The government wanted the Avon engine to be built at Standard's Fletchampstead plant and, because of the tight labour situation in the city, expressly prohibited further growth in motor-vehicle production. Any expansion of Standard's car-making activities, therefore, required the company to search for a resource base beyond Coventry. A suitable 136 acre site near Kirkby was offered by Liverpool City Council but, once the Korean emergency receded, the Avon project was cancelled, bringing to an end Standard's projected move northwards. This example of government intervention was a foretaste of what lay in store for both Standard and Rootes later in the decade.[26]

By the early 1950s the British motor industry had more than recovered from the war and the following two decades were characterised by very substantial expansion. Output for 1950 was already 30 per cent above the 1937 figure and, with the exception of the Korean War period, growth was almost continuous, reaching a peak of 1,867,640 units in 1964. Despite fluctuating thereafter, production in 1970 was still around 88 per cent of the 1964 level. These trends were mirrored in Coventry where the output of vehicles fell, as table 7.3 indicates, from almost 28 per cent of the UK total in 1951 to 22.5 per cent in 1970. In 1959 BMC, Ford and Vauxhall, none of which had an assembly presence in the city, together had sufficient spare capacity to account for all Coventry's output. Coventry was becoming a centre of marginal importance for volume-produced passenger cars and in a relative sense was already in decline at a time when its output was reaching record proportions.[27]

Although both Rootes and Standard remained part of the 'big five', as the five major producers became collectively known after the creation of BMC in 1952, their position in the production league was lower than was economically sound, as shown in table 7.4.

BMC's share of total output declined slowly. Ford continued with the impressive progress achieved between the wars, while Vauxhall managed a modest improvement in its position. By contrast, Standard exhibited a marked decline and Rootes struggled doggedly to retain a 10 to 13 per cent share of output and, taken together, the overall trend for the two Coventry volume producers was ominously downwards.

Market penetration was as important to the motor manufacturers as relative production figures, and this became a matter of particular concern in the late 1960s and early 1970s as foreign car imports surged into Britain to take 14.3 per cent of the market in 1970. As table 7.5 indicates, Rootes struggled to hold its market share which averaged between 10 and 12.2 per cent between 1954 and 1970. Standard's performance was even more worrying, falling from 11 per cent in 1954 to a mere 5.9 per cent in 1970.

Considering that the whole period was one of vast expansion in the domestic market it is evident that both firms were in decline. Low product levels and poor market share were indicative of weak firms, but in addition both companies displayed a poor record on profits and rates of return on capital. Because of differences in economies of scale, product mix and accounting practices, profitability in the motor industry is often notoriously difficult to measure. A further complication is that while small falls in capacity usage normally have only a minor effect on costs they can exert a disproportionate impact upon profit levels. Despite these qualifications, it is clear from table 7.6 that profitability in the car-manufacturing industry improved during the decade after 1945, even outstripping the growth in company profits as a whole. The next five years saw considerable volatility in profit margins. The post-war peak was reached in 1960 after which, using Rhys's index, profits fell consistently until 1968 when another sharp rise helped to recover some of the lost ground.[28]

Table 7.3
Output of cars in Britain and estimated output in Coventry with Coventry output as a percentage of UK production 1951–70

Year	UK output	Coventry output	Coventry output as % of UK output
1951	475,919	133,265	27.9
1952	448,000	111,835	24.9
1953	594,808	137,830	23.1
1954	769,165	182,720	23.7
1955	893,560	205,225	23.0
1956	707,594	151,655	21.4
1957	860,842	162,000	18.8
1958	1,051,551	223,010	21.2
1959	1,189,943	256,545	21.5
1960	1,352,728	276,170	20.4
1961	1,003,967	182,100	18.1
1962	1,249,426	244,670	19.5
1963	1,607,939	294,670	18.3
1964	1,867,640	372,370	19.9
1965	1,722,045	320,351	18.6
1966	1.603,679	319,990	21.0
1967	1,552,013	325,966	21.0
1968	1,815,936	351,100	19.3
1969	1,717,073	324,850	18.9
1970	1,640,966	369,550	22.5

Sources: SMMT Data; Mallier and Rosser, 'Economic Decline in Perspective', appendix 3, p. 26; BL Data: 14th Report from the Expenditure Committee, sess. 1974–75, *The Motor Vehicle Industry*, HC 617 (1) (London HMSO, August 1975), p. 194.

In turning to an examination of individual companies it is apparent that the two Coventry firms fared badly in comparison with their main rivals. Rootes accumulated losses in six years out of ten during the 1960s amounting to a total of just over £21 million. Standard was largely profitable during the 1950s, though Turner claims that had it not been for the successful tractor division income would have been significantly reduced and the company's financial position much less secure. Indeed, by the time of the Leyland takeover the firm was in deep trouble. The transfer of the Banner Lane plant to Massey Harris of Canada increased Standard's vulnerability, since it was left totally dependent upon cars sales. In 1961

Table 7.4

Production by the 'big five' as a percentage of total vehicle output in Britain 1946–70

Year	BMC	Ford	Vauxhall	Rootes	Standard	Others
1946	43.4	14.4	9.0	10.7	11.6	11.0
1950	39.4	19.2	9.0	13.5	11.1	7.5
1955	38.9	27.0	8.5	11.4	9.8	4.4
1960	37.5	30.0	11.0	10.5	8.0	4.0
1962	37.5	29.5	11.5	11.5	6.0	4.0
1964	37.0	28.5	13.5	12.6	7.5	2.7
1966	a37.6	29.0	10.7	10.7	7.6	4.2
1968	a33.6	30.5	13.5	10.4	7.6	4.4
1970	a35.8	27.3	10.8	13.3	n/a	0.5

Note: Figures for Jaguar and Rover have been excluded.

Sources: Maxcy and Silberston, *The Motor Industry*, p. 117; A Silberston, 'The Motor Industry 1955–6', *Bulletin of Oxford University Institute of Economics and Statistics*, vol. 27, pt. 4 (1965), p. 28. Rhys, *The Motor Industry: An Economic Survey*, p. 312.

Table 7.5

UK market penetration by firms 1947–70, %

Year	BMC/ BL	Ford	Vauxhall	Rootes/ Chrysler	Standard	Imports
1947	40.1	18.4	11.2	10.9	13.2	-
1954	38.0	27.0	9.0	11.0	111.0	-
1965	44.5	27.3	11.8	11.9	-	5.1
1966	45.21	25.1	11.2	11.8	-	7.4
1967	40.7	25.3	13.2	12.2	7.8	8.3
1968	40.6	27.3	1.31	10.2	7.3	8.3
1969	40.2	27.3	13.1	10.2	7.3	8.3
1970	38.1	27.5	10.0	10.5	5.9	14.3

Sources: Rhys, The Motor Industry: An Economic Survey, pp. 19–20; Hood and Young, Chrysler UK, p. 138; Coventry Evening Telegraph (various editions).

these were extremely disappointing and a deficit of up to £3 million was anticipated. At one stage losses reached £600,000 a month and but for the Leyland intervention the company might well have gone into liquidation. Under the Leyland umbrella, and with an upturn in the market between 1962 and 1964, Standard's financial situation improved greatly with profits rising to a peak of £6 million in 1968. In essence, both Rootes and Standard were too small to survive as independent producers in the highly competitive volume car market and had little choice but to seek partners through merger or takeover.[29]

Table 7.6
Pre-Tax Profit (Loss) in the UK Motor Industry 1952-70, £m

Year	BMC	BLMC	Standard	Rootes/ Chrysler	Ford	Vauxhall
1952	5.2	-	1.6	3.4	9.6	5.3
1953	12.3	-	1.6	2.2	15.7	9.9
1954	17.9	-	2.2	3.5	19.0	12.4
1955	20.3	-	3.3	3.3	18.1	10.8
1956	11.7	-	0.8	1.7	10.0	7.4
1957	11.2	-	0.8	(0.6)	20.1	(2.3)
1958	21.0	-	-	3.4	24.7	1.1
1959	15.7	-	4.0	3.9	32.2	13.5
1960	27.9	-	2.2	4.4	33.7	14.1
1961	10.1	-	(1.5)	2.9	22.2	14.5
1962	4.2	-	(1.5)	(0.9)	17.0	16.0
1963	15.4	-	-	(0.3)	35.0	17.3
1964	21.8	-	-	1.8	24.0	17.9
1965	23.3	-	4.0	(0.2)	8.9	17.7
1966	21.8	-	3.5	(3.1)	7.4	13.7
1967	(3.28)	-	-	(10.5)	25.4	12.0
1968	-	37.9	6.0	3.9	43.0	12.2
1969	-	40.0	3.5	0.6	38.1	1.6
1970	-	4.0	-	(10.0)	20.6	(5.1)

Note: Standard's profits from 1965 are estimates based on figures contained in the Standard Board Minutes in the MRC at Warwick University.

Sources: Dunnett, *The Decline of the British Motor Industry*, p. 39; Hood and Young, *Chrysler UK*, p. 98; Rhys, *The Motor Industry: An Economic Survey*, p. 361.

Table 7.7
Profit /(loss) per unit (£)

	1945	1950	1961	1968	1970
Vauxhall	100	80	20	35	(33)
Ford	65	45	53	59	47
BMC	50	35	6	38	(22)
Standard	30	30	(21)	–	–
Rootes	23	–	7	17	(46)

Source: Rhys, *The Motor Industry: An Economic Survey*, p. 363.

Moving beyond corporate profits to those earned per unit sold, the relative weakness of both Rootes and Standard is again evident from table 7.7, with the latter company in particular finding it hard to achieve a satisfactory return on sales. In 1953 Standard's profit per vehicle was as low as £13, less than one-third that of Ford. Two years later, the figure had risen to £35, but even in 1962 the firm was losing £10 on every Herald produced. Falling profitability was also reflected in low rates of return on capital, but this was a near universal feature of the British motor industry. Although care must be taken in measuring rates of return across different companies, it is clear from table 7.8 that among the volume manufacturers Rootes was the weakest performer, with Standard also trailing badly. The turning point for Rootes came in 1952 when the rate of return peaked at 40 per cent before dropping precipitously for the remainder of the decade. These years saw the start of Rootes's decline with low sales, low returns and inadequate investment.[30]

Sufficient statistical evidence has been marshalled to outline the broad areas in which Coventry's volume producers lagged behind in the motor industry. The reasons for this sluggish performance are not easily disentangled. Among those suggested are poor returns to scale because of lack of size, inadequate investment, weak model design, comparatively high costs and prices, trade union influence on the shop floor, inadequate management and government economic policy. It is clear, however, that no single explanation is adequate and that the problems of both Rootes and Standard emanated from the complex interaction of a number of variables. Moreover, causality was further complicated by the reinforcement effect which decline itself promoted.

Studies by Silberston, Rhys, Bhaskar and, more recently, by Church, Foreman-Peck, Bowden and McKinlay, have examined the obstacles to the achievement of economics of scale in the motor industry. These have demonstrated that the output necessary for minimum economies of scale has increased over time for all processes involved in car manufacture.[31]

Table 7.8

Rates of return /(loss) on capital 1954–63 (per cent)

Year	BMC	Ford	Vaux-hall	Rootes	Stand-ard	Leyland	Average
1954	32	44	43	23	23	16	34
1955	29	25	28	17	24	19	26
1956	17	13	14	9	5	22	14
1957	11	24	(2)	(2)	6	17	12
1958	26	25	4	10	13	15	19
1959	20	28	23	12	18	15	22
1960	28	24	22	14	9	24	23
1961	11	15	12	4	-	12	12
1962	4	11	16	(8)	-	7	8
1963	15	21	16	1	-	15	16

Source: Maxcy and Silberston, *The Motor Industry*, p. 276.

For firms such as Rootes and Standard, predominantly concerned with final assembly, the relevant targets rose from 100,000 units in the early 1950s to 250,000 in the late 1960s. A consistent growth in output was essential in order to control unit costs and maintain profit and investment levels. The shortfall in production at the Rootes and Standard plants over the period 1951 to 1970 is indicated by table 7.9. It is quite apparent that both firms failed to obtain anything like the economies of scale necessary for efficient production. The fact that in the volume side of the industry, small is neither beautiful nor profitable was recognised by the Standard board in 1958 when a target of 250,000 units was set to be achieved within three years.[32] This was not realised, and in fact 1961 saw a substantial drop in production with a correspondingly adverse effect on costs. As we have noted, the Herald sold at a loss with output falling well below the 2,000 a week needed to yield a profit. The company's overall break-even point in 1961 was 95,000 vehicles but this was undershot by nearly 30 per cent.[33] Production figures at Rootes were somewhat higher but still failed to reach the figures necessary for significant economies of scale.[34]

The importance of size helps to explain why both Rootes and Standard featured so prominently in the spate of mergers which occurred in the motor industry during the 1950s and 1960s, culminating in the formation of the British Leyland Motor Corporation in 1968. One of the principal reasons why Standard remained a relatively small-scale producer of motor-cars during the 1950s was its concurrent interest in manufacturing Ferguson tractors. Some 750,000 tractors of various designs

Table 7.9
Estimated output of cars by Standard and Rootes 1951-70

Year	Standard	Rootes	Rootes (CKD) a
1951	54,606	58,400	-
1952	36,000	58,340	-
1953	44,400	76,100	-
1954	79,300	84,500	-
1955	85,500	102,700	-
1956	56,800	75,000	-
1957	54,100	88,300	-
1958	77,100	130,300	-
1959	86,400	150,000	-
1960	107,500	120,830	23,142
1961	66,807	84,845	11,172
1962	86,533	123,138	19,830
1963	107,284	118,400	19,099
1964	105,528	120,743	17,436
1965	103,851	104,452	17,349
1966	98,016	109,875	13,332
1967	117,927	112,019	24,772
1968	102,595	106,000	38,964
1969	90,711	89,829	49,344
1970	95,711	88,871	-

a: CKD = Complete Knock Down

Sources: SMMT Data, various years; BL Data; Fourteenth Report from the Expenditure Committee, The Motor Industry, 1975, p. 194.

were produced at Banner Lane between 1948 and 1960.[35] In 1953, however, Harry Ferguson sold his interests to Massey Harris of Canada, makers of agricultural implements. Standard's relations with its new partners proved somewhat stormy. Massey Harris (later known as Massey Ferguson) became convinced that profits from the tractor side were being used to subsidise Standard's car division, and also had doubts concerning the Coventry firm's ability to control its costs. It became clear in 1957 that the Canadians were attempting to gain control, not just of the Banner Lane tractor plant but of Standard as a whole, by the purchase of shares through nominees. When this manoeuvre was revealed Masseys were forced to make a formal offer for Standard which was duly repulsed, but relations between the two firms were so irreparably soured that the Banner Lane facilities were sold to the Canadians for £12 million in 1959.[36]

Realising the nature of its difficulties due to its ambivalent relationship with Massey Harris, Standard was also involved in merger talks with Rootes and Rover (twice), both of which were equally keen to acquire partners in order to improve their production facilities and the range of their products. These negotiations collapsed, primarily on the issue of the composition of the boards that were to control the new companies perhaps because there were too many egos to satisfy. This left Standard quite isolated and in the late 1950s the company used some of the proceeds from the Banner Lane sale to create its own integrated, if geographically disparate group. Beginning earlier with the purchase of Beans Industries of Tipton in 1956 to give much-needed foundry provision, the company subsequently acquired the Fisher and Ludlow body-making plant at Tile Hill in Coventry, and also the Birmingham firm of Mulliners which for some years had been almost entirely engaged upon the manufacture of Standard bodies. Alforder Newton of Hemel Hempstead, suppliers of suspension and steering units, was also brought into the group, as was Hall's Engineering of Liverpool. A rather loose conglomerate was constructed under the name of Standard Triumph International in 1959, but Standard remained too small and poorly integrated to achieve real efficiency. It was fortunate that the company retained an outstanding reputation for its sports cars for it was probably this which attracted the Lancashire-based producer of commercial vehicles, Leyland Motors, into a takeover bid. Leyland had been attempting to enter the car side of the motor business for some time and, given Standard's financial problems in the early 1960s, any reasonable offer was likely to generate a positive response so that it was no surprise when the two firms merged in 1961.[37]

Rootes were also seriously concerned at their relatively modest production facilities in the 1950s. Thomas Tilling was taken over in 1950 and its premises switched almost immediately to manufacturing the new Rootes two-stroke, three-cylinder diesel engine. This was followed three years later by the purchase of the Coventry-based Singer Company, whose output had dwindled to a mere fifty cars a week. The Singer marque was retained and appeared in a new model, the Gazelle, as part of the firm's policy of badge engineering. In the same decade Rootes countenanced the idea of getting control of Standard. When Black left the company talks were entered into with Alick Dick, Black's successor, but after a period came to nothing. Billy Rootes, though, went as far as encouraging Massey Harris to sell Standard when and if the Canadians acquired the company, but again this proved fruitless. The company was clearly desperate to increase the scale of its operations and to find a partner that could lift its position in the industry and so it was in the early 1960s that Rootes became involved with Chrysler of America. The American corporation had been searching for a European base for some time and before it eventually bought into Simca and Rootes, had made unsuccessful approaches to both Standard and Leyland. Initially, Chrysler could not afford to bid outright for Rootes and so settled for purchasing the greater part of the firm's capital, but only a minority of the equity, which nevertheless saved it from impending bankruptcy. As Rootes profitability continued to decline it is scarcely surprising that as paymasters the Americans should become anxious to assume overall control. This ultimately occurred in 1967 after agreement had been reached between Chrysler, Rootes and the Industrial Reorganization Corporation. Despite its criticisms when in opposition of Chrysler, the Labour administration had little alternative but to agree to the takeover. The firm's uncertain future made the Minister of Technology, Anthony Wedgwood Benn, unwilling to consider public ownership, while no British car manufacturer was in a position to provide alternative assistance, and the complete failure of Rootes would have thrown many thousands out of work.[38]

In the early 1960s Jaguar tackled its need for additional production facilities by taking over the assets of the ailing Daimler company, to be followed by Guy Motors of Wolverhampton, and eventually Coventry Climax, and Meadows Engines. In 1966, however, Jaguar was itself absorbed into BMC to create British Motor Holdings. Alvis, Coventry's other quality-car producer, merged with Rover and both were subsequently taken over by Leyland as a defensive measure to balance BMC's acquisition of Jaguar. This meant that by 1966–67 almost all of the United Kingdom-owned sectors of the British motor industry had been divided into two large and disparate groups, BMH and Leyland. It was obvious by the late 1960s that the domestic motor industry was rapidly losing ground to overseas competitors such as Fiat and Volkswagen and so the Labour government became convinced that if British interests were to survive, the two conglomerates should merge into one large unit. Under the auspices of the Industrial Reorganization Corporation (IRC) and Lord Kearton, and after a considerable period of debate, the two firms were brought together in 1968 to form the British Leyland Motor Corporation. Hopes were high for a new phase of success for the British motor industry but these proved badly misplaced.[39]

Closely linked with the economies-of-scale explanation is the contention that investment levels in Coventry's motor industry after 1950 were below those necessary to promote high output and profitability. The motor industry enjoyed additional net investment in almost every year down to 1970, though three distinct phases can be identified. The first occurred between 1950 and 1953 as new investment became essential to cope with rising domestic demand and to replace old equipment. The second, lasting from 1956 to 1958, was more significant in scale and scope, while the third between 1960 and 1964 brought the industry's total capacity to 2,400,000 units per annum.[40] The investment cycles of Rootes and Standard loosely conformed to the first two upsurges but were spasmodic in nature and on a relatively smaller scale than those of Ford or even Vauxhall. Standard invested heavily in new transfer machines in 1956 and four years later spent over £5 million in opening a new assembly hall at Canley, raising production capacity to 250,000 cars a year, which under normal working operations would have been expected to run at about 75 per cent efficiency. New investment plans were harboured at the time of the Leyland takeover, but with the severe losses in 1961 and 1962 these had to be ruthlessly pruned in an effort to reduce costs and ease the firm's cash-flow problem. It was not until four years later that any significant new investment occurred when, under the Leyland umbrella, £25 million was put into plant and equipment to facilitate increased production of the Triumph 2,000. A year later a further £900,000 was expended upon six In-Line transfer machines and another £330,000 on new equipment to make cylinder heads for the Triumph 1,300 and Herald models.[41] As a consequence of this investment, and astute management, Leyland succeeded in turning the Canley plant into a producer of high-quality cars which were well able to compete with their Ford and BMC equivalents. However, the fact remains that for too long Canley was underfinanced and there can be little doubt that this was a fundamental cause of the failure to achieve satisfactory economies of scale and sufficient levels of profitability.

The picture was almost identical at Rootes. Profits were simply too meagre to enable the company to embark upon a systematic programme of new investment. By the time the firm was taken over by Chrysler, the Ryton plant was reported to be in a very bad state, with inefficient production methods and suffering from excessively high costs. The three assembly lines were described as cramped and inflexible with the Alpine and Humber tracks working well below capacity in comparison with the Minx, which could not produce fast enough to satisfy consumer demand. Yet, given the nature of the available machinery, it was virtually impossible to switch the other two to Minx production except at a very high cost, which of course the firm could ill afford.[42]

New investment in the motor industry over the decade 1946–56 generally came from retained earnings rather than depreciation allowances. Standard's level of retained earnings, as table 7.10 indicates, was some way below the industry average and so the company ploughed back far less than the majority of firms over this period, though by contrast its provision for depreciation was higher than most.[43] A major reason for this was a policy of maintaining high dividends despite low profitability. By the late 1950s Standard had increased its funds raised on the market to approximately £12 million, a relatively high figure for the industry at that period. Recourse was also made to securing overdrafts from Barclays Bank. In 1954 the firm's overdraft facility with the bank stood at £7 million, where it remained for several years before climbing to £9 million in 1961. When Leyland assumed control of Standard, reducing the company's heavy overdraft was made a priority.[44] Rootes's profit levels in the post-war decade were only marginally superior to those of Standard, but it, too, pursued a policy of high dividends. Thus, despite having a higher rate of capital retention and a slower rate of depreciation, the overall level of internal funding available to Rootes was lower than Standard's which in turn helps to explain why investment levels were poor. However, Rootes made comparatively modest use of the financial institutions and in the mid-1950s its liquidity position was quite healthy, while the value of its assets ranked third among the 'big five'. Thereafter, with rates of return generally declining in the industry and Rootes's deterioration being exceptionally fast, little new investment was forthcoming until the advent of Chrysler.[45]

Market penetration and model development undoubtedly suffered as a consequence of inadequate production, profit and investment levels, so that even in periods of sustained expansion of demand at home and abroad, difficulties in the supply side made themselves felt. Equally, there were problems of quality control and in maintaining flows of spares. Neither Rootes nor Standard made the running in the car market and both simply had to follow the lead set by their larger competitors which, given their poor economies of scale, meant that for most of the period under discussion they were relegated to the position of price takers rather than price leaders. Thus, in order to maintain sales Rootes and Standard were unable to market their vehicles at a price high enough to ensure a satisfactory rate of return. Turning to model development, Standard's policy after 1945 was to manufacture smallish family saloons under its own marque and to use the Triumph badge for sports cars of various types. In practice too many poorly-developed products were pushed on to the market, only to fail. The Roadster and the Renown have already been alluded to, but a similar disaster was the Triumph Mayflower, known as the 'Watchcharm Rolls' because of its razored edge. The car was built on the whim of Sir John Black who, after a trip to America, thought that such a small car would appeal to American women, and yet no market research whatsoever had been carried out. In the event this small, underpowered vehicle proved unsuitable for American roads and distances and had to be withdrawn from the market in 1954, with less than 44,000 being produced during the six years of its life. The consequence of this policy was that such ill-prepared products sold only in small quantities at little or no profit and it was not until the 1960s that some sort of order and standardisation was brought to the firm's offerings.[46]

By 1957 Standard's saloon cars were rather unimaginative in design, epitomised by the reliable but bulbous Vanguard, which at that time was having to be sold off at rock-bottom prices in the North American market simply to get rid of unwanted stock. It was because of this sagging performance and poor market share that a breakthrough was attempted with the development the Triumph Herald. Alick Dick, who had replaced Sir John Black as managing director in 1953, was adamant that the new vehicle should be designed in several variants – saloon, coupe, convertible, estate and van, and that it should be equally saleable in home and foreign

Table 7.10
Funds available, internal and external 1947–56 (£,000)

	Retained earnings	Deprecia- tion	Total	Long term capital raised	
Austin (1947–51)	5,552	2,294	8,347	2,580	1948
Morris (1947–50)	2,000	2,213	4,219	-	-
BMC (1952–)	19,494	11,498	31,029	4,117	1954
Ford	39,257	20,462	59,719	-	-
Rootes (1949–)	7,024	4,102	11,126	5,848	1949-54
Standard +	3,126	13,849	16,975	7,385	1948, 1954, 1955
Vauxhall	19,336	14,950	34,745	17,680	1954, 1955, 1955
Total	96,356	69,868	114,224		

Note: In addition a further £1,560,000 had been raised in 1945 by the issue of ordinary shares.

Source: Maxcy and Silberston, *The Motor Industry*, p. 217.

markets. However, designing and manufacturing a popular and profitable car did not prove easy. Without a fully integrated plant the different parts of the bodywork were made in separate factories and brought to Canley for final assembly where they were bolted together rather than welded, as was normal practice in the industry. This technique allowed the various models of the car to be built quickly and minimised tooling expenses. When the Herald was launched it was generally well received by the motoring press and public. Apart from its technical and design features, the Triumph marque helped to give it an up-market sports image. However, complaints were soon voiced that the bodywork was deficient with water leaks appearing in the bolted sections and road dirt finding its way into the engine. There was also some criticism that the engine was too small to power the car effectively.[47] In its early days the Herald's future was, therefore, rather uncertain, but great effort was made by the company to improve construction techniques and quality control, and to ensure that delivery dates were met. By 1965 the Herald enjoyed the highest resale price of any small car available on the British market and a year later, when the 1,300 version was introduced, supply could barely keep pace with demand.[48] Standard deserve credit for the efficient way in which the Herald's teething problems were tackled, but the impression remains that the initial assembly process involved a number of significant weaknesses, though the firm's planning was undoubtedly constrained by its slender resource base. Abroad the car was not quite so successful. Sales were moderately good in France and Italy, but outside Europe there was disappointment. It had really been designed for European driving conditions and was not particularly well suited to other markets. In Australia there was difficulty in generating even a modest degree of consumer interest. The Herald's image in South Africa was reported in 1961 to be poor, while in the United States prices had to be substantially reduced in 1962 in an effort to boost sales.[49]

Most Triumph sports models sold well abroad, particularly in the United States where the success of the TR4 and the Spitfire in the mid-1960s elevated the company from third to second in the import league. This even forced Renault, one of Standard's main rivals in the American market, to cut its prices in order to remain competitive.[50]

By 1965, however, the company's overall foreign sales had improved considerably with exports to America and Europe running at 23,000 and 21,000 units respectively, much of which was due to the growing popularity of Triumph sports cars.[51] Laudable though these efforts were, the sad fact remains that with sales being in such small numbers the profits made from the sports cars were insufficient to sustain adequate levels of overall profitability.

Rootes's lack of profitability and investment also manifested itself in poor model development. By the early 1960s all three of the company's Ryton-produced cars, the Alpine, the Humber Limousine and the Minx were ageing rapidly, and of these only the Minx made a profit. The Minx was an extremely successful car and in the medium-sized market outsold all its rivals except the Ford Cortina, but the profitability of one vehicle was insufficient to offset the losses sustained by the rest of the range. Moreover, there was no possibility of Rootes introducing new cars without very high levels of capital injection, money which it simply did not have. The company was thus heavily penalised for being too small and unprofitable in the volume side of the industry, a vicious spiral of decline from which it became increasingly difficult to escape.[52]

Before examining the more general problems which afflicted the Coventry motor industry, it is necessary to pause briefly to consider developments among the city's quality producers. At the end of the war this part of the market was covered by Jaguar, Daimler, Lanchester, Alvis, Armstrong Siddeley and Rootes through the Humber marque. The quality market had always been small and highly competitive with too many firms and models chasing too few customers. The output of individual companies, and in total, remained modest and in the 1950s failed to match the growth rates of the volume producers, causing some firms to diversify their investments and others to leave the industry altogether. The last Lanchester car was manufactured in 1956 and four years later Armstrong Siddeley also ceased production, while in the same year Daimler was absorbed by Jaguar. In the case of Armstrong Siddeley motor vehicles represented only a small part of the firm's total operations, and car output probably failed to realise sufficient funds to encourage model development programmes so that it was only a matter of time before this side of the business was dropped. Similarly, despite its long pedigree in the car trade, by the 1950s Daimler had developed far more profitable activity in the manufacture of aircraft engines and buses and, indeed, it is doubtful if total car output during that decade exceeded 20,000 vehicles, including those made under the Lanchester name. Shifts in government policy in the late 1950s largely demolished Daimler's aircraft division, leaving it with relatively modest car and bus interests so that the takeover by Jaguar made good business sense.[53]

The pattern at Alvis was rather similar. After the war the company maintained a high armaments and aircraft profile, mainly because these offered a more satisfactory return on capital than motor vehicles. Behind a public reaffirmation of its intention to resume car manufacture the company had serious doubts as to whether specialist and expensive vehicles would survive in the chilly economic climate of the post-war world. Nevertheless, a decision to re-enter the car market was taken with the commissioning of the low-budget TA 14, which by August 1946 had attracted some 900 firm orders. In the late 1940s the Alvis board rejected a proposal to manufacture a small luxury car on the assumption that consumer demand was insufficient to support another quality vehicle. Several new Alvis models were eventually introduced, though they appeared in such small numbers as to be hardly visible. Gradually, car-making was relegated to a minor part of the company's activities and between 1945 and 1967, when motor production ceased, only 21,535 vehicles had left the Coventry works. By 1956 Alvis was largely concerned with aero-engines and armoured vehicles, areas in which it has established a considerable international reputation for quality and expertise, so that it came as no surprise when car production was ultimately abandoned.[54]

While Alvis slipped quietly and with dignity out of the car market, Lea Francis left under something of a cloud. The firm continued to manufacture high-quality expensive cars in the post-war years, but in such small numbers that profits were minimal. Although the vehicles performed well in competitions and races, commercially they were unsuccessful and by 1956 the company's financial position began to weaken. Net profits for that year stood at only £16,000 and 1957 saw the start of the slide into eventual bankruptcy. Results for the financial year ending 31 January 1957 revealed a net loss of £2,441 which two years later had increased to £56,121, due largely to the ending of a government contract. Moreover, to make matters worse a bank overdraft of £51,000 was being carried. By 1961 this had risen to £74,000 and so desperate did the cash-flow situation become that valuable plant and equipment was sold to finance the daily running of the company. Despite its plans for new model development Lea Francis was forced into receivership in 1963 and motor production ceased.[55]

In sharp contrast to its rivals, Jaguar's luxury saloons and sports cars not only gained international recognition for styling and technical development, but also sold in large numbers. In 1951 Jaguar manufactured some 6,600 vehicles and by the end of the decade this had virtually trebled. Until its absorption into BMC in 1966 the company remained under the shrewd control of its founder, William Lyons, who personally made great effort to stimulate foreign sales, particularly in the USA. He promoted demonstrations in many parts of the world and encouraged participation in races and competitions to help ensure that the Jaguar marque, as distinct from SS cars, became widely known in the post-war world. As a result, Jaguar cars generally fared well in export markets, and in the twenty years after 1947 nearly 52 per cent of total output found its way abroad, with North America taking the major share. In 1967, an outstanding year for foreign sales, 50 per cent of exports found their way to America, 17 per cent to the European Economic Community and 8 per cent to the European Free Trade Area, with the remainder being distributed throughout the rest of the world. Some 85 per cent of all Jaguar E-Types manufactured in 1968 were sold in America, where their already competitive price was greatly aided by the devaluation of sterling in the previous year.

Jaguar's post-war turning point was perhaps the introduction in 1948 of the XK120 with its now legendary twin overhead-camshaft engine. With this and subsequent models a reputation was achieved in the 1950s for high-quality fast cars which was reinforced by repeated success in the Le Mans, Sebring and other international races. Jaguar's models remained remarkably stable throughout the 1950s, though a policy of continuous refinement meant that by the early 1960s the company was able to modernise its range with the minimum of disruption through the introduction of the Mark X, E-Type and XJ6. Behind this outward panache lay a careful policy of financial rectitude. The company never distributed more than 12 per cent of its trading profit in dividends and was therefore able to reinvest and increase its capacity as required. It was this which enabled Jaguar's fixed assets to triple between 1950 and 1960. Pre-tax profits increased slowly during the early 1950s, but by 1958 stood at £1,487,981 before rising spectacularly over the next twelve months to £2,603,969. Although profits fell in 1960, the upward movement was resumed in the following year, which was generally regarded as a bad period for the industry as a whole, and from then until the BMC merger hovered annually around £2–2.5 million.[56] It could be argued that prices were kept too low and that profits were artificially depressed, but Lyons was keenly aware of the intense competition from Mercedes and other foreign companies. Consequently, his policy appears to have been one of tight control over production levels in order to ensure a small market scarcity so that the prestige value of Jaguar cars was maintained, while at the same time effort was made to keep costs and prices within acceptable limits.

Reverting to a more general level of analysis, much has been made in the literature of the impact of government economic policies upon the motor industry's overall pattern of development. An important element in this discussion concerns the 'stop-go' measures of the 1950s and 1960s, which were used to control repeated balance-of-payments difficulties through the management of aggregate demand in the economy as whole. One popular target of government was hire-purchase regulations, and between 1952 and 1970 these were changed on no fewer than seventeen occasions, one result being that minimum deposits fluctuated from a low of 15 per cent in 1952 to a peak of 40 per cent in 1966 and 1968. General financial controls governing the purchase of cars changed every ten months over a period of two decades, creating uncertainty for consumers and for manufacturers attempting to plan their production, marketing and investment schedules.[57]

At first glance there appears to have been a strong positive correlation between fluctuations in total car output and Treasury attempts to manipulate the economy. With end of the Korean War the Conservative government embarked upon a period of expansion so that economic restrictions were loosened. Production increased until 1955 when a deterioration in the balance of payments brought the introduction of 'stop' policies, including a rise in hire-purchase and minimum-deposit rates. The Business Allowance was also abolished. These measures achieved their intended deflationary aims. They contributed, for example, to a decline in national car output of 21 per cent between 1955 and 1956. The corresponding figures for Rootes and Standard indicated a much greater local impact with falls of 27 per cent and 33.5 per cent respectively. This reduction in the general tempo of economic activity was prolonged by the onset of the Suez crisis in 1956 which led to a further package of measures, including the introduction of petrol rationing. An upswing began in the following year helped by growing American export demand, and in 1958, perhaps with the forthcoming general election in mind, the government declared the crisis over and restrictions were scaled down. Car production increased rapidly to meet growing home sales and in 1959 an output of 1.4 million vehicles was achieved, with both Rootes and Standard sharing in the boom. Yet by the end of 1960 the balance of payments was again in serious deficit so that national economic strategy was reversed once more. This was reflected in Coventry where motor vehicle output fell by 34 per cent between 1960 and 1961. With the exception of Jaguar, every motor firm in the city registered a decline in production. In the case of Rootes and Standard this amounted to 36 and 39 per cent respectively, which in real terms meant a total drop of almost 93,000 units. Output for the industry as a whole declined by 25.7 per cent so that the smaller volume producers, represented by the two major Coventry firms, appear to have suffered a disproportionate under-utilisation of capacity during the crisis period. The balance of payments remained unstable throughout the 1960s. Under Reginald Maudling's 'dash for growth' between 1962 and 1964, total car production rose to a peak of 1,867,640 units and that for Coventry firms to 372,370 units. By 1964 the external account was moving towards fundamental disequilibrium and over successive years the domestic economy was squeezed, first under the stewardship of James Callaghan and then by his successor as Chancellor, Roy Jenkins. For the motor industry the picture was one of declining national output with the 1964 peak not being regained until the following decade.[58]

In comparison with the growth of output achieved by foreign producers, the 1960s was a period of decline for the British motor industry, though how far this was the consequence of repeated changes of government economic policy is conjectural. The motor manufacturers and traders complained loudly and often that alternating periods of expansion and contraction rendered market forecasting extremely difficult and disrupted production and investment schedules. Although these arguments have a convincing ring, there is little firm evidence that changes in Treasury policy brought about the cancellation or deferment of investment plans. In their important 1978 study, Jones and Prais did not find any statistical evidence to prove that market demand in the United Kingdom has been significantly more unstable than elsewhere, but pointed instead to the industry's general inability to expand output as a major cause of its long-term relative decline. However, frequent changes of economic policy almost certainly affected smaller firms most severely through a disproportionate underutilisation of capacity and might well have eroded the will to invest. In this respect, Rootes and Standard might well have been disadvantaged in comparison with the majors, such as Ford and BMC.[59]

A related argument is that government regional policy forced the motor companies to expand their operations in areas of high unemployment, often far removed from the industry's traditional heartlands, with adverse effects upon costs and profitability. All the volume producers were anxious by the late 1950s to acquire new capacity, increase production and improve their overall performance. The government shared these objectives, but was also keen to reduce unemployment levels in the older industrial regions of Britain and so began to adopt a more active interventionist position with regard to the geographical location of new manufacturing development. By refusing to grant Industrial Development Certificates, necessary to expansion, the Midlands and the South East and by offering a battery of grants and loans as incentives, the government leaned very heavily on the motor firms to develop their activities in the north of England, Scotland and Wales. In response, Ford opened a new plant at Halewood and Vauxhall at Ellesmere Port. Standard increased its existing operations at Speke on Merseyside, while Rootes, having been refused permission to develop further at Ryton, moved furthest of all to Linwood near Paisley some 16 miles south of Glasgow.[60]

The dispersion policy had some logic. The Liverpool–Manchester nexus appeared attractive, offering sound road, rail and harbour facilities as well as a plentiful supply of labour. Standard already possessed a working base in Liverpool. This was the Hall's Engineering Motor Division, which had been purchased for £2 million in 1959 to provide much needed body capacity for the Herald and was later used to produce the TR4, 5 and 6 sports models. Thus, Standard was no stranger to the area when in 1967 it opened a new body plant on Merseyside, about one mile from the original Hall's factory, by then known as Speke No.1. The new plant proved an almost unmitigated disaster, never operating at more than one-third of its eventual productive capacity. Although it has not been possible to conduct a cost–benefit analysis of this move northwards, there seems little doubt that it increased Standard's cost, very significantly and helped further to undermine the company's already precarious financial position. With its low production and productivity rates and high incidence of strikes, Speke was to prove a running sore to British Leyland throughout the 1970s so that its eventual closure came as no surprise to the business community.[61]

Thanks to the work of Young and Hood much more is known of the consequences of Rootes's move to Linwood. The Clyde Valley had a number of attractions. These included a readily available labour force, though untrained in track work, excellent dock facilities and steel from the new strip mill at Ravenscraig near Motherwell which would supply Pressed Steel, already at Linwood, with the raw materials for body-making. Yet there were several obvious and immediate problems, particularly the stretching of overextended supply lines the and distance from markets. Throughout its life no more than 15 per cent of Linwood's total output was sold within 150 miles of the plant, which naturally added to distribution costs for the remaining 75 per cent. This was further complicated by transhipments of engines, components and finished bodies north and south, and by the need to hold larger than normal stocks of supplies as a hedge against possible transport delays. Finally, key personnel had to be transferred to Scotland which resulted in duplication of certain key management and other services. Thus, the expense of moving to Linwood was considerable. The company itself estimated that a similar expansion in Coventry would have cost £1.2 million compared with the £2 million which was eventually expended. Government financial assistance was relatively generous, amounting to £9.6 million in 1961–62, with further loans and grants being inherited through the acquisition of the Pressed Steel complex in 1966. Additional aid also came from the regional employment benefit scheme introduced by the Labour government in the late 1960s. Yet the fact remains that Linwood never made a profit. The plant failed to operate at anywhere near efficient capacity and its basic model, the Imp, with its expensive aluminium rear-engine design, entered the market too late, since by 1962 there had been a movement away from very small to medium-sized cars. In terms of sales, the Imp fared badly in comparison with the BMC Mini, which was sold at a price which did not cover full production costs. The main conclusion to be drawn is that the move to Scotland brought little or no benefit to Rootes's combined operations and, indeed, it has been calculated that between 1963 and 1970 the excess of costs over benefits amounted to an astonishing £6,440,000.[62]

It is too simplistic to argue that had the expansion associated with Linwood and Speke occurred in Coventry, Rootes and Standard would have automatically enjoyed greater financial success. When the two projects were being advanced in the late 1950s, labour was in very short supply in Coventry, so that any locally-based development would have necessarily involved recruiting migrant workers which would probably have added a further twist to wage costs. More important, perhaps, was the fact that both firms were commercially weak, especially Rootes. There is no reason to believe, for example, that the Imp, with its design faults and late appearance, would have been any more attractive to the motoring public had it been made at Ryton rather than Linwood. Government regional policy was well intentioned so far as the economy as a whole was concerned, and although its implementation brought particular problems for Coventry's two volume car-producers there is no reason to suppose that this was the fundamental cause of their corporate problems.

In explaining the failing health of the Coventry Motor industry, especially from the mid-1960s, much attention has focused upon the role of the trade unions. The affluent Coventry car-worker has often been condemned as epitomising an 'I'm all right Jack' attitude. His behaviour on the shop floor was allegedly irresponsible in relation to piecework bargaining; his attitude towards labour relations was said to have been politically motivated and his interest in output and productivity limited solely to personal financial gain. Such a narrow view of the workforce and its representatives will not suffice. Given the complex nature of shop-floor organisation and bargaining, the role of gang leaders, shop stewards and union officials was not easily separated from that of management. For example, at both Rootes and Standard and, to a lesser extent, Jaguar the shop stewards frequently exercised a quasi-managerial function and in the process helped to fill a vacuum in the formal management hierarchy. That the Coventry car-worker was highly paid and nearly 100 per cent union organised is undeniable, but whether he was the stereotyped selfish militant depicted in the tabloid press is far more questionable.[63]

Wages in Coventry's motor and engineering industries at the end of the war were among the highest in the country. This trend continued throughout the 1950s and 1960s when the city's engineering wage levels stood at 35–40 per cent above earnings for comparable labour in the rest of Britain. As late as 1969 this differential was calculated to have been as significant as 36 per cent.[64] In the generally buoyant conditions in the motor industry as a whole, and with labour in short supply, management was prepared to accept a trade-off between wages and production. Expansion also gave greater strength and confidence to the trade union movement and officials became increasingly willing to use their bargaining power in pursuit of higher wages and better working conditions for their members. In addition, productivity in the car factories rose sharply, faster in fact that the rate for British industry as a whole during the 1950s, and so further nudged earnings in an upward direction. It should be emphasised however, that during the mid-1960s, when wage drift in British industry was at its height, earnings rose fastest in shipbuilding and chemicals. Thus, the Coventry motor manufacturers were not unique in allowing wage levels to gravitate upwards and, ironically, by 1965 the highest payers in the city were Alvis and Armstrong Siddeley whose interests in cars had virtually come to an end.[65]

Labour costs are one area of industry where management might be expected to exercise a high degree of control, yet this does not appear to have been the case in Coventry until the 1960s, the reasons for which must be sought in the gang and piecework bargaining systems that developed after 1945. The gang system enshrined the idea of payment by results and in effect became a substitute for management in the control of production. It was widely regarded as a self-regulating mechanism for the achievement of high output, productivity and earnings. Moreover, the relative absence of supervisory staff in the car factories meant that in order to keep production flowing gang leaders, who were invariable shop stewards, had to assume quasi-managerial functions. It has therefore been correctly argued that between 1945 and 1952 the right to manage the shop floor was in essence ceded by management in return for the promise of peaceful industrial relations and rising output through a series of agreements involving both sides of industry.[66]

During the Second World War the gang system had become firmly entrenched in the main Coventry car factories. The tightness of the labour market allowed the gangs to assume an important role in the running of the shop floors, but, as will be discussed later, the system varied between firms and was by no means uniform even if the structure and form at Standard is often held up as the prime example. As early as 1944 Sir John Black advised his fellow employers in the CDEEA of the need to evolve a coherent policy towards the workforce, suggesting initially that rates of pay should be high, but at a fixed rate. When his ideas were rejected, Black made it plain that he would pursue his own labour policy and was subsequently expelled from the CDEEA. There remains suspicion, though that Black may have deliberately engineered the situation to free Standard from the CDEEA's constraints.

The gang structure and system engendered by Black owed much to Standard's tradition of welfarism, dating back to the First World War when the company inaugurated a bereavement fund, as well as establishing child-care arrangements for women workers, a canteen and recreational facilities. In 1936 Black took the initiative in founding the Standard Employees' Special Fund to provide sickness and death benefits, life insurance and pensions for those with at least fifteen years' service. The firm appears to have believed that such schemes encouraged loyalty among the workforce and was also perhaps compensation for the tough management style associated with the firm in the 1920s and early 1930s. Black also recognised that trade unions had become a force to be reckoned with and that a positive approach might help in improving Standard's position in the 'big six'.

Black's strategy was to formalise a policy described as Responsible Autonomy through institutionalising both the unions and the gangs in an agreement that hopefully would lead to high ouput, high productivity, profits and wages with piecework as the cash nexus driving force. In 1945 there was a plethora of gangs at Standard's plants with bonus rates ranging between 175 per cent and 250 per cent above basic rates. Three years later this chaotic system ended. The concordat signed between the firm and the unions in 1948 reduced the number of gangs at Canley from 104 to 15 and scaled down the number of grades from sixty-eight to eight with the working week being reduced from 44 to 42 ½ hours. A minimum bonus of 100 per cent was guaranteed compared to the CDEEA's minimum of 25 per cent, though in practice this was closer to 60 per cent. All bonuses were based on the gang's actual performance with all workers receiving an immediate 20 per cent increase in wages that guaranteed all workers, including those at Banner Lane, who were organized in one large gang, a minimum weekly wage of £5. This was an immense deal, especially as all labour was to be hired through local union offices and in effect ceded a tremendous amount of power downwards to the workforce. Under the principle of mutuality, stewards were responsible for negotiating the price of jobs with the rate-fixers and for the distribution of workers between jobs as well as for manning levels and track speeds. Basically foremen and supervisory staff were marginalised, with near total control of the shop floor lying in the hands of the stewards and the gang leaders who frequently were one and the same person. A serious consequence of this was that management was weak at lower and middle levels so that when disputes arose it tended to capitulate quickly, simply to keep the tracks running and cars rolling out the gate.

Neither Rootes nor Jaguar adopted the Standard model. Permanent union recognition did not occur at Ryton until 1950 after which managerial power was devolved to the stewards, who had responsibility for all booking in and out of work, loading levels and the pace of the track. The Ryton plant became known eventually as a self-governing republic, piecework being the surrogate foreman with management virtually abdicating its responsibility and not seeming too worried about the state of the shop floor as long as the production lines flowed.[67] Jaguar provided a third variant on workplace organization. There the gangs were relatively small in size and limited in authority. The shop floor was not allowed to dictate the pace or work so that, for example, loading and manning levels were closely supervised by management. Yet Jaguar enjoyed relative industrial peace until the late 1950s when the introduction of new models necessitated major changes in work patterns and job specification. Stoppages over new piece-rates did occur in 1961, but were of short duration and had very little impact on output. Much more serious at that time were bottlenecks on the supply side caused by delivery problems among the component firms. Nevertheless, the company was concerned about its labour relations and work practices and commissioned the management consultants Urwick, Orr and Partners to investigate these and offer advice. Their findings concluded that the workforce was in general co-operative, if somewhat reluctant to accept changes in work practices. This was perhaps explained by the particular character of Jaguar's shop-floor employees, who were distinguished by their exceptionally high level of skill which in turn gave them particular status and a significant measure of economic independence. In the 1960s demand for Jaguar cars began to assume a seasonal nature which weakened trade union influence and caused marked fluctuations in take-home pay. This brought feelings of insecurity among the workforce as earnings could be £30 one week and £15 the next. However, despite the fact that compared with Ryton, inter-union feuding within the plant was low, the stewards were not collectively strong enough to force a solution to this particular problem. Indeed, Clack has argued that while the shop stewards fulfilled a number of quasi-managerial functions aimed at avoiding labour disputes, the overall union structure at Jaguar was too disparate for effective organisation. It is also worth noting that the company's own labour-relations machinery was rather primitive, for it was not until the 1960s that a manager was appointed to this area of work when Harry Adey, chairman of the Joint Shop Stewards' Committee, moved from one side of the negotiation table to the other. Prior to this, labour relations was only one of the many portfolios borne by the works manager.[68]

The structure, strength and role of the gangs and the unions varied so much between plants that it is difficult to arrive at firm conclusions concerning the general efficacy of workplace organisation. There is no doubt that the post-war agreements institutionalised the gangs as an integral part of Coventry's negotiating framework, and was presented as a system of labour relations which was beneficial to both management and workers. In terms of output and production, the system did not catapult either of the city's volume producers to leading positions among the 'big five', though given the structural defects of both Rootes and Standard that was never a serious proposition. When the system was first introduced it did lead to a high degree of co-operation between management and labour. It also had the useful spin-off of saving considerable expenditure on supervisory staff so that, for example, foremen eventually became of only marginal importance in the car factories. At its best in the 1950s and 1960s, Coventry's system of workplace organisation brought harmonious labour relations in a joint attempt to push up output and earnings, but it also carried a number of inherent problems. Firstly, the gang system did little to alter workforce attitudes and within a short time of the 1948 accords even the hiring of labour came under a cloud at Standard, with strong rumours circulating that employment was often obtained unfairly. Black did try hard to wrest this function back from the unions but failed abysmally. The gangs in many cases created their own empires even engaging in bitter wrangling over the more lucrative jobs, with jurisdictional and territorial disputes being common. In other words, the gangs never really developed a factory-wide view of operations, but rather one based on sectionalism. Attempts were frequently made to de-man gangs by the members themselves, to increase the earning power of the remaining members. Similarly, efforts were made to recruit very low-paid operatives into gangs so that the more highly-paid members could cream off the top bonus, and this despite the whole system being geared initially to narrowing differentials. The essential problem lay in the cash nexus because under the piecework system all new jobs, no matter how trivial or how little they differed from earlier variants, had to be recalculated so that they yielded a price not lower than its predecessor. So once a gang had mastered a new technique it was easy to push up monetary reward. Underlying the philosophy of the gang system was the continuation of inter-union rivalry from the interwar period, with Rootes suffering more than Standard from this. At Rootes there was serious rivalry between the AEU and the TGWU in the 1950s with no JSSC to hold the ring between them. Additionally, there were Communist and non-Communist factions who quarrelled almost continuously; indeed, there was no JSSC committee in Rootes until 1960 when one was established to try to bring a degree of order to inter-union relations, let alone labour relations in general. The end result of both inter-gang and inter-union disputes was that narrow and limited horizons led to a failure on the part of both labour and management to take full cognisance of the wider problems of both Rootes and Standard, when both firms were heading into decline. Finally, claims that the gang system led to unduly high production costs have been made, although evidence is hard to come by. Nevertheless, the employers felt that this was the case in the 1960s and early 1970s, which led after bitter struggles to the introduction of Measured Day Work, designed not only to get a grip on costs, but also to restore managerial prerogatives on the shop floor, but this is the subject of a later chapter. It may well be, however, that the low levels of investment, the extent of overmanning, and low productivity were far more potent sources in pushing up costs than high wages *per se* and, indeed, events at British Leyland in the 1970s lend some credence to this view.[69]

It has been suggested that such a high level of shop-floor control made Coventry car firms more strike-prone than their competitors in other parts of the country, but again the evidence tends to refute this. Table 7.11 shows that disputes at Rootes and Standard, where the gang system was exceptionally strong, were no more common than at other companies and that both had a better record on strikes than Jaguar, where the system was at its weakest among the Coventry manufacturers. The majority of Coventry strikes, both official and unofficial, were of short duration. Standard developed a reputation in the late 1950s for being strike-prone but until 1954 the company had few disputes worthy of note. In 1956 it was involved in a major dispute over redundancies which eventually involved the withdrawal of more than 3,000 men. However, this strike accounted for most of the working days lost through industrial action during the 1950s, while many of the short-term strikes in the late 1950s and early 1960s involved white-collar staff rather than direct production workers.[70] Care should be taken not to minimise the cumulative effect of successive disputes of limited duration, particularly between 1966 and 1968 when the columns of the local press conveyed a dismal picture of an industry plagued by lost production from strike action, some of which involved only a few workers but which nevertheless brought whole factories to a standstill. It has been argued, however, that management was not beyond manipulating strikes as a method regulating output and that some disputes were seen as beneficial since they prevented undue stockpiling when demand was slack. Labour relations did deteriorate in Coventry in the 1960s, but the bargaining system was not necessarily the main cause of this. It is more likely that the sense of decline in the industry, coupled with job insecurity and fluctuations in earnings, were at the heart of the problem.[71]

Much has been said indirectly in this analysis about management performance, but any overall assessment of this is fraught with difficulty. With hindsight it is easy to blame management for failing to rationalise the structure of the motor industry, for ceding too much power to the unions and for not investing enough, though these are criticisms which should not be applied to Coventry alone. Coventry motor firms did produce several outstanding managers, such as William Lyons at Jaguar. Lyons stands in sharp contrast to his great rival, Sir John Black, whose post-war direction of Standard appears to have been much less successful than it was in the 1930s and the wartime years. Black's behaviour became increasingly erratic, explained, perhaps, by of his failing health. Important management decisions were sometimes taken with little reference to the Standard board.

Table 7.11
Strike liability of individual firms 1946–64

	Of all strikes	Per cent of striker days	Of 1963 employment
BMC	44	41	32
Ford	11	25	24
Rootes	8	5	5
Standard	4	9	4
Pressed Steel	7	6	11
Rover	8	5	4
Jaguar	9	6	3
Others	7	3	17
	100	100	100

Source: H. Turner, G. Clack and G. Roberts, *Labour Relations in the Motor Industry* (Macmillan, London, 1967), p. 231.

This included, for example, the negotiations surrounding the Ferguson tractor deal when agreements were struck and the company's directors simply informed of the results. Black was personally responsible for the decision to manufacture the Renown Roadster and the Mayflower models. None of these vehicles proved particular successful, thus casting serious doubt upon his ability to assess market trends. Black did achieve an imaginative management coup with the labour agreements of 1945–48, though to some extent this was perhaps motivated by personal animosity towards members of the CDEEA and was not entirely the product of sound business principles. In the circumstances, Black's forced resignation in 1953 came as no surprise. He was succeeded as managing director by Alick Dick, a doctor's son who, because of his outstanding management potential, had graduated through the ranks of the firm at a very rapid rate. Dick had the intellectual capacity and experience to analyse Standard's problems with insight and clarity. Regular board meetings were introduced and even a casual reading of the minutes reveals his methodical approach to management and high level of personal interaction with his fellow directors. Dick successfully guided Standard through its various mergers and was also responsible for the important programme of model rationalisation which resulted in the Herald and Triumph 2,000 ranges. Dick's influence was of critical importance in keeping Standard afloat until the Leyland merger, though credit for turning round the company's finances should probably be given to his successor, Stanley Markland, who arrived at Canley in 1961.[72]

Rootes's weaknesses have already been discussed and these were quickly recognised by Chrysler when it assumed control of the company in 1967. The Americans, though perhaps over-keen to introduce modern Detroit-style management systems, found themselves forced to appoint a number of key executives in order to strengthen the management team. New financial controllers were established in an effort to achieve a much higher degree of cost control and all members of the Rootes family, other than Lord Rootes, were obliged to resign from the board. It is likely that any other group taking over the company would have behaved in a similar fashion, though it has been argued that Chrysler's approach to the existing management was unnecessarily harsh.[73]

By the mid-1960s Coventry's motor industry was much changed from what it had been in 1939. Its position as a leading centre of car manufacture and assembly had been greatly eroded, while at the quality end of the trade only Jaguar had prospered. The boom days of the 1950s were over and the growing level of competition in the industry was increasingly felt. Although concern was expressed about the future, it was widely believed by 1968 that the worst was over and that under the newly created BLMC the situation could only improve. There was a degree of optimism, but who could have foreseen what lay in store in the 1970s?

Notes

[1]   A. Mallier and M Rosser, 'Industrial Decline in Perspective: the car industry in Coventry'. Staff Seminar Discussion Paper No. 47, Dept of Economics, Coventry (Lanchester) Polytechnic, January 1982, p. 6.

[2]   Ibid., pp. 6–8.

[3]   The Times, 31 March 1959.

[4]   Financial Times, 8 November 1950

[5]   CDEEA, Minutes 27 May 1950

[6]   Ibid., 2 May 1950; Richardson, Twentieth Century Coventry, p. 98.

[7]   A. Mallier and M. Rosser, 'The Economic Base of Coventry', Staff Seminar Discussion Paper No. 33, Dept of Economics, Coventry (Lanchester) Polytechnic, 1981, pp. 3–5.

[8]   Ibid., p. 11.

[9]   Day, Alvis, p. ll.

[10]   Whyte, Jaguar, pp. 118–28.

[11] W. Lanchester and A. Mason (eds), *Life and Labour in a Twentieth Century City*, p. 39.

[12] MRC, Mss 226/ST/1/1/10, Standard Directors' Minutes, 21 March 1946; P. Dunnett, *The Decline of the British Motor Industry* (Croom Helm, London, 1980) pp. 31–44.

[13] Jaguar Cars, Annual Reports and Accounts 1945–50.

[14] MRC, Mss 226/ST/1/1/10, Standard Directors' Minutes, 18 December 1946.

[15] Dunnett, *The Decline of the British Motor Industry*, p. 36.

[16] MRC, Mss 226/ST/1/1/10, Standard Directors' Minutes, 22 February 1946.

[17] Dunnett, *The Decline of the British Motor Industry*, p. 37.

[18] MRC, Mss 226/ST/1/1/10, Standard Directors' Minutes, 21 March 1946.

[19] R. Langworth and G. Robson, *Triumph Cars* (Motor Racing Publications, London, 1979), p. 307.

[20] Jaguar Cars, Annual Reports and Accounts, 1945–51.

[21] Maxcy and Silberston, *The Motor Industry*, p. 112; Dunnett, *The Decline of the British Motor Industry*, p. 41.

[22] MRC, Mss 226/ST/1/1/10, Standard Directors' Minutes, 2 July 1946.

[23] Jaguar Cars, Annual Reports and Accounts 1946–52.

[24] Dunnett, *The Decline of the British Motor Industry*, pp. 39–40; MRC, Mss 226/ST/1/1/11, Standard Directors' Minutes, 26 February 1951.

[25] Society of Motor Manufacturers and Traders Data (various years).

[26] MRC, Mss 226/ST/1/1/11, Standard Directors' Minutes, 22 May 1951, 22 July 1951.

[27] *The Times*, 31 March 1959.

[28] G. Rhys, *The Motor Industry, An Economic Survey* (Butterworth, London, 1970), pp. 358–63.

[29] G. Turner, *The Leyland Papers* (Eyre and Spottiswoode, London, 1971), p. 43; MRC, Mss 226/ST/1/1/13, Standard Directors' Minutes, 25 January 1961, 6 July 1962.

[30] S. Young and N. Hood, *Chrysler UK: A Multinational in Transition* (Praeger, New York, 1977), p. 96.

[31] Maxcy and Silberston, *The Motor Industry*, pp. 64–7. Rhys, *The Motor Ind-ustry: An Economic Survey*, p. 212; K. Bhaskar, *The Future of UK Motor Industry* (Kogan Page, London, 1979), pp. 19–28; R. Church, *The Rise and Decline of The British Motor Industry* (MacMillan, London, 1994). J. Foreman-Peck, S. Bowden, A. McKinley, *The British Motor Industry* (Manchester University Press, Manchester 1995).

[32] MRC, Mss 226/ST/1/1/12, Standard Directors' Minutes, 25 December 1958.

[33] MRC, Mss 226/ST/1/1/13, Standard Directors' Minutes, 25 January 1961.

[34] Mallier and Rosser, 'Industrial Decline in Perspective', pp. 12–15.

[35] Rhys, *The Motor Industry: An Economic Survey*, p. 22; E. Neufield, *A Global Corporation: A History of the International Development of Massey Ferguson Ltd.* (University of Toronto Press, Toronto, 1969), p. 784.

[36] Rhys, *The Motor Industry: An Economic Survey*, p. 22.

[37] MRC, Mss 226/ST/1/1/11–12, These mergers are heavily documented over several years.

[38] Rhys, *The Motor Industry: An Economic Survey*, pp. 26–7; Young and Hood, *Chrysler UK*, pp. 73–103; S. Morewood, *Pioneers and Inheritors; Top Management in*

162   THE COVENTRY MOTOR INDUSTRY

the *Coventry Motor Industry 1896–1972* (Centre for Business History and Policy, Coventry Polytechnic, Coventry 1990), pp. 119–56.
[39] Rhys, *The Motor Industry: An Economic Survey*, pp. 28–9.
[40] Ibid., pp. 358–64.
[41] T. Donnelly and J. Critchley, Data and Information File on the Standard Motor Company, unpublished, Dept of Politics and History, Coventry (Lanchester) Polytechnic, 1984.
[42] J. Ensor, *The Motor Industry* (Longmans, London, 1971). p. 98.
[43] Maxcy and Silberston, *The Motor Industry*, p. 177.
[44] MRC, Mss 226/ST/1/1/12, Standard Directors' Minutes, 19 April 1961.
[45] Young and Hood, *Chrysler UK*, pp. 75–103.
[46] Langworth and Robson, *Triumph Cars*, pp. 188–190; MRC, Mss 226/ST/1/1/2, Standard Directors' Minutes, 20 December 1960.
[47] Langworth and Robson, *Triumph Cars*, pp. 188–90
[48] Ibid.
[49] MRC, Mss 226/st/1/1/12, Standard Directors' Minutes, 3 May 1961, 6 March 1962, 11 October 1963, 6 July 1963.
[50] Donnelly and Critchley, Data and Information File on Standard Motor Company.
[51] Ibid.
[52] Ensor, *The Motor Industry*, pp. 98–100.
[53] Whyte, *Jaguar*, pp. 153–5; Mallier and Rosser, 'Industrial decline in Perspective', pp. 8–11.
[54] Day, *Alvis*, pp. 91–112.
[55] Price, *Lea-Francis Story*, pp. 130–31.
[56] Jaguar Cars, Annual report and Accounts, 1956–67; *CoventryEvening Telegraph*, 31 December 1947, 21 February 1949, 19 December 1964, 14 April 1968; T. Donnelly and D. Clark, Data and Information File on Jaguar Cars, unpublished, Department of Politics and History, Coventry (Lanchester) Polytechnic, 1984.
[57] Dunnett, *The Decline of the British Motor Industry*, p. 77.
[58] Ibid., pp. 60–65 and 87–95; J. Foreman-Peck et al., pp. 194–204.
[59] Ibid., D.T. Jones and S.J. Prais, 'Plant Size and Productivity in the Motor Industry: Some International Comparisons', *Oxford Bulletin of Economics and Statistics*', vol. 40 (May 1968).
[60] Dunnett, *the Decline of the British Motor Industry*, pp. 76–81.
[61] Ibid., p. 176.
[62] Young and Hood, *Chrysler UK*, chs 3–6.
[63] S. Tolliday, 'High Tide and After: Coventry Engineering Workers and ShopFloor Bargaining'. We are grateful to Dr Steve Tolliday for providing us with a copy of his paper and allowing us to quote from it.
[64] K.G.C. Knowles and D. Robinson, 'Wage Movements in Coventry', pp. 1–12; W. Brown, 'Piece Working in Coventry', pp. 1–29; R.A. Hart and D.I. Mackay, 'Engineering Earnings in Britain 1914–68', *Journal of the Royal Statistical Society* no. 138 (1975), pp. 32–50.
[65] Tolliday, 'High Tide and After', p. 6.
[66] Ibid., Richardson, *Twentieth Century Coventry*, pp. 114–15.
[67] Ibid., pp. 117-19; Tolliday, 'High Tide and After', pp. 13–17.
[68] Richardson, *Twentieth Century Coventry*, pp. 120–23; T. Donnelly and d. Thoms, 'Trade Unions, Management and the Search for Productivity in the Coventry Car Industry', in C. Harvey and J. Turner (eds), *Labour and Business in Modern Britain* (Cass, London, 1989).
[69] Tolliday, 'High Tide and After', pp. 25–33; Friedman, *Industry and Labour*, pp. 219–26.

[70]   H. Turner, G. Clack and G. Roberts, *Labour Relations in the motor Industry* (Allen and Unwin, London, 1967), pp. 230–34.
[71]   Tolliday, 'High Tide and After', pp. 230–34.
[72]   This paragraph is based on the Standard Directors' Minutes from 1940–68 held at the Modern Records Centre, University of Warwick.
[73]   Young and Hood, *Chrysler UK*, p. 99; Morewood, *Pioneers and Inheritors*, pp. 119–56.

Chapter 8

The End of the Boom

By 1980 Coventry's economy was in sharp decline. The halcyon days of the boom-town image – high wages and almost no unemployment – had gone. All of the city's major industries had contracted, in some cases, such as aero-engineering and machine tools, at an alarming rate. Over the decade to 1981 Coventry's population fell by 6.5 per cent to just under 313,000 with unemployment reaching nearly 17 per cent of the labour force. The causes of this reversal of fortune are not easily isolated. However, the dismal performance of the British economy under successive administrations, structural change in the economy as a whole and the more general problems of the motor industry, all made a significant contribution. This was exacerbated by Coventry's legacy of having achieved fast growth on a very narrow industrial base and its associated failure to diversify into new areas of technology.[1]

With the advent of a Conservative government in 1970, economic policy, cushioned by a balance-of-payments surplus of nearly £1 billion, became more expansionary with budgetary stimuli being applied in successive years up to and including 1972. Although the growth rate did improve to around 6 per cent per annum, the balance-of-payments surplus was frittered away and the external account moved into the red. This, coupled with an over-rapid expansion in the money supply, fuelled inflation which was worsened by the sudden and dramatic increase in the price of oil imposed by the OPEC nations in 1973. Even before the impact of the oil price-rise was felt, the Heath government was forced to reduce activity levels in the economy through the introduction of a voluntary prices and incomes policy designed to bring inflation under control, and this was later strengthened by statutory measures. Expenditure cuts were introduced in 1973 and hire-purchase controls were restored. The following year brought a general election and the return of the Labour administration which, despite its quick abandonment of a compulsory prices and incomes policy, soon found itself defending sterling and fighting inflation through the mechanism of the Social Contract. This was a voluntary incomes policy negotiated with the TUC, supported by the Treasury's more traditional economic weaponry. Inflation peaked at approximately 25 per cent in 1975 and although this was more than halved by 1979, it was at the expense of a much reduced rate of economic growth. Despite the expansionist policies pursued during the early period of the Heath government, in general the UK economy performed no better in the 1970s than in the previous decade.[2]

It is against this rather dismal background that Coventry's economy, and indeed that of the West Midlands as a whole, must be viewed. For several decades the West Midlands industrial conurbation was widely regarded as a barometer of the health of the national economy. During the 1970s, however, the region declined badly in comparison with other parts of Britain. This was not a sudden fall into recession but rather an acceleration of a trend which had begun in the 1960s when labour productivity and investment levels regularly fell below the UK average.[3] Coventry was not immune from the overall regional trend and its economic malaise was dramatically reflected in widespread factory closures and rising unemployment.

Concern over Coventry's economic plight was first brought to prominence in 1968 when a series of Lord Mayor's Conferences was held to investigate the city's difficulties and future prospects. As we shall see, attention focused upon the problems of motor and aircraft manufacture, the adverse impact of government regional policies and the relative absence of both the new 'science'-based and service industries. The decline of the aircraft industry was regarded as particularly serious. Coventry's aero-engineering industry emerged from the war with a greatly enhanced reputation, so that a bright future was predicted for it. Post-war governments accepted that Britain would require a substantial aircraft industry for both civilian and military purposes. One of the civilian aircraft considered for priority development was the Coventry-built AWA Apollo. However, this aircraft appeared a year later than its major rival, the Vickers' Viscount, and proved to be inferior in terms of speed and carrying capacity. The government's announcement in 1952 that it could not support the Apollo was a major setback for Baginton, and during much of the 1950s the works was forced to concentrate upon the production of military aircraft which had been designed elsewhere. Until 1957 the emphasis at Baginton was upon service and repair work so that Coventry's importance as a centre of aircraft design and manufacture gradually receded. In order to retrieve the situation at Baginton, permission was obtained from the parent company, Hawker Siddeley, to develop both military and civilian versions of a new aeroplane, the Argosy, but this project proved to be an expensive flop. One of the most severe blows for the British aircraft industry, the Coventry segment in particular, was the cancellation in 1964 of the HS 681, TSR2 and Hawker P1164 projects, all of which were at an advanced stage of development. This prompted further rationalisation within the industry and in 1965, following the merger of Bristol Siddeley Engines and Rolls-Royce, it was decided to close the Baginton plant. Between 1962 and 1967 some 11,000 jobs were lost in Coventry's aircraft industry, with only 4,000 new ones being created in motor vehicles. This served to narrow the industrial base even further and to push up unemployment, which by 1968 stood at 5.8 per cent of the labour force.[4]

An increase in service-sector employment would have helped to compensate for Coventry's job losses in manufacturing industry. However, jobs disappeared faster in manufacturing than they were created in services. One major reason for this is that despite its size – Coventry is the ninth-largest city in Britain – it is neither a county town nor the principal administrative centre of the West Midlands, of which it had been part since 1964. Moreover, the principal regional offices of the public utilities, financial institutions and distribution organisations have tended to gravitate towards Birmingham and since Coventry is in general merely a customer for their services, they have brought few jobs to the city. These problems have been exacerbated by the fact that since the war, the ownership of Coventry's major industries has become concentrated in some fifteen major companies, most of which are either multinationals or British conglomerates. With the exception of Alfred Herbert, until it was taken over by the National Enterprise Board, none of these had their head offices in the city so that the administrative posts which naturally accompany large-scale manufacturing firms have benefited other areas, though of course this was not unique to Coventry. The expanded services have largely been in local government, education and health, and these have mainly absorbed women workers. Without the benefit of a substantial service sector, employment in Coventry by 1970 was heavily dependent upon a few large interrelated companies which were themselves highly vulnerable to economic recession. Space precludes a detailed analysis of the industrial problems which have emerged since the 1970s, though it is worth mentioning that between 1975 and 1982 Coventry's fifteen largest firms shed a total of around 55,000 jobs, rendering the city a microcosm of de-industrialization. The rate at which labour was declared redundant was remarkable, amounting to a drop in employment of 46 per cent between 1974 and 1982, compared with 27 per cent for Britain as a whole and 32 per cent for the West Midlands.[5]

Before turning to the specific reasons for the demise of motor manufacture in Coventry, it is necessary to place this decline within the more general context of the industry as a whole. If the 1960s was a decade of disappointment for British motor companies, the 1970s were to prove traumatic. Table 8.1 suggests that Anthony Barber's expansionary policies brought national car output, and that for Coventry, to their respective peaks in 1972 and 1971. Thereafter, the general trend was downward, with Coventry's decline being particularly rapid so that by 1979 the city's 'big three' accounted for just 11.4 per cent of total British output.

Much has been written on the problems of Britain's car industry in the 1970s, including the crisis year of 1975–76, when government intervention became necessary to save both BL and Chrysler from financial collapse. In 1975 reports by the Commons Expenditure Committee and the Central Policy Review Staff pointed specifically to the low profitability, production and productivity records of British assembly plants compared with their European and Japanese rivals. The marginal nature of profitability in the industry is clear from table 8.2. Even in monetary terms, BL's profits for 1973 were below those achieved by its four constituent companies in 1964. Indeed, at 1973 prices profits for 1964 were almost double those reached nine years later. It was also noted that the industry suffered from a number of structural weaknesses, including too many manufacturers, resulting in excess capacity and model development, while overmanning, poor labour relations and weak

Table 8.1

Output of cars in the UK and estimated output from the three largest producers in Coventry 1971–80.

Year	UK output	Chrysler Talbot a	Jaguar	BL b	Total Coventry output	Coventry output as a % of UK output
1971	1,741,440	265,280	29,512	95,711	390,503	22.4
1972	1,921,311	263,452	22,336	100,804	386,592	20.1
1973	1,747,321	265,413	27,787	95,625	388,825	22.2
1974	1,534,119	261,801	30,710	89,919	382,430	24.9
1975	1,267,695	230,602	26,686	64,181	321,469	25.3
1976	1,333,449	144,580	30,433 c	94,448 c	269,461	20.2
1977	1,327,820	147,770	24,095	49,449	221,314	16.6
1978	1,222,949	129,736	25,684	47,229	202,649	16.5
1979	1,070,452	64,112	13,988	43,933	122,033	11.4
1980	923,794	108,753	13,228	27,424	149,405	16.1

a: Includes Linwood production figures.
b: Comprises basically the old Standard Triumph Plants.
c: Figures for 15 months.

Sources: BL Data; Peugeot Talbot Data; Fourteenth Report from the Expenditure Committee 1974–75; *The Motor Vehicle Industry* (HMSO, London, 1975), p. 94.

Table 8.2
Pre-tax profits /(loss) in the UK motor industry 1970–77, £m

Year	BL	Chrysler	Vauxhall	Ford
1970	4	(10.7)	(9.7)	25.2
1971	32	0.4	1.8	(30.7)
1972	32	1.6	(4.3)	46.8
1973	51	3.7	(4.1)	65.4
1974	2.3	(18.7)	(18.1)	8.7
1975	(76.1)	(35.5)	(2.5)	40.8
1976	70	(31.9)	(8.4)	140.2
1977	3	(8.2)	5.2	263.1

Sources: Dunnett, *The Decline of the British Motor Industry*, p. 39; Annual Reports of both Chrysler and BL 1970–78.

marketing were identified as other key factors which undermined Britain's international competitiveness. The comparatively low productivity levels of British motor-vehicle factories was a central issue in the 1970s debate on the future of the industry. Table 8.3 demonstrates that this lag was often very considerable, though the reasons for this remain a matter of considerable and ongoing controversy. Dunnett has argued that such failure was the logical outcome of low investment, productivity and profits in the previous decade, and on the same theme the CPRS drew attention to the fact that some British models were as much as ten years old.[7] The Commons Expenditure Committee argued that poor capitalisation was the principal cause of the industry's weak financial record and it is clear from table 8.4 that in, general, British investment levels were considerably below those of the main European producers. Variations in product mix and investment cycles render it difficult to compare the performance of different firms and plants at any one time. However, after examining a number of companies, the Expenditure Committee did conclude that a correlation existed between the value of assets available, the value added per man and the value of gross output per man.[8] Table 8.5 reveals the extent of differences in capitalisation, a pattern which the committee took to be the major reason for the much superior economic performance of the European motor companies. Newer equipment was less susceptible to technical failure, more consistently accurate, faster and cheaper to run, all of which had a concomittant impact on costs, productivity and reliability of the finished product. The CPRS agreed with many of the points raised by the committee, but argued that overmanning, a slower pace of work and poor maintenance, rather than inadequate investment, were often the real causes of low productivity. It was emphasised that, even when similar or

Table 8.3
Employees and productivity: unit sales per employee

Company	1973	1974	1975	1976
BL	5.2	4.9	4.5	5.0
Ford UK	9.5	8.6	8.0	9.5
Chrysler UK	11.7	10.3	9.8	8.8
Vauxhall	8.6	8.6	8.5	8.0
Renault	14.5	15.4	15.3	14.7
Peugeot	12.4	12.3	11.1	12.4
Mercedes	4.3	4.4	3.7	3.8
Volkswagen	10.6	10.4	13.8	14.2
Opel	14.8	12.9	14.3	15.3
Volvo	5.6	4.9	4.9	5.2
Fiat	6.7	8.3	8.2	6.4

Source: Bhaskar, *The Future of the UK Motor Industry*, p. 63.

comparable equipment was used, productivity in British plants was lower than on the Continent. The net result, said the CPRS, was that it took almost twice as many hours to assemble a vehicle in Britain as it did in the rest of Europe.[9] This criticism was particularly directed at BL, and was later given added credence by Michael Edwardes's statement that, despite substantial injections of new capital, productivity at the Rover plant at Solihull was the lowest within the group as a whole. The general conclusion drawn by the CPRS was that British facilities were either heavily overmanned or that because of slower work speeds similarly manned lines were only half as productive as comparable tracks elsewhere. In other words, high levels of investment did not automatically guarantee high production of productivity.[10]

The reports of the Expenditure Committee and CPRS converged closely in identifying bad labour relations as one of the British motor industry's fundamental weaknesses, emphasising in particular the damage caused to production by the exceptionally high incidence of labour disputes. The number of man days lost in the industry averaged 3,575 between 1969 and 1974, while table 8.6 indicates that between 1972 and 1974 a total of some 843,000 vehicles were lost through labour disputes. Interruptions to production in any one stage of car manufacture frequently had serious knock-on effects which brought assembly to a complete halt. The CPRS noted that for every man hour lost by a man on strike at BL in 1974, another two or three hours were forfeited as a result of consequent lay-offs.[11] Labour problems were not unique to any particular firm or factory, but tended to be worse in larger plants employing upwards of 10,000 operatives, than in smaller establishments. Several causes of labour disputes were identified. There was said to be a deep and widespread feeling of uncertainty which generated a lack of confidence among the

Table 8.4
Capital investment records 1970–77, £m

Company	1970	1971	1972	1973	1974	1975	1976	1977
BL	67	50	42	67	108	92	114	149
Ford UK	68	49	32	42	52	52	56	81
Vauxhall	21	19	6	13	26	9a	25a	25a
Chrysler UK	18	4	3	5	1	7	15	28
Volkswagen	107	107	98	102	327	165	229	445
Opel	47	61	42	61	68	na	na	na
Renault	101	89	86	84	117	na	na	na
BMW	42	34	63	63	40	42	na	na
Daimler/Benz	191	189	152	138	180	223	186	238
Peugeot	na	na	na	na	na	na	na	na

a: Estimates.
na: Not available.

Source: Bhaskar, *The Future of the UK Motor Industry*, p. 91.

Table 8.5
Relationship between value added per man and fixed assets per man in terms of gross output per man in 1974 (£)

Company	Value added per man	Gross output per man	Fixed assets per man
Opel	5,875	14,747	3,612
Daimler Benz	5,207	12,672	2,694
Volvo	4,886	14,790	4,662
Ford Germany	4,883	14,186	3,608
Saab	4,637	19,972	3,141
Renault	4,133	12,928	2,396
Ford UK	3,901	11,397	2,657
Chrysler UK	2,765	9,968	1,456
Vauxhall	2,560	7,975	1,356
Fiat	2,259	8,142	3,160
BL	2,129	6,539	920

Source: Fourteenth Report of the Expenditure Committee: *The Motor Vehicle Industry*, 1974-75 (HMSO, London, 1975), p. 36.

Table 8.6
Number of vehicles lost due to internal labour disputes, '000

Company	1972	1973	1974	Total
BL (estimated)	149	157	131	437
Chrysler	31	76	22	129
Ford	28	129	89	246
Vauxhall	4	24	3	31
Total	212	386	245	843

Source: Bhaskar, *The Future of the UK Motor Industry*, p. 70.

workforce in the ability of management to reverse the industry's decline. Apprehension fuelled mistrust and further weakened the lines of communication between management, the stewards and shop-floor operatives. These problems were said to have been exacerbated by the introduction at BL and Chrysler of Measured Day Work in place of piece-rates, while the large number of unions involved in wage bargaining and their insistence upon the maintenance of differentials created special negotiating difficulties. The CPRS concluded that the conduct of labour relations in the motor industry was badly in need of reform but that this could only be achieved when the underlying causes of insecurity were removed.[12]

Import penetration has frequently been cited as a prime cause of decline in the British sector industry, though on close inspection this rather lacks conviction. As we saw earlier, imports took less than 10 per cent of the domestic market in 1969, but rose consistently thereafter reaching 40 per cent in 1975 and accounting for almost half of total sales by 1977.   The main reason why foreign producers made such a dramatic entry to the home market was that British firms were unable to expand output sufficiently to satisfy rising demand, especially during the boom period of 1970–73.   Moreover, international trade in motor vehicles was assisted by Britain's accession to the European Economic Community and by falling tariff barriers negotiated under the Kennedy Round. During the 1950s and for most of the 1960s domestic consumers had been relatively content to wait and 'buy British' when new cars were in short supply. By 1970 this attitude had changed. European and Japanese companies had greatly increased their productive capacity and were able to export to the UK in ever-rising quantities. As a consequence, during periods of supply shortage after 1970 motorists increasingly turned to imports so that it became acceptable, and even fashionable, to drive a foreign car. In general, imported vehicles were of sound quality, well designed and well suited to British road and driving conditions, while sales and service facilities usually maintained a high level. In addition, it is important to note that when British manufacturers rationalised their distribution outlets many of the dealers who had been dropped had little alternative but to turn to foreign franchises if they wished to remain in business. Although initially foreign vehicles were more expensive than their British equivalents, sometimes by as much as 20 per cent, this differential was eroded after 1973 as price controls were lifted and domestic inflation accelerated, so that by 1975 Britain was a net importer of cars for the first time since the war.[13]

The mid-1970s was a crisis period for Coventry's economy as both BL and Chrysler were forced to seek government assistance in order to remain solvent. Although the problems of the two companies had certain similarities, there were also important differences so that it becomes necessary to treat each firm as a separate case study. Much of Coventry's industrial experience in the 1970s must be considered against the background of the Leyland–BMH merger of 1968 and the problems which emanated from it.   Local opinion was generally in favour when the merger was announced. It created an extremely potent economic force in the city, with some 27,000 jobs spread between Standard Triumph (11,000), Jaguar (7,000), Morris Engines (5,500), Alvis (1,000), Pressed Steel Fisher (1,000) and Self Changing Gears (500).[14] Frank Chater, District Secretary of the AUEW, considered that the new entity would increase the competitiveness and,   therefore, the general wellbeing of the British motor industry, a view shared by many other prominent local trade unionists.[15] Such sentiments outweighed the reservations of those workers in the smaller plants who suspected that they would be early casualties in any programme of rationalisation.[16]

At the time of the merger the new company's Coventry plants were operating at virtually full capacity so that little attention was directed towards its general economic viability. BLMC was a patchwork of companies which had themselves evolved from mergers or takeovers during the 1960s. The implications of these amalgamations had yet to be properly digested and the whole group remained a poorly co-ordinated empire overburdened by an excessive number of plants, models, works and dealers. For BLMC to have become truly competitive would have required an extensive rationalisation programme. While Ford had a total of four plants and a highly integrated engine-making and body capacity, BLMC's operations were spread between some sixty plants. Some of these were small and inefficient, but more significant was the fact that co-ordination between the constituent elements of the group was of a very limited nature. Most of the weaknesses lay in the former BMC plants, typified by the expensive transportation of completed bodies from Birmingham to Oxford where the engines were fitted and final assembly completed.[17] A further complication was the outdated nature of much of the model range. The Mini, Triumph 1,300, Jaguar XJ6 and a number of other cars were likely to retain their popularity for some years, but others, including the Herald, Morris Oxford and Rover 3.5 luxury saloon were beginning to show their age.[18] BLMC's chairman in 1968, Donald Stokes, was well aware of the difficulties which lay ahead, and although new model development and a modicum of plant rationalisation were sanctioned, the overall pace of change was too slow and by 1974 the company was slipping badly. In that year profits were extremely disappointing as market share fell to 31 per cent compared with 41 per cent six years earlier. It has been argued that the company's failure to rationalise made this decline almost inevitable. Turner and Williams have both concluded that Stokes was personally responsible for retaining BLMC's manufacturing structure, principally because he was unwilling to initiate large-scale redundancies even though the IRC advocated 42,000 redundancies out of total workforce of 180,000 employees. Stokes became known as a creator of jobs, but this paternalism was to limit severely the parameters within which company policies were formulated and was to store up many problems for the future.[19]

Space precludes a full discussion of BL's collapse, but given the inherited problems of the firm, the lack of successful model development in the volume passenger-car sector and the weak financial situation, there does seem to have been a certain inevitability about it. Between 1968 and 1974 profits totalled only £74 million, a pitifully small sum for such a large company, and yet £70 million was paid out in dividends, with very little capital being allocated to new plant and machinery. In 1975 the Ryder Report stated bluntly that even if all of the firm's profits had been retained, together with the additional £49 million raised by a rights issue in 1972, this would still have been inadequate to accommodate BL's capital requirements. Moreover, the amount set aside for depreciation was derisory and this, combined with a heavy run-down of working capital, meant that profits were artificially inflated. The financial position eventually deteriorated so badly that suppliers were forced to wait up to four months for settlement of bills and moves were made by the company to defer payment of taxes. By 1975 BLMC's balance sheet recorded the staggering loss of £76 million.

Failure to rationalise the company's structure and to introduce a sound investment programme rank high among the explanations for BL's failing profitability, but as Karel Williams has argued, an inability to respond adequately to market demand may have been the more significant influence. In this analysis BL's decline was product-led, though this was itself partly the result of a weak investment strategy. Between 1968 and 1973 the company had a total of £312 million or an average of £45 million a year available for investment from ploughed-back profits. Such small sums could not finance new production facilities on any scale, especially at a time when the tooling and development costs of new models were increasing rapidly. At 1974 prices the expenditure required for a new car body was in the order of £75 million and £150 million for a new engine. Thus, all that BL could afford was the introduction of new body shells using existing equipment and levels of technology. In 1969 the company was relatively well covered in the market for small and large cars and also in the area of sports vehicles, but it was exceptionally weak in its range of medium-size family saloons. The market strategy adopted involved the introduction of new vehicles and the upgrading of selected existing ones to compete against the Ford Escort and Cortina. None of the new cars – the Maxi, Allegro and Princess all of which were poorly developed – sold well enough to reverse the company's declining share of total sales, partly because they competed against each other as well as other makes. The Maxi failed to secure more than 3 per cent of the domestic market, while the Marina and Allegro peaked at 6.4 per cent and 5.3 per cent respectively, both of which were well behind the double figures achieved by the Cortina and Escort. Regardless of their limited success, the most significant point for Coventry about these new cars was they were built elsewhere, for this further undermined the city's long-term viability as a volume producer of motor vehicles.[20]

BL's policy towards the development of its Coventry factories from the group's formation until the crisis of 1975 appears to have been somewhat ambivalent. In essence, the Coventry plants represented the company's specialist car division and over time some attempt was made to achieve a degree of integration between Jaguar, Triumph and the Rover works at nearby Solihull. A number of policy statements, however, between 1968 and 1972 made it clear that none of the city's assembly plants was considered large enough for volume production in the popular end of the market.[21] Major development programmes were announced in 1972 and 1973 which attracted a great deal of local interest. Although continuing as a production centre for sports cars and high-performance saloons, Canley was to move towards the manufacture of engines and transmission equipment. Rationalisation and a more integrated system of production were to be achieved by transferring manufacture of the larger Triumph models to the Rover works at Solihull and the vacated accommodation was used for the establishment of a divisional spares centre at Canley. Alvis was to be drawn further into the group by supplying engine blocks for the new Rover SD1 which was scheduled for launch in 1975. The object of the exercise was to streamline the Jaguar, Triumph and Rover Divisions, while at the same time boosting output of the first two from a combined total of 150,000 units to over 250,000.[22] Joint Management Teams were created to help facilitate these changes, but Jaguar was effectively left free to develop its own identity.[23] Finally, to reflect BL's commitment to Coventry, the head of its international marketing division established his headquarters in 58,000 square feet of office space close to the city's mainline station.[24] In practice these initiatives promised more than they delivered. Canley's output remained small and by 1974 its days as a centre of car production were clearly numbered. Manufacture of Triumph models was also very limited and it was reported in 1972 that the factories concerned were showing no return on investment, when the expected rate had been in the region of 25 per cent.[25] The inescapable truth is that Canley was reduced to a secondary role within the company, a position that not helped by the fact that the sports cars produced there under BL such as the Stag, the Toledo and the Dolomite Sprint were all plagued with reliability problems and in the case of the Stag, it had to be withdrawn altogether from the American market. Finally, Jaguar with its fluctuating output figures struggled to retain its high reputation for its saloons and sports variants, but there were growing worries about its quality control and the increasing unreliability of its products.

As part of its attempt to bring a degree of commonality to its plants, BL sought to end piecework and to replace it with Measured Day Work, which was also intended to reassert managerial control of the shop floor and to bring an end to the gang system. Following the appointment of Pat Lowry as industrial relations director, BL made it clear that MDW was, in the company's view, the best way to organise a modern car plant. The arrangement was said to provide greater control over wage drift, eliminate continual bargaining, facilitate more rapid introduction of technical change and encourage labour mobility without the need for protracted shop floor negotiation. Moreover, MDW was intended to lead to greater output supervision, including track speed and loading levels, and to provide scope for economies in clerical and administrative staff. The principal advantage to the work force was said to be less reliance on bonus payments, which would help to minimise fluctuations in total earnings as well as reducing sectional divisions between workers and inequalities in pay between direct and indirect workers. Despite some labour resistance, this change was introduced fairly smoothly at the Birmingham and Oxford plants, but engendered a great deal of bitterness in Coventry, leading to industrial unrest at both Triumph and Jaguar. When the plan was first suggested in 1968, Mr Eddie McGarry, the influential shop stewards convenor at Canley, was quoted as saying that 'We have decided that in no circumstances will we tolerate any interference with the present approach of payment by results or piecework systems unless the proposed changes are mutually agreed at domestic level.'[26] There had been little change of attitude by 1971 when senior shop stewards described the prospects of MDW as 'absolutely nil'.[27] The response of the workforce at Jaguar was equally hostile and it was only after repeated industrial disputes at Canley and Brown's Lane, including an eleven-week strike at the latter, that a settlement was achieved under the Secure Earnings Plan. The issue generated a similar protracted struggle at Chrysler. When negotiations failed, the company announced unilaterally that it would introduce MDW regardless of the union position. Attitudes hardened quickly with the workers voting against the firm's proposals and refusing to implement revised schedules. Chrysler eventually produced the incentive of an increased wage offer, placing its workers at the summit of the Coventry earnings league. The introduction of MDW proved to be no panacea. Neither Chrysler nor BL were properly prepared for it managerially, with neither firm having sufficient trained staff to police the shop floor. Of equal seriousness, Chrysler's industrial engineering department proved itself incapable of organising production efficiently, to the extent that within a short period a form of mutuality was restored with the workers being left to establish their own pattern of work. Now that that their power over rate and bonus bargaining had been seriously eroded, shop stewards simply turned their attention from purely financial matters to issues concerned with safety, status, pensions, holidays and other fringe benefits and sought to improve these. There was no significant improvement in labour relations, especially at Chrysler where some 500 strikes were recorded in the early 1970s. Equally, the stewards quickly relinquished their quasi-managerial functions as these were now part of management's prerogatives. No longer did they bother to book in work or chase up materials or parts, tasks which were left to newly-appointed superiors who had been given little training for their new roles. The revised system is said to have reduced personal incentives for the workers in that however hard they worked the money remained the same. Increased labour manning on the tracks, though, was welcomed as it reduced physical stress, but a higher proportion of poor work was permitted to pass down the track as it no longer had any impact on wages. Many have argued that in the short term the introduction of MDW was strongly demotivating to the workers and this, when allied to job insecurity and closure threats, perhaps helps to explain why labour relations were so poor in Coventry's main car plants in the mid 1970s. MDW had failed to deliver the stability its supporters sought.[28]

When BL approached the government for financial aid in 1974 it was granted an overdraft facility of £50 million, but in return an investigating team under Sir Don Ryder was set up to investigate and analyse the company's problems and to make recommendations to promote its future viability. Ryder estimated that £900 million needed to be injected into the firm between 1975 and 1978 and suggested that just over half should come from long-term loans and the remainder from government equity and bank loans. It was also anticipated that a further £500 million would be required during the period from 1978 to 1981. These sums appear massive but in fact underestimated BL's true investment needs. Surprisingly, Ryder did not recommend factory closures but did stress the importance of increased product rationalisation involving the use of common components, structures and suspensions where possible. The report pointed to the advantages of a more centralised management structure based on four divisions – cars, international products, trucks and buses. Above all, however, Ryder highlighted the need for improved labour productivity and a reduction in the overall number of bargaining units, arguing that without these the company's future was extremely uncertain In Coventry, Jaguar was to continue much as before but it was envisaged that car assembly at the Canley plant would be phased out and the factory turned over to engine, transmission and component manufacture.[29] When it was published, the Ryder Plan was immediately attacked as being hopelessly optimistic, particularly because so much of its diagnosis and prognosis was based on the company's own financial and production estimates. It was a plan that paid little heed to the harsh realities of the car industry, even going as far as believing that BL would continue to hold 30 per cent of the domestic market, and which paid little heed to the necessity of cost-effectiveness in production. Almost as soon as the plan had been published it was attacked as being hopelessly unrealistic and was labelled as a lame duck. Between 1975 and 1979 BL's share of the domestic car market plummeted from 32 per cent to approximately 20 per cent.[30] There was little improvement in productivity and the high levels of overmanning identified in the report continued almost unabated.[31] The suggested production targets were abandoned as early as 1977. The Ryder Plan had failed and in that year Michael Edwardes was recruited to salvage the company's future.[32]

Between the publication of Ryder's report and 1977 there arose a great deal of uncertainty in Coventry about the future of BL plants, leading to a high degree of concern among not only the workforce but also members of the City Council. In 1974 BL forecast a bright future for its factories in the area, but locally there was a growing awareness that Coventry had become merely a part of a very large international enterprise. The apprehension which emanated from this was articulated by the leader of the council when he noted that 'Decisions about employment in Coventry's motor industry used to be taken locally. Now they are taken nationally and in some cases internationally.'[33] These views gained added credence in 1976 when it was announced that some models were to be phased out and others, including the Triumph Dolomite, transferred from Coventry to other BL plants. It was planned that by 1980 Canley would have become almost entirely a power-train plant. This decision involved the transfer of some thousands of employees to the Solihull works, but the company went to considerable lengths to stress that compulsory redundancies would not be required. A massive retraining programme was promised in order to enable the remaining Canley operatives to switch to engine and gearbox manufacture.[34] Despite these assurances it became clear that BL's plans for Coventry were not expansionary. The council became deeply concerned that only one major BL marque, the Jaguar, would remain in Coventry and this was seen as a grave threat to employment in the city as well as a distinct blow to civic pride. BL responded by offering assurances that none of its manufacturing plants in the city would close and that job opportunities would remain much as before. However, the company also emphasised that since none of its factories had sufficient capacity to achieve substantial economies of scale it would not be possible in the future to manufacture a volume produced car in the city. Although BL vehemently denied that Coventry would become a production backwater, much of local opinion was not convinced, believing that the company's major activities would increasingly gravitate towards Birmingham and Oxford.[35]

Much has been written elsewhere on the impact of Michael Edwardes on BL as a whole and so the immediate focus will be on how his policies affected Coventry. Edwardes's arrival brought a new air of stark realism to BL. The Ryder-inspired centralised management structure was soon abandoned and the car division split up and returned to specialist companies – Austin-Morris, Land Rover and Jaguar, Rover and Triumph. Decisions were taken to press ahead with new model development which ultimately bore fruit in the shape of the Metro, Maestro and Montego. More importantly, Edwardes introduced a number of reforms concerned with production capacity, manning levels and labour and labour relations, thorny issues which had been avoided by successive management teams even though managerial perogatives were supposedly reinstated through the introduction of MDW. When the Edwardes Plan was revealed it was relatively well received by both shop stewards and the workforce, though whether they were entirely aware of its implications seems doubtful.[36] The decision to move production of the TR7 sports car from Speke to Canley and promise of several hundred new jobs helped to cushion the initial impact in Coventry of the Edwardes rationalisation scheme. The closure of Speke was resisted by the Liverpool labourforce but, despite Eddie McGarry's statement that 'We are not going to pick the bones of the Speke carcass', the transfer of work went ahead. Similarly, Canley's medium term future appeared to be secure when it was later announced that assembly of the new Acclaim, a joint venture with Honda of Japan, would be located at the plant.[37] All proved a false dawn, however. In view of BL's continuing financial difficulties, Edwardes proceeded with plant rationalisation at a rapid pace, announcing the close of thirteen factories, one of which was Canley, in September 1979. Production of the TR7 was to move to Solihull and the Acclaim to Oxford, leaving Canley with the loss of 5,500 jobs, to say nothing of those in related industries. The closure had important implications for the remaining BL plants in the city, particularly Alvis, Coventry Climax and Self Changing Gears, all of which were outside mainstream car manufacturing and, in the search for extra funding, prime candidates for early privatisation.[38] The news of Canley's fate prompted John Butcher, Conservative MP for Coventry

South East within whose constituency the plant lay, to suggest that 'Canley was paying for the whole of the group's problems', while William Wilson, Labour Member for Coventry South West, added that the closure was a 'contradiction of the assurances given a year ago on the plant's future existence'.[39] BL argued that despite these and other protests the closure policy was necessary as part of an overall strategy to rescue the firm by restoring its profitability. At its peak Canley had given employment to 13,000 people, but by late 1981 this had fallen to just under 2,000, distributed between product engineering (1,500), sales and marketing (550) and Unipart (200). Canley's demise was followed by the closure of the old Morris Engines plant at Courthouse Green and the smaller Clay Lane and Torrington Avenue works, while both Alvis and Coventry Climax were sold to the private sector.[40] BL's total workforce in Coventry shrank from 27,268 in 1975 to 8,221 a mere seven years later. The Coventry outposts had paid ultimate price for being too small and, therefore, expendable within BL's corporate planning.[41]

When BL was first created Sir William Lyons expressed considerable reservations concerning Jaguar's ability to retain its special identity within such an amorphous conglomerate, and by the mid-1970s it appeared that his fears had been realised.[42] Lyons was succeeded as chairman and chief executive by Lofty England, but at Donald Stokes's insistence he was joined in 1973 by Geoffrey Robinson who had been running the BL's Innocenti plant in Italy. Robinson proved an extremely able managing director, but his stay with the company was relatively short for in 1975 he succeeded Maurice Edelman as Labour MP for Coventry North West.[43] Between 1968 and 1974 Jaguar's fortunes fluctuated yearly as sales rose and fell. For example, 32,589 cars were sold in 1971 but in the following year this declined to under 23,000. Sales again increased sharply in 1974 but declined consistently thereafter until by 1981 they stood at only 14,353.[44] England and Robinson both nurtured expansionary plans for the company and shortly after his arrival Robinson announced that with the aid of new investment worth £60 million it was planned to raise output to 60,000 vehicles a year by the end of 1975. These hopes evaporated in 1974 when the whole programme was frozen while the Ryder team investigated BL. The Ryder Report recommended that Jaguar should lose its separate identity and be merged as part of the new BL car division. As a result, the board was disbanded and in effect the post of chief executive disappeared leaving Robinson with little alternative but to tender his resignation.[45]

William Lyons's creation now appeared to be losing its way. Management was dispersed with the Brown's Lane and Radford plants being under separate control and with their heads reporting individually to the executives responsible for BL's power-train and assembly divisions. The impression developed that no one had ultimate responsibility for Jaguar. In addition, the morale of the labour force was further weakened by rumours that BL planned to close the Brown's Lane factory and shift production to Birmingham. The decision to erect a new paint shop at Castle Bromwich rather than Coventry and the removal of the Jaguar service works to Birmingham appeared to confirm the truth of this speculation. Inadequate funding was eventually reflected in shortages of materials and components which brought a further slump in production. Vehicles became difficult to acquire and their reputation for quality and reliability also began to suffer. By 1980 Michael Edwardes realised that Jaguar was a luxury which BL could ill afford.[46]

In an attempt to retrieve the company's financial situation, John Egan, a graduate of the London Business School, was recruited from Massey Ferguson to become Jaguar's first chief executive since 1975. Egan's role was to rehabilitate Jaguar by raising output, productivity, competitiveness and quality. Given the nature of the company's product, the first task was to identify and resolve complaints about the vehicles themselves. When it was discovered that over half of these emanated from bought-out components, suppliers were encouraged to improve the quality of their goods by receiving contracts which required them to meet all warranty costs inclusive of labour. The labour force was reduced by about a third as part of an internal programme of rationalisation and reorganisation but despite this production rose by roughly the same figure between 1981 and 1983, with output per man increasing from an average of 1.5 to 3 cars per annum.

The cachet surrounding Jaguar ownership is a vital part of the company's marketing strategy, particularly in highly competitive foreign markets, and this depends heavily upon performance and general reliability. The improvement in quality which appeared in the early 1980s was due in large measure to an imaginative scheme of quality control monitored by shop-floor workers themselves. The trade union response to this initiative was highly positive and it was soon noted that operatives were working with a greater degree of care, purpose and precision. The success of this scheme was partly responsible for a sharp improvement in sales to the United States, which consumed approximately half of Jaguar's total output. In 1982 American sales reached 10,349 vehicles, double the figure for the previous year.[47] Jaguar's commercial success brought a return to private ownership in August 1983 when its shares were eight times oversubscribed on the London Stock Exchange.[48] Jaguar's recovery will be given more attention in the next chapter.

The near collapse of Chrysler UK in the mid-1770s compounded the problems which were already undermining Coventry's industrial economy. Chrysler had been in financial difficulty for some years as sales consistently failed to meet expectations and seemingly endless labour disputes added to costs and delays in production. The causes of this predicament were located in the inheritance from Rootes and the parent company's own weaknesses which combined to restrict investment and model development. In addition, these problems were exacerbated by the introduction of American management techniques which in many ways were unsuited to the traditions of industrial relations in Britain. In comparison with Ford and General Motors, Chrysler entered Europe relatively late and, without the funds to establish a new manufacturing base, was forced to buy into existing operations. The French government allowed Chrysler to take over Simca after its own attempts to save the company had failed. The Americans also acquired Barrieros, a small Spanish family company mainly concerned with assembling imported Simcas, which was experiencing problems in its own domestic market as a result of intense competition from Seat, a subsidiary of the Italian Fiat organisation. Rootes was the third element in Chrysler's European manoeuvres, while Mitsubishi of Japan was also brought into the group. Only Simca of these new acquisitions was really capable of producing cars efficiently and in large numbers, so that the new empire was a collection of relatively unprofitable firms held together by the weakest of the major American motor-vehicle companies. A rapid integration of the Simca and Rootes operations was essential if Chrysler's European outposts were to be placed on a sound manufacturing and commercial basis. The failure to achieve this reflected the parent company's own financial problems and its firm belief that the group's constituent elements should be self-financing.[49]

Chrylser's position in Britain was weak from the beginning and it continued to deteriorate alarmingly throughout the 1970s. The small profits earned between 1971 and 1973 were outweighed by deficits in other years so that from 1968 until 1975 the firm accumulated total losses of £68.3 million, while its market share dropped from 12.7 per cent in 1967 to 6.6 per cent in 1975.[50] Yet this trend was unexceptional within the context of the British motor industry. Chrylser's record was no worse, for example, than that of Vauxhall, another American subsidiary company. However, in this instance, the crucial difference was that Vauxhall enjoyed the financial support of the giant General Motors corporation. Chrysler's problems in Coventry were very similar to those experienced by Rootes. In particular, it proved impossible to obtain really significant economies of scale, for even the combined output of both Ryton and Linwood only reached 350,000 units, well below that necessary to achieve optimum costs. Young and Hood have argued that this line of analysis needs to be qualified since smaller companies may offset their size disadvantage by retaining production of particular vehicles for an extended period of time and by having a more limited range of models and derivatives. To some extent this was the strategy adopted by Chrysler, but it seems likely that such a policy required a high utilisation of capacity, continuity of output and favourable sales levels, objectives which the company was not able to achieve with the necessary degree of consistency. BL was profitable when working at 65–70 per cent capacity but the comparable figure for Chrysler was 75 per cent. The company's higher break-even point meant that Chrysler was under constant pressure to maintain high levels of output and sales so that when these dropped sharply in 1975 its balance sheet recorded a very substantial deficit.[51]

Chrylser's initial investment policy towards its British subsidiary was highly positive. Gilbert Hunt was recruited from Massey Ferguson and as managing director was given responsibility for planning and supervising a major programme of modernisation. In contrast to Simca, Ryton's production lines were in need of a thorough overhaul. The three old-fashioned assembly tracks were scrapped and replaced by a single long gate line, capable of turning out a variety of cars, thereby providing a much greater degree of flexibility than was previously available. New equipment was installed at a cost of some £17 million at the nearby Stoke factory, while at Linwood the adjacent Pressed Steel works was purchased for £12 million and integrated into a completely redesigned car plant, costing another £20 million.[52] Until 1970 by far the greater proportion of Chrysler's European investment went into the UK. However, the parent company made it clear that once the initial round of investment had been completed, subsidiaries were expected to generate their own funds for self-sustaining development. Yet it soon became apparent that the British operation was unable to produce such resources and so any advantage gained from the early capital injections had been eroded by 1973, leaving the monetary value of investment no higher than a decade earlier. The company admitted in 1975 that its aggregate investment in Britain was low and that the value of its fixed assets per employee was among the lowest in Europe. Although the equipment used at Ryton was relatively modern and compared favourably in age with that operating elsewhere in the British motor industry, the same could not be said of Stoke where the plant's antiquity and technological obsolescence increasingly caused the machinery to break down and production to be brought to a stop. In 1975 the Stoke works was cruelly described as a museum for vintage equipment.[53] Stoke's reliance upon ageing machine tool equipment is indicated by table 8.7.

Table 8.7
Age of machine tools used in the Arrow and Avenger power-trains 1975

	Arrow		Avenger	
Age (years)	Number of machines	Per cent	Number of machines	Per cent
Under 8	52	2.9	196	66.6
8–13	287	16.0	9	3.1
14–23	1,150	63.9	72	5.8
24–33	51	2.8	0	0
Total	1,799	100	294	100

Source: Young and Hood, *Chrysler UK*, p. 161.

Despite some early success in new model development, Chrysler's limited investment input led eventually to a range of vehicles characterised by a rather outdated appearance. In an attempt to increase turnover, and against the national trend, prices of the Minx and Imp were lowered in 1969. Yet Chrysler's market share continued to decline, reaching a low point of 8 per cent. Hope then appeared in the form of the Avenger, introduced in 1970 to compete in the market for medium-sized cars where the company was not represented. The Avenger was to join with the larger Chrysler 160 to form the company's two-car range. The 160 was to be joint operation with Simca involving the manufacture of engines in France and bodies in Britain and with final assembly taking place in both countries. This arrangement was designed to alleviate the problems arising from capacity shortage and to enable a serious threat to be mounted against the larger Ford models. However, the Chrysler Corporation's own financial crisis in 1969 meant that the British version of the 160 never materialised, though the Ryton-built Avenger was an immediate and outstanding success and in 1970 outsold the Escort and the Mini, pushing the company's market share back towards 14 per cent. But the important point is that the Avenger was the only new car Chrysler introduced in Britain and by 1975 it was beginning to show its age compared with Ford's new Cortinas, Escorts and Capris. In addition, Vauxhall had updated its Viva range, launched the Chevette and was preparing to bring out the new Cavalier, while BL had given facelifts to the Allegro and Marina. It is not surprising that in the face of this intense competition Chrysler's market share should dwindle.[54]

In contrast to its poor sales performance at home, Chrysler's export record in the 1970s was relatively healthy. The firm managed to export a growing proportion of its output at a time when the other two American subsidiaries in the UK, Ford and Vauxhall, were showing the opposite trend. In 1975 the export–output ratio stood at over 70 per cent compared with 42 per cent for the British motor industry as a whole. However, this success needs to be qualified since it largely involved Complete Knockdown Kits (CKDs) destined for Iran. Very few cars found their way to continental Europe and in 1975 sales to EEC countries amounted to no more than 4 per cent of total exports. The reason for this poor record in Europe remain unclear, though there were suggestions in 1975 that the Chrysler Corporation's overall marketing policy discriminated against UK-built cars in order to allow Simca a clearer run at the Continental market and so prevent the two subsidiaries from competing against each other to the disadvantage of both. In particular, it was alleged that Chrysler's Belgian dealers were allocated sales quotas for UK and Simca vehicles in the ratio 1:7. The Avenger enjoyed some success in the American market where it sold as the Plymouth Cricket and was instrumental in raising exports to the United States from 3,200 units in 1970 to 28,000 in the following year. However, complaints of poor quality and erratic delivery led to the Avenger being replaced in America by the Mitsubishi Colt, leaving the UK subsidiary with only one major export outlet, Iran. Rootes had negotiated an agreement with the Iranian National Industrial Manufacturing Company in 1967 to establish a plant near Tehran for the assembly of CKD Minx and Hunters. The contract was to last until 1980 and mainly involved the Hunter family saloon, known in Iran as the Peykan. By 1974 total CKD exports to Iran were running at 80,000 units per annum, accounting for about 30 per cent of the company's car output and generating nearly 3,000 jobs in Coventry. The profitability of this deal remains a subject of debate. Young and Hood argue that the unit revenue from Iranian sales was approximately 17 per cent below the equivalent figure for the home market and so it may well be that the main benefit from this contract was a contribution towards fixed overhead and other production costs in Britain.[55]

Labour relations problems were almost a running sore in the British motor industry by the early 1970s. The Coventry press suggested that disputes at Chrysler's plants were perhaps more noteworthy than those elsewhere because they took place against a background of falling market share and trading losses, and so further emphasised the precarious financial situation of both the UK subsidiary and the parent American company. Industrial disputes cost Chrysler over 129,000 vehicles between 1972 and 1974, a very substantial loss for a small firm struggling to maintain its market share. Lack of space, however, prevents a full analysis of the causes and impact of industrial unrest at Chrysler and, as a detailed discussion of these is available elsewhere, recapitulation need centre only on the salient points. It has been suggested that the fundamental reason for industrial unrest at Ryton and Stoke hinged on the company's failure to appreciate the nature of Coventry's system of labour relations and its attempt to impose American-style management techniques on an already insecure labour force. The introduction of MDW has already been discussed, but the various disputes surrounding it and other disputes and strikes such as the 'shoddy work' dispute and the electricians's strike and other equally bitter labour-relations battles, gave Chrysler the reputation of a firm being torn apart by appalling labour relations. Both sides eventually realised that what amounted to industrial warfare could not be allowed to continue and belated efforts were made to improve communications and create a more harmonious atmosphere through the introduction of joint management–union committees. Ironically, the company's more detailed plan for the conduct of industrial relations was unveiled during the course of an unofficial strike at the Stoke plant. Chrysler's Employee Participation Programme was a progressive document which offered significant benefits to shop-floor workers. It involved the establishment of a series of Plant Employee Representation Committees (PERC) to discuss and review with management the ongoing operations of the plants. Each PERC would appoint two of its members to higher-level committees to discuss output, manning, recruitment and quality-control issues. Additionally, PERC delegates would sit on the Chrysler Employee Representatives Committee (CERC) which would assess with management the company's policy and direction. Two worker representatives were to be elected from the CERC to the company board, though their precise function was never closely defined. Finally, joint committees, drawn from employee CERC representatives and management, were to be set up to regulate wages grading structures and to appoint referees to help settle disputes. These proposals were highly innovatory and laudable, but they came too late to arrest the company's decline.[56]

The financial position of Chrysler UK was extremely serious by 1975 and rumours of a 'pull out' or 'sell out' were rife in Coventry. There was only enough work to keep the Ryton plant occupied for eleven days between early October 1974 and the following January. As losses mounted and reserves were run down, the company was kept afloat by bank loans and financial assistance from its American parent, which together amounted to £104 million. Senior Chrysler Corporation executives warned at a Detroit press conference that 'In an operation where the possibility of continued losses remains, extraordinary action which could result in non-recurring losses may be necessary to protect the company's interests.'[57] It was clear that the disposal of Chrysler UK was under consideration, though in Coventry it was widely believed that this was the first move in an attempt to secure aid from the British government using the workforce, dealers and customers as pawns. As Harold Wilson put it, 'the government was presented with a pistol to their head'. MPs from the areas most likely to be affected by Chrysler's collapse pressed for some type of government rescue operation. Yet to take over Chrysler was far from an attractive financial proposition since liabilities, redundancy payments losses and development costs were estimated at £170 million and all that would be obtained in return was a car company too small to be viable on its own. Moreover, to save Chrysler conflicted with the new industrial policy agreed only a short time earlier at Chequers between the government, the CBI and the TUC that public money was not be used to support 'lame ducks'.[58] Indeed, with an estimated 25 per cent overcapacity in the industry there was a strong case for allowing Chrysler to fold.

The Wilson government could not be described as doctrinaire. Pragmatism was its watchword and so, too, was its ultimate decision to step in and rescue Chrysler. At first a number of senior ministers, including Denis Healey and Eric Varley, were determined to allow the company to go under; Michael Foot, Secretary of State for Employment, even drew up plans for a generous scheme of redundancy payments. Without access to Cabinet or departmental papers it is difficult to be precise as to the reasons for the government's eventual change of heart. It is clear, however, that opposition to closure became increasingly more vocal and that this was allied to a greater awareness on the part of government as to the social and political costs which such a policy would have involved. A Cabinet subcommittee was set up to salvage what it could from the Chrysler demise but as negotiations broadened, the debate gradually moved from close-down to rescue. Firstly, the whole Scottish Office team led by the formidable Willie Ross threatened to resign if Linwood was abandoned, and the prospect of losing safe Labour seats to a rampant Scottish National Party was a particularly unwelcome thought. Secondly, Michael Foot shifted his position in favour of a rescue because of the need to preserve work at a period of rising unemployment generally and because of the economic fact that the end of Chrysler UK would have cost some 55,000 jobs adding between £150 and £160 million to social security payments. Thirdly, closure also had serious implications for the balance of payments since many of the firm's dealers would almost certainly have taken up foreign franchises and thus added to the growing volume of imported cars. Fourthly, there was the loss of exports to Iran, and the Shah made it clear that if Chrysler's Iranian contract was cancelled or put in jeopardy the prospects for other British firms attempting to develop their interests in the country could be harmed. The Cabinet was itself divided. The Industry Minister, Eric Varley, was the most ardent supporter of a policy which would have allowed Chrysler to go under, but he was gradually isolated as Wilson and Healey changed sides and others prevaricated. Only Tony Benn among Cabinet ministers favoured nationalisation. A rescue package was agreed but it was at the expense of the government's industry policy which then lay in shreds.[59]

To facilitate a rescue package two new important elements were agreed. The government signalled its intention not to take an equity holding in the company, thus placing the risk and responsibility for the firm entirely on the shoulders of the Chrysler Corporation. In return, the firm offered to inject £12 million into Ryton if the workforce there was willing to agree to the transfer of the Avenger line to Linwood in return for the introduction and assembly of the C6 Alpine from Poissy in France, thereby saving Ryton from extinction. The prospect of keeping both assembly plants open left the government with little choice but to make an offer of assistance. The financial arrangements which were eventually concluded committed the government to provide £162 million over four years from 1976 to 1979, broken down as follows: £72.5 million for possible losses, £55 million in loans for future capital investment and £35 million as a guarantee for a further medium-term loan from the banking sector. For its part, the Chrysler Corporation guaranteed £28 million of the £55 million with the remaining £27 million secured on the assets of Chrysler UK. The medium-term loan of £35 million was also counter-guaranteed by the parent company. Additionally, Chrysler's overall commitment consisted of £32.5 million to cover possible losses, a further £19.7 million for the waiver of loans and interest payments and the £12 million required for bringing the Alpine from France. According to Don Lander, the chairman of the British operation, the company was now secure and could look to the future with renewed confidence.[60]

The rescue agreement involved the loss of some 8,000 jobs, mainly at Ryton and Stoke, and a number of major changes in work organisation. Ryton was to become an assembly centre for front-wheel-drive vehicles, such as the Alpine, with rear-wheel-drive cars being built entirely at Linwood, while the Stoke factory was to prepare the CKDs for Iran and continue in its role as the main machining operation for the UK. Through the mechanism of a Declaration of Intent the government tried to ensure that new models would be introduced to the UK plants and that integration would proceed as quickly as possible in order to ensure that British factories did not become mere assembly points for Chrysler's French-built vehicles.[61] The deal brought audible sighs of relief in Coventry, though in the wider economic community there was criticism that, by bailing out the lamest of lame ducks when there were other far more deserving cases, the government had spectacularly sabotaged its own industrial policy. Furthermore, the rescue had left the UK motor industry still suffering from excess capacity and, once committed, the government was in danger of being forced into providing Chrysler, or indeed other firms, with additional financial aid. There was also resentment in some quarters that taxpayers' money had been used to help save an American multinational during a period when the Treasury was imposing cuts upon education, health and other social services, a sentiment not helped by a comment in the Wall Street Journal that British funds had turned Chrysler from an economic albatross into a financial angel.[62] These and similar criticisms were essentially a reflection of the widely-held belief that Chrysler UK was unlikely to achieve long-term viability.

The structural changes outlined in the rescue plan began in 1976. The run down of labour proceeded very quickly and by 1982 the workforce stood at 9,000, or 62 per cent of the earlier total. Production integration saw the assembly of the Alpine at Ryton and some of Simca's machining being located at the Stoke plant. But these changes had only a modest impact upon Chrysler's financial health and despite improvements in productivity and labour relations the British operation did not return to profitability until 1983, by which time it had been taken over by Peugeot of France.[63] Nevertheless, sufficient progress had been made by July 1978 for the government to approve Chrysler's new plans for future development in Britain. It was therefore a major shock when a month later the Chrysler Corporation announced that it had agreed to sell its British subsidiary to Peugeot. The sale was condemned by MPs from both sides of the House and united members as politically far apart as Renee Short and James Prior. Trade union reaction was equally critical and Clive Jenkins of the Association of Scientific, Technical and Managerial Staff attacked the

Table 8.8
Pre-tax profit /(loss), Chrysler/Peugeot Talbot 1975–83 (£m)

1975	(33.5)
1976	(42.9)
1977	(21.5)
1978	(20.2)
1979	(41.1)
1980	(75.0)
1981	(91.0)
1982	(54.7)
1983	3.4

Source: Annual Reports and Accounts Chrysler UK, Talbot 1975–83.

fact that decisions affecting the jobs of so many British and other European workers were taken without consultation or compassion by a small clique of businessmen in Detroit.[64] The American Corporation justified its policy as part of a general scheme of rationalisation and retrenchment designed to stem losses at home which, it was claimed, had greatly hindered its own research and development programmes. In fact Chrysler sold foreign holdings in Britain, France, South Africa and Australia which realised some $8 million. The British Cabinet was unhappy at the deal for, apart from general political and economic considerations, the Americans had reneged on that part of the original rescue plan which required government approval if more than 20 per cent of the operation was to be sold to another foreign concern. Both government and trade unions soon realised, however, that there was no alternative but to accept what was in effect a *fait accompli*. The main concern of the workforce was that wages and jobs should be maintained and that, providing this was achieved, ownership of the firm was largely immaterial.[65] In practice, the French were cool on guarantees of employment and made it clear that job security depended upon the success of the its newly-acquired British holdings.[66]

Under the deal concluded between the two companies, Peugeot assumed responsibility for £400 million of Chrysler debts, paid the Americans £230 million and gave them 15 per cent of Peugeot-Citroen stock in return for Chrysler UK and Chrysler France. This gave the Peugeot-Citroen group approximately 18 per cent of the European market with sales of over 2 million vehicles a year, making it larger than Volkswagen, Fiat or Renault. At the time of the takeover it was suggested that the French were only interested in the Simca production facilities and Chrysler UK's dealerships and that the British plants were a not wholly welcome part of the total package.[67] It was not surprising, therefore, that the Coventry workforce should be apprehensive about the French company's immediate intentions. The appointment of George Turnbull, a Coventrian, as chairman of the UK car division, renamed Talbot after an old Rootes's marque, was a positive and reassuring step. Turnbull was and remains a highly respected figure throughout the motor industry and had previously enjoyed success with Standard, BL and the Hyundai Motor Company of South Korea. Pledges were given on the continuation of the Iranian deal, trade union recognition and on further integration between the British and French factories. The Alpine was duly transferred from France and subsequently updated, and the newer Horizon and Solara models were introduced at Ryton from Poissy. In the early 1980s the Ryton plant employed 1,350 men, produced some 35,000 vehicles a year, consisting of 16,000 Horizons, 11,500 Solaras and 7,500 Alpines. Productivity at the plant rose from twenty-five cars per employee per annum in 1979 to forty-one in 1983 and, backed by aggressive sales campaigns, market share had been pushed back up to 8 per cent. Overall, the signs looked promising, although there remained a nagging fear that Peugeot's sojourn in Coventry might be brief, but that would depend on decisions taken in Paris rather than Detroit.[68]

Notes

[1] Mallier and Rosser, 'Economic Base of Coventry', p. 106. We are grateful to Drs M. Healey and D. Clark for allowing us sight of a draft of their paper, 'Industrial Decline and Government Response in the West Midlands: the Case of Coventry'.

[2] For a discussion of the British Economy in the 1970s see S. Pollard, *The Wasting of the British Economy* (Croom Helm, London, 1982).

[3] For a discussion of recent trends in the West Midlands economy see J. House (ed.), *The UK Space: Resources and Environment* (Weidenfeld and Nicolson, London, 1982); P.A. Wood, 'West Midlands Leads the Downward Trend', *Geographical Magazine*, vol. XLIX (1976), pp. 2–8; S. Taylor, 'De-industrialisation and Unemployment in the West Midlands', *Political Quarterly*, vol. 52 (1981), pp. 64–73.

[4] Lancaster and Mason (eds), *Life and Labour in a Twentieth Century*, pp. 43–7.

[5] Healey and Clark, 'Industrial Response and Decline'.

[6] Central Policy Review Staff, *The Future of the British Motor Industry* (HMSO, London, 1975), pp. 5–6.

[7] Fourteenth Report of the Expenditure Committee: *The Motor Vehicle Industry*, HC 617 (HMSO, London 1975), p. 34.

[8] Ibid., pp. 34–46; K. Bhaskar, *The Future of the UK Motor Industry* (Butterworth, London, 1979), pp. 85–9.

[9] CPRS, *The Future of the British Motor Industry*, p. 79.

[10] Ibid., p. 91.

[11] CPRS, *The Future of the British Motor Industry*, p. 99.

[12] Ibid., pp. 96–102; K. Bhaskar, *The Future of the UK Motor Industry*, pp. 70–75; Dunnett, *The Decline of the British Motor Industry*, pp. 140–46.

[13] Ibid., pp. 124–8.

[14] *Coventry Evening Telegraph*, 12 January 1968.

[15] Ibid., 18 January 1968.

[16] Ibid.

[17] Ensor, *The Motor Industry*, pp. 117–18.

[18] Ibid.

[19] K. Williams, J. Williams and D. Thomas, *Why are the British Bad at Manufacturing?* (Routledge, Kegan Paul, London, 1983), p. 227.

[20] Ibid., pp. 227–59; Friedman, *Industry and Labour*, pp. 230–31.

[21] *Coventry Evening Telegraph*, 12 June 1968, 8 October 1968.

[22] Ibid., 14 December 1972, 14 May 1973.

[23] Ibid.

[24] Ibid.

[25] Ibid., 16 May 1972.

[26] Ibid., 23 October 1968.

[27] Ibid., 16 October 1971.

[28] Tolliday, 'High Tide and After', pp. 34–8.

[29] Dunnett, *The Decline of the British Motor Industry*, pp. 134–5.

[30] Williams, et al., *Why are the British Bad at Manufacturing?*, p. 258.

[31] Dunnett, *The Decline of the British Motor Industry*, pp. 234–5.

32 For a critique of the Ryder Plan see Bhaskar, *The Future of the UK Motor Industry*, pp. 175–7.

33 *Coventry Evening Telegraph*, 29 April 1976.

34 Ibid.

35 Ibid.

36 Bhaskar, *The Future of the UK Motor Industry*, p. 113; *Coventry Evening Telegraph*, 11 December 1978.

37 Ibid., 16 February 1978, 10 September 1979.

38 Ibid., 11 September 1979, 1 November 1979.

39 Ibid.

40 Ibid., 6 September 1982.

41 Ibid., 2 July 1981.

42 *Sunday Times Magazine*, 5 December 1982.

43 Whyte, *Jaguar*, p. 168.

44 Ibid., p. 241; BL Data.

45 Whyte, *Jaguar*, p. 172.

46 *Coventry Evening Telegraph*: 15 May 1975, 10 December 1975, 5 August 1976.

47 This section has been based on The Money Programme, BBC TV 27 February 1983; *Guardian*, 2 December 1983, 9 October 1984; *Sunday Times*, 7 November 1983; *New Society*, 12 January 1984.

48 *Guardian*, 6 August 1984.

49 Ensor, *The Motor Industry*, pp. 96–8.

50 Chrysler UK Annual Reports and Accounts 1968–76.

51 Young and Hood, *Chrysler UK*, pp. 153–4.

52 Ensor, *The Motor Industry*, pp. 100–101.

53 Young and Hood, *Chrysler UK*, p. 160; *Coventry Evening Telegraph*, 26 November 1975.

54 Ensor, *The Motor Industry*, pp. 102–3; *Coventry Evening Telegraph*, 24 October 1975.

55 Young and Hood, *Chrysler UK*, pp. 141–8

56 Ibid., pp. 217–46; *Coventry Evening Telegraph*, 30 October 1975, 1 November 1975, 14 November 1975.

57 Ibid., 29 October 1975.

58 Young and Hood, *Chrysler UK*, pp. 285–88; *Sunday Times*, 14 December 1975; *Coventry Evening Telegraph*, 12 December 1975.

59 *Sunday Times*, 14 December 1975.

60 Young and Hood, *Chrysler UK*, pp. 285–8; *Coventry Evening Telegraph*, 16 December 1975.

61 Dunnett, The Decline of the British Motor Industry, pp. 162–3.

62 Young and Hood, *Chrysler UK*, pp. 241–92.

63 Chrysler UK and Talbot Motor Company Ltd., Annual Reports and Accounts 1976–83.

64 *Coventry Evening Telegraph*, 11 August 1978.

65 Ibid., 15 August 1978.

66 Ibid., 22 December 1978.

67 Ibid., 12 February 1981; Dunnett, *The Decline of the British Motor Industry*, p. 165.

[68] Talbot Motor Company Ltd, Annual Reports and Accounts 1979–83; *Coventry Evening Telegraph*, 12 April 1983, 2 October 1983, 9 April 1984, *Sunday Times*, 13 April 1983, 8 January 1984; *Financial Times*, 9 September 1983; *Guardian*, 23 February 1983, 7 March 1984.

Chapter 9

Renaissance or False Dawn?

The late 1970s and early 1980s witnessed the nadir of Coventry's economic fortunes in the latter half of the twentieth century, with the city having a distinct air of gloom surrounding it. Not for nothing, though, is Coventry's civic symbol the phoenix and, like that fabled bird, the city has slowly restructured its economy, moving away from its shrinking manufacturing base into services. By the early 1990s, out of a total workforce of 118,300, manufacturing accounted for only 30 per cent of employment, while public administration and education, and distribution, hotels and restaurants took up 30 per cent and 19 per cent respectively. Banking, finance and insurance took up a further 15 per cent, with the remainder scattered between other services, transport and communications, agriculture, energy and water. All of this was in sharp contrast to the heady days of dominance by machine tools, aerospace, electrical engineering and cars at the end of the Second World War.[1] Within manufacturing itself there was a structural shift, with the growth of hi-tech companies, due to both domestic growth and direct foreign investment from firms in the European Union, Australia, the United States and Japan. Despite this shift, however, the car firms still loomed large when it came to direct employment, with Jaguar employing around 4,000, Peugeot 4,500, Alvis almost 700 and Rover just over 450, giving a total of slightly over 10,000.[2] In addition to the assemblers, the city's twenty-four main component manufacturers employed 3,890 people; the largest, the Torrington Company and Hills Precision, with 434 and 400 employees respectively.[3]

Though shrunken in size compared with its heyday, Coventry's car industry gradually pulled itself away from the dark days of the late 1970s, and stabilised, but not without periods of serious uncertainty. However, this must be contextualised within the automotive industry as a whole and also with regard to the fate of Rover down to its takeover by BMW. As has been pointed out elsewhere, the car industry changed markedly from the late 1970s. The days of Fordist mass production with quantity rather than quality being the driving force were replaced by the concept of lean production, which was ultimately embraced by all Western European producers in their attempts to emulate Japanese methods of production. Space precludes a full discussion of this Eastern concept but its salient features can at least be outlined. According to Kochan and Lansbury, the key elements in lean production *inter alia* are 'the application of simultaneous engineering, the zero buffer principle, total quality control, continuous incremental improvement, integrated supply chains, team work and the use of the "pull" system of production'.[4] Building on their initial successful export drives, Japanese cars continued to penetrate the UK market even though by agreement their share was limited to 11 per cent. Not content with exporting but seeing the UK as an excellent potential launch pad for a sustained attack on European markets as a whole, Nissan, welcomed by the Conservative Government, arrived in Britain in 1984 and opened a factory near Sunderland and was subsequently followed by Toyota and Honda.

The Japanese producers entered an industry that was trying to rationalise itself and improve its productivity and quality in attempts to make itself competitive in Britain, let alone in Europe or globally. The 1980s were characterised by a fall in UK production from 1,328,000 in 1977 to a low of 887,679 in 1982, with the 1977 figure not being achieved again until the following decade. Exports, too, plummeted from 741,788 units in 1977 to 186,158 almost a decade later. As exports sagged badly, imports rose. Indeed, in 1979 imports exceeded UK-produced sales for the first time in more than fifty years. This was due partly to the demise of Rover and the use made by Ford, and Peugeot in particular, of pulling in vehicles from their Continental plants in the 1980s. In addition to rising imports the configuration of market leadership altered. The collapse of BL allowed Ford to become dominant in market share in the early 1980s even though its percentage lead over the others fell in the early 1990s, but of equal importance has been the growing force of second division players such as Volkswagen, Peugeot and Renault, who have made their presence felt strongly in UK markets.[5] The 1980s and early 1990s, especially with the recession of 1979–81 and 1989–91, were difficult years for the UK car industry as new methods of production were sought in the search for competitiveness. When the period began, the prospects for Coventry's car workers looked grim and it is against this background that their performance must be judged.

Despite the arrival of Michael Edwardes with his ruthless reform of labour relations, no less aggressive managerial clear-out and macho style, BL's performance proved no better than under his predecessors. Output continued to fall, dropping from 747,000 units in 1977 to 519,000 in 1982, while employment fell from 192,000 employees in 1978 to 108,000 four years later.[6] Productivity continued to drop until 1980 when it turned upwards to reach 4.81 vehicles per employee compared to 4.19 in 1976. While BL management maintains that much-needed labour reform helped boost productivity, others have argued that such an upswing was inevitable given the drop in labour relative to output and was only to be expected in the wake of large-scale redundancies and the closure of marginal plants such as Speke No.1, Canley and Solihull. Nevertheless, market share continued to fall and was to do so for years to come. By the mid-1980s it had dwindled to 17 per cent, with neither the Montego nor Maestro models, which were conceived in the Edwardes era, making any serious impact on the market, both failing to gain more than 5 per cent market share in their respective sectors, thus leaving the firm too dependent on the Metro.

Though Edwardes quit BL in 1982, he had recognised BL's deficiencies in investment, technology and design and realised that it was impossible to run a modern car company on the basis of one successful model, and so the alliance with Honda was gradually extended beyond producing the Honda Acclaim under licence. This, indeed, was tacit recognition that no longer could BL compete against the major producers on equal terms, but needed to embark on a niche strategy, which really only gained force under Graham Day, who took over the firm in 1986. On the back of the Acclaim agreement in 1984 was the Rover 200, which was almost a clone of the Honda Ballade, but nevertheless 125,000 were built. Two years later followed the Rover 800 and the Honda Legend, a joint development effort, which was subsequently followed by the Rover 200 and 400 series in 1989 (to replace the Montego and Maestro models), the outcome of continued joint development and cross sourcing of components.[8]

The tie-up with Honda benefited both parties. It allowed the Japanese firm an easy route to expanding its operations in Europe and eventually allowed it to gain a 20 per cent stake in Rover, with the latter gaining a similar stake in Honda UK. Additionally, it paved the way for Honda to announce in 1985 its intention to open its own operation at Swindon. Rover's gain from the relationship was significant, but it also had its downside. There is no doubt that Rover benefited from working with a Japanese partner, as it allowed the concept of continuous benchmarking to become more firmly established for key activities. Even though the total workforce was cut by a further 70 per cent from the 1982 figure, output was stabilised at around 500,000 units per annum. Engineering productivity doubled, product development cycles halved and there was a new invigorating emphasis on quality. Work processes were altered to allow the development of a cross-functional multi-skilled labour force. The downside is that the relationship proved unequal; Rover became too dependent on Honda's design and engineering expertise, which was a reflection of its own internal weaknesses. Despite the boost from Honda, market share continued to drop to only 13.6 per cent in 1989. In retrospect, perhaps Edwardes's best move as boss of Rover was to link with Honda, otherwise the firm may not have survived as long as it did as a separate entity.[9]

Edwardes was succeeded in 1982 by Sir Austin Bide, but it was not until the advent of Graham Day four years later that further change made itself felt. A Canadian by birth and a lawyer by training, Day came to BL from British Shipbuilders where he had successfully completed a policy of rationalization, earning the admiration of the then Prime Minister, Margaret Thatcher. Day had a reputation for being a hard taskmaster as well as possessing a sharp business brain. He was convinced that, with an annual output of scarcely half a million vehicles, there was no way that Rover could compete as a large-volume producer and so it was decided to move upmarket and try to create the image of a British Volvo or Mercedes, which was in fact a strategy that had been mooted inside the company nearly fifteen years earlier, by its one-time finance director, John Barber. 'Profit was given priority over market share.'[10]

Having privatised large parts of British Shipbuilders, Day, who ditched the lugubrious name BL in favour of Rover Group as part of upmarket image-building, was intent on following up an earlier privatisation of parts of Rover such as Jaguar, Istel and Unipart and got rid of Leyland Trucks and Freight Rover. Essentially, Day was giving priority to concentrating on Rover's core business. All in all, by the late 1980s, eighteen subsidiaries had been disposed of, reducing the core workforce to less than 40,000 employees.[11] Rover, too, was on the market.

Rover could scarcely be described as a favourite of successive Thatcher governments, which were continually looking for a reason and an opportunity to unload it to the private sector. An opportunity then presented itself in 1985 when GM first showed interest. GM's subsidiary Bedford Trucks had been seriously hit by the collapse of world truck sales which had adversely affected the sales of all commercial vehicle producers. The crux of the problem was that there was vast excess capacity in the market and putting BL/Rover and Bedford together had its own logic. Moreover, GM was interested in acquiring the four-wheel-drive Land Rover and Range Rover and marketing them vigorously in the United States. News of their negotiations leaked and, after Roy Hattersley, Deputy Leader of the Labour Party, raised the matter in the House of Commons, there was a typical British jingoistic backlash of outrage at the prospect of the two remaining jewels in the crown, Land Rover and Range Rover, falling into the hands of an American multinational. The project was dropped quietly as GM withdrew.

For several years Ford Europe had been concerned about the advances made in European markets by Japanese imports and was looking both to consolidate and strengthen its position through linking up with BL. After initial discussions with Norman Tebbit, a former Secretary of State for Industry, though still a Cabinet Minister, an approach was made to his successor at the DTI, Leon Brittan, who gave permission to talk to BL. There is no doubt, as Adeney says, that Whitehall was excited at the potential offloading of the ailing concern, but there was both anger and resentment in BL at the prospect of revealing highly confidential commercial information to a competitor on the instruction of government. Though the talks were secret they were leaked to the Opposition who demanded a government enquiry as to what was going on. What made this sensitive was that it appeared on the surface that the government was prepared to sell off chunks of British industry to America and, coming so soon after the Westland Helicopter affair which was resolved controversially in favour of the American Sikorski Company, news of yet more secret talks were highly embarrassing to the Cabinet which, in an act of face-saving, ended the negotiations.[12]

In the event, Rover was sold off in 1988 to British Aerospace. When the announcement was made by Lord Young, claims were made that such a union would bring synergy between the two firms with parallels being drawn with Saab. How this was to be achieved between a small-niche playing, struggling car manufacturer and a company whose own efficiency was in great doubt, was highly debatable and, in the event, such synergy proved illusory with Rover being sold on to BMW in 1994. Essentially, the government got rid of its problems. BAe offered £150 million for Rover and asked for a further £800 million to write off debts This was granted but, upon investigation by the EU, was reduced to £549 million, a blow softened by Lord Young's 'sweetener' of £44 million in the form of tax concessions. The government could claim that by selling to BAe it had kept Rover in British hands, even though BAe lacked the necessary resources to fund Rover's corporate investment plans, all the more so as Rover was incapable of generating such funds on its own. At the time of privatisation, Rover's capital debts amounted to almost £3 billion. The selling price, including deferred payments, was £148 million. For this BAe gained significant property in London and the Midlands and Rover's stocks of vehicles, valued at over £440 million. BAe's net gain, including regional aid and tax breaks, was £397 million. Finally, as part of the deal, BAe gave an undertaking not to sell Rover for at least five years.[13] Between Graham Day's arrival and the sale of Rover under the tutelage of his successor, George Simpson, to BMW in 1994, great effort was put into trying to modernise the company, improve sales, gradually adopt lean production techniques, gain the confidence of the workers and forge new relationships with suppliers. During the Edwardes era negotiation was virtually by diktat with unions being bypassed, as they were over his plan and the sacking of Derek Robinson, a senior shop steward at Longbridge who had challenged both his authority and his plan. Sadly, Edwardes's policy left a serious communications vacuum between management and workers, which was eventually recognised in the mid-1980s, when factory surveys revealed high levels of disaffection and insecurity on the shop floor. To try to overcome this and at the same time continue managerial control by softening the approach, the workforce was set in groups of twelve to fifteen under the control of a supervisor, who gave 'zone briefings' on a regular basis. This initiative failed. It was management-inspired, and one might speculate that it was neither accepted nor trusted by the workforce; it was abandoned within two years – a Japanese implant that bit the dust. Although significantly reduced in power, the unions still remained the true representatives of the workers.[14]

Burgeoning competition in the market, though, meant that Rover could not function without the active co-operation of its workforce. New initiatives such as Rover Learning Business were introduced in an attempt to make the company a learning organisation. With an annual budget of £35 million, all members of staff, regardless of status, were given £100 to spend as they liked. John Moles from Personnel used his fund to take a course in German, Dariush Jamfar spent his on doing an A-level in Law and Mazin Khayat from Gaydon took a course in pottery.[15] Managers were also sent on a range of engineering, business and management courses at several Midlands universities including those of Coventry and Warwick.

The culmination of these processes was the signing of the New Deal between the company and the unions in 1992. This was not a marriage between new-found lovers, but one of dire necessity. The principles affecting labour in the lean production approach was an appreciation that unless there was co-operative change in the firm in the light of depressed world markets in the early 1990s, survival would be hard. The opening page of the document drew staff's attention to the challenges to Land Rover from Japanese, American and even European producers. Moreover, there was the growing challenge, not only of Japanese imports, but also from the transplant factories of Nissan, Toyota and Honda in the UK. Lessons were drawn from the success of Japanese transplants in America, where ten domestic plants were closed in the 1980s, even though the three American majors, Ford, GM and Chrysler had reasons for plant rationalisation other than Japanese competition. The end result was that, if Rover was to compete, it had to be competitive in efficiency, quality, productivity, flexibility and employee contribution.[16]

The unions, mainly the TGWU, realised that there was little alternative but to be pragmatic and accept the principles of lean production. In return, Rover offered a commitment to no compulsory redundancies, a single- status sick-pay scheme and employee benefits. The TGWU's attitude was basically one of co-operation rather than confrontation with management in the hope that it could influence events and policies rather than be driven by them. It made serious attempts to bring the workforce on board while reassuring operatives that this was not a Nissan- or Toyota-style operation and that unions would still play a genuine representational role on their behalf.

The word 'Quality' is emphasised time and again in the New Deal document and, if Rover was to succeed, then this concept had also to be applied to component and parts suppliers. Lean production taught that assemblers, manufacturers and suppliers should attempt to avoid adversarial confrontational bargaining, in favour of long-term agreements and partnerships. This was not simply a structural change in the bargaining process, it was part of Rover's attempts to introduce Total Quality Improvement, not only within itself but also with its associated companies, which ultimately would lead to total customer satisfaction. In 1984 an independent market survey on customer satisfaction placed Rover fifteenth out of fifteen companies surveyed. The lesson was not lost. Internally, different parts of the firm were challenged to view each other as customers, taking the view that if relations were to be reformed, then it would make sense to take cognisance of the text 'physician heal thyself'. Part of this programme involved careful recruitment and induction programmes for new staff, with senior management taking much more visible responsibility for projects and working in a cross-functional manner with all those involved until completion. Communication procedures were speeded up and staff were made aware of the cost of quality.[17]

Rover's annual spend on components by 1990 was in the order of £3.1 billion, 80 per cent of which was spent in the UK. Following Japanese practice, Rover from the mid-1980s reduced the supplier base from 1,200 to around 260. The suppliers were seen as being in a unique position to enhance customer satisfaction, either through self-development or, more often, being assisted in this by Rover which would send in its own experts. Much of the drive for this came from attempts to adopt advanced 'just in time' systems which would allow the late configuration of cars to customers' specifications and also reduce inventories. This programme, which became known as Rover 2000, was pursued avidly with booklets being given to suppliers and seminars held to explain the processes of supply-chain mapping, the division of supply time into stages, such as the type of activity, process time, waiting time, validation time, travel time, storage time and how performance would be rated. This programme was given, deservedly, a high profile and high publicity, but what was achieved? [18]

Rover retained a production capacity of half a million vehicles and its productivity improved, reaching thirty-five vehicles per employee by 1993. Much of this was due to genuine improvement coming from new investment and reformed working practices but this needs to be seen against a background of a declining workforce, which by 1993 had fallen to just over 30,000, and also nearly £3.5 billion of public funding from 1975.[19] Despite all efforts and genuine improvements in quality, Rover's market share continued to fall, reaching 13 per cent in the early 1990s, with car sales totalling only 325,000 units in 1993. On the surface these figures look reasonably good, given the car market at that time, but the sad fact is that year upon year Rover's market share fell almost routinely from the 15 per cent it held in 1988. A breakdown of the sales figures indicates that the crucial weakness lay in the car divisions, particularly in the mid-range in domestic markets as shown in table 9.1.

Table 9.1
Sales of Rover Cars 1988–93

Model	1988	1993
Metro	86,064	58,650
Montego/Maestro	100,053	12,250
200/400 Series	50,254	112,233
800	29,000 (1989)	17,345

Source: Strategy Update in Rover Group, EIU European Motor Business, First Quarter, 1994, p. 74.

Basically, had it not been for sales of Land Rover and Range Rover, the position would have been worse.

Hard times in the home market forced Rover to look overseas, where it tried to rebuild a dealership network in nearby Europe, trying hard to present an upmarket image emphasising 'Britishness'. On the surface there was some success, with exports reaching over 30 per cent of total sales. To boost overseas sales, however, and remembering the necessity of a careful pricing policy in a market where prices are often considerably below those in Britain, export vehicles were selling at an average price of US$6,000 dollars compared with US$10,000 in the UK, which suggests that Rover was pitching its prices to boost market penetration, with UK consumers appearing to subsidise exports.[20]

Trying for overseas markets made sense for Rover, whose problem domestically was that, despite all the firm's efforts, it still carried a lot of baggage from its troubled past in the market-place. It was still regarded as a product of not very exciting vehicles of mediocre quality, even if the truth was different, and by the end of 1993 there was renewed debate as to whether a small operator could survive alone in a market that was destined to consolidate, making it hard for small independents to survive. But who would buy Rover?

At that time BMW did not seem a natural purchaser of Rover. The German car manufacturer had always worked in the upper segments of the market and was recognised as one of the powerful brands in the world when compared with Rover. In the early 1990s BMW, like others of its ilk, found both its American and European markets hard going. In the former its market share was under pressure and falling due to fierce competition from the Honda Acura and Toyota's Lexus models. At home, amid talk of a European recession, competition was equally strong, and with both the growing concentration within the industry, as well as the increasing fragmentation of the market through the demand for quality small cars and for large off-road four-by-four vehicles which were increasingly popular with the wealthier section of society, BMW was potentially vulnerable and needed a partner.

As BMW was scanning the market BAe found itself short of capital not only for developing Rover, to whom it had never given adequate funds, but also for its core defence business. BAe did offer Rover to Honda but, though prepared to raise its stake in Rover to 47 per cent, the Japanese concern did not want a majority shareholding. Although originally rejected by BAe, BMW's second offer of £800 million was accepted, as well as its willingness to take on £900 million of net debt and off-balance sheet finance. On the surface Rover looked an ideal partner. The two brands did not compete against each other and when combined gave a full range of products.

For the sum paid, which was equivalent to the cost of developing a new model, the Bavarians not only doubled their European market share to 6.4 per cent in one fell swoop but gained control of Europe's leading producers of four-wheel-drive sports/utility vehicles in Land Rover and Range Rover, an easy way of penetrating the small-car market without damaging the BMW brand image, access to a low-cost production base in which labour costs were 30 per cent lower than in Germany, instant acquisition of Honda's know-how in engineering and production, front-wheel-drive technology and the excellent K series engine as well as seventeen brands. BMW in return gave a commitment to invest $500 million a year up to the year 2000 and promised to safeguard jobs and work with local suppliers provided they could supply quality components. Finally, BMW expressed the view that it hoped it could work with Honda but the Japanese, feeling betrayed, would have none of it, having seen their European strategy wrecked almost overnight, and prepared to go it alone.[21]

Initially, BMW left its British protégé very much to its own devices and in 1995, the first full year of ownership, 500,000 units were produced with 54 per cent of these being exported. Yet there were reports that Rover had registered a deficit of £158 million. All was not well and in the following year John Towers resigned as chairman and was replaced by Walter Hasselkus with Tom Purves of BMW becoming sales and marketing director.[22] Essentially, BMW felt it was getting little in return for its money and so began to take a more interventionist line in guiding its British subsidiary towards a brighter future. It could be argued, though, that this late move reflected BMW's failure to realise the depth of Rover's problems from the outset. In September 1996 it was reported that BMW was concerned about spiralling costs, continuous revision of production schedules and appalling build quality even at Land Rover. Such views were not well received by Rover executives and workers, but it was clear that the honeymoon was over.[23] The Bavarians, though critical, were not negative. Besides bringing in a management team more in line with its own culture, BMW went ahead with construction of a £750 million factory at Land Rover, announced its plans to build a £400 million engine plant at Ham's Hall, gave a commitment to progress with the new Mini and successfully launched the Freelander Discovery. While acknowledging the strength of the Mini as a brand, BMW recognised that there were major problems in the car division with the 200, 400 and 800 models looking old and boring compared with rivals in the market. The company intended to ruthlessly rationalise the model range, and move from three to two platforms. The new cars envisaged were not to be BMW clones but distinct front-wheel drives and British-looking even if there were commonalities in product development and a shared four-cylinder engine with many shared parts under the skin. The problem was how the gap between the advent of the new cars and the current lacklustre range was to be bridged.[24]

Sadly, the following two years brought little improvement in Rover's plight. Though there was a continued drive for cost-cutting and higher productivity and new investment, apart from Land Rover, the picture was dismal with the car factories in March 1998 functioning at only 62 per cent capacity, although the firm did produce 395,000 cars plus 128,000 units at Land Rover with 68 per cent of output being exported. Even so, the firm continued to predict that by 2000 Rover would have overtaken British Petroleum and BAe as the country's largest export earner.[25]

By 1998 Rover's position had become critical. Market share fell below 10 per cent, while abroad, exports were hit by the high value of sterling. BMW in fact called for a devaluation of sterling, which brought a sharp riposte from the Chancellor, Gordon Brown, that the real problem lay in Rover's poor productivity record rather than in the exchange rate.[26] Matters came to a head in July 1998 when the company announced that it wanted 1,500 job losses at Longbridge to offset the impact of an overvalued pound. Moreover, the company made it clear that an increasing quantity of components would be purchased outside Britain and this would reach a figure of 30 per cent compared with the current imported average of 15 per cent. These measures were intended to protect the business in the short term without threatening long term investment.[27] In addition to job losses, management made it clear that a much greater level of labour flexibility to boost productivity was required. Comparisons in the press showed that Rover's workers produced only thirty-four vehicles per employee and were near the bottom of the European league in labour productivity.

Such comparisons though are almost meaningless. Admittedly, Rover did lag, but to compare Longbridge with Sunderland, Eisenach, Melfi and Burnaston is to compare chalk and cheese. All four are relatively new greenfield sites with almost state-of-the-art technology, whereas Longbridge is best described as a ramshackle collection of buildings whose technology is such that 'You wouldn't even get a factory like that in the Third World' according to Kumar Battacharyya. Nevertheless, such figures were sufficient to concentrate the workforce's mind when BMW proposed a new deal. Basically, the choice was to agree to changes in work practices accept redundancies or Longbridge could close, especially as Rover was technically

Table 9.2
Vehicles produced per employee per annum

Company	Location	Output per employee per annum
Nissan	Sunderland	98
GM	Eisenach	77
Fiat	Melfi	70
Honda	Swindon	62
Ford	Dagenham	62
Toyota	Burnaston	58
GM	Luton	39
Rover	Longbridge	34
Voltswagan	Emden	28
Peugeot	Sochaux	25

Source: *Guardian*, 22 October 98.

bankrupt, heading for an estimated £500 million loss in 1998. The deal on offer to the workforce stipulated that the basic salary of £16,000 per annum would remain but overtime would be phased out and become negligible. The pay rise for 1998 would be kept to 3.5 per cent, but would be reduced to 0.8 per cent the following year. The revolutionary part of the offer was the demanded flexibility in working hours that would put Rover workers into line with their BMW counterparts in Reginsburg or Munich.

The current working week of thirty-seven hours spread over five days from Monday to Friday with any extra hours, including Saturday morning paid as overtime would be changed. The new working pattern meant that workers could be asked at busy times to work up to seven hours a week extra for no pay, with the worked time to be taken as holiday at a later date. Overtime would only be paid for hours worked above the total, short notice or sickness cover. Allocated work not completed on time would necessitate a compulsory Saturday shift at normal pay. The new arrangements were to be phased in over three years. Beginning in January 1999 workers would work a thirty-seven-hour week (four 9.25-hour shifts on a rotating basis); in the following year the working week would drop to thirty-six hours before settling at thirty-five hours a week in the subsequent year at the same basic salary. Workers would be paid for thirty seven hours and the extra time 'banked' to be worked for no pay at a later date to meet production schedules as requested.[28] This deal was accepted because there was no choice. Tony Woodley of the TGWU made it clear to the workforce that the BMW board in Munich had already voted to close Longbridge and would have done so had it not been for the personal intervention of Bernd Pichetsreider who had put his reputation on the line in the hope that a deal could be achieved and Longbridge saved.[29]

Obtaining a deal from the workforce, though, was not enough for BMW. The Bavarians went further, asking for another tranche of redundancies, and amid the launch of the Rover 75, built at Cowley, demanded a subsidy of around £200 million from the UK government to help finance the badly-needed £1.7 billion investment programme required at Longbridge if new vehicles were to be produced. The company posed the question that if funds were available for greenfield sites, why not for modernising brownfield sites.' Without government funding BMW could give no guarantees on Longbridge's future. The government in return responded by saying it would look favourably upon a request for state aid, but within the confines of EU regulations on state subsidies.[30]

By early 1999 it became clear that Longbridge's fate was not the sole cause of concern for BMW. In the European markets it was wilting under pressure from competition from VW's Audi range and at the same time appeared to become aware of the growing consolidation in the industry, with the recent merger between Daimler Benz and Chrysler, and Ford's acquisition of Volvo to complement its Jaguar range. Essentially, BMW looked vulnerable to a predator, a position that was not helped by being saddled with Rover. Essentially, the Quandt family became impatient with Rover's performance and Pichetsreider had little alternative but to resign. It was thought initially that he would be replaced by the more hardline Wolfgang Reitzle who was considered much less sympathetic to the British subsidiary. He, however, was unacceptable as chairman to the German union representatives on BMW's supervisory board and he, too, had to resign at the same meeting as his rival. A new chairman was appointed in the person of Professor Joachim Milberg, a respected engineer and pragmatic man, in an effort to restore stability after such boardroom bloodletting. Another victim was Walter Hasselkus who in his own words 'fell upon his sword', appearing to shoulder personally much of the blame for Longbridge's poor performance.

The outcome of this was that the promise of a new Mini was reinforced. Disappointingly, facelifts for the 200 and 400 series were signed off, but not a replacement vehicle which Longbridge needed to survive.[31] No sooner was the ink dry on this document than BMW was warning of further major job-losses of up to 2,500 workers. Much more seriously, BMW stated bluntly that it was considering building the 200 and 400 series replacement in Hungary rather than Longbridge. It could be argued that this was a tactic designed to exert leverage on the UK government to produce a generous subsidy, but Hungary has its attractions as a centre for car-building as Audi, Ford and GM have found out. The Hungarian government vowed to more than match any subvention offered in Britain. Furthermore, wages at £2,300 a year were 70 per cent lower than at Longbridge and a further package involving skills, training, tax breaks and a greenfield site added to Magyar attractiveness.[32]

The UK government offer of aid came in March 1999 with a subsidy amounting to £118 million, well below the £240 million BMW expected. It was immediately rejected by the BMW board. All in all, the poverty of the sum relieved the pressure on BMW as it appeared to indicate that 'there's a view that if this is the extent of the British government's caring about UK industrial jobs, then BMW is no longer under the social and political pressure it thought it was'. In the event, BMW made it clear that while it wanted to build in Birmingham it could go elsewhere, so forcing the government's hand to up its offer to £200 million. Bavarian brinkmanship had worked and Longbridge's immediate future was secured.[33]

Despite the promises made at the time of the sale of Chrysler's UK plants to Peugeot, the early 1980s saw considerable uncertainty in Coventry over the company's medium- to long-term plans for its newly acquired UK subsidiary. It was feared that having acquired the Chrysler dealerships, the UK plants would be closed and the market supplied from France. Turnbull's appointment, though, did appear to be a positive move and he harboured plans for an almost independent Ryton supplying a range of cars different from those of the parent company. How this was to be achieved is unclear, but it would have put Coventry based products in direct competition with Peugeot's, imported directly from France.[34]

Peugeot, as discussed earlier, had taken several positive steps to boost its Coventry operation. Linwood was inevitably closed, the Alpine was brought from France for assembly at Ryton, as were the Solara and Tagora models. The latter, though technically a good car mechanically, arrived too late to make an impact and competed directly with the Peugeot 505 in the British market. In the event only 19,000 were produced before it was withdrawn entirely. Rising market share proved elusive and the firm struggled to hold its position of having only 5–6 per cent of the UK market. Losses continued to mount in the first four years of the company's history, rising from £20.2 million to £91 million in 1981 and then falling to £54.7 million in 1982 before showing a modest profit of £4.9 million in 1983.[35]

Though George Turnbull felt that the corner had been turned, the firm remained vulnerable. Firstly, the Ryton plant was in dire need of new investment. Secondly, the entire model range was ageing rapidly and needed replacing. And thirdly, the entire operation was too dependent on the Iran deal. The fall of the Shah and the ensuing revolution in Iran imperilled the export of Paykan kits. Exports fluctuated considerably. The modest profit of 1983 was due in no small measure to the 85,000 kits sent out compared with only 35,000 the previous year. The break-even point on the contract was 50,000 kits. The subsequent Iran–Iraq war caused further confusion with the Iranian, reneging on payment in 1985. Production of kits that year fell to 1,700 a week and at one stage 35,000 kits were stacked up at Newport docks awaiting shipment. The end result, although the deal was renegotiated, was that losses on this contract in the first six months of 1985 crashed to £130.6 million.[36] The Iran deal ended three years later by which time it had become almost irrelevant to company performance.

Being the UK subsidiary of a French enterprise, involving mainly the assembly of kits imported from France, rendered the Coventry operation vulnerable to events on the other side of the Channel. This crystallised in 1984 when there was savage inter-union infighting in the firm's plants at Poissy. The impact of such labour trouble caused a serious shortfall in supplies of body panels, gearboxes and other parts which enforced a nine-day lay-off. Additionally, it was felt that the scenes of violence shown on British television would harm the company's image in the UK and, finally, it was felt that the French management would be reluctant to invest in the UK if this was perceived as exporting French jobs. Indeed, in 1983 the firm's Whitley design centre was sold to Jaguar and the work transferred to Paris. There was a feeling of expendability.[37]

Survival depended on new investment at Ryton and a new model. There was disappointment at the failure to secure a role in building the Peugeot 205, but French paymasters considered this a 'French' car and so it would seem out of place with a British badge.[38] Peugeot did give pledges to Ryton that its future was secure seeing that in the early 1980s labour productivity was rising at an annualised rate of 8 per cent and the workforce was stable with quality improving.

Turnbull left the company in 1984, being replaced by Geoffrey Whalen, Ryton's personnel director, but the major boost came with the announcement that Ryton would build the Peugeot 309 saloon, a follow-up on the 205, and that output would rise from 750 vehicles a day to a maximum of 1,250. The important point is that this brought with it some £30 million of new investment. This was viewed by some as a feather in Geoffrey Whalen's cap, but others more cynically saw it as the parent company laying out a fairly small amount of capital in the UK as a hedge against further unrest in the French plants.

Eventually, 309s were exported to Holland and Belgium and caused the factory to run at near full capacity.

By the middle 1980s there had been a very big change in the quality of labour relations. The opening year of the decade saw a near-demoralised workforce fearful for its jobs. The early signs of change came when Turnbull inaugerated team briefings in an attempt to involve the workforce more in the firm. Though such exercises are totally inadequate in themselves, the theme of worker involvement was pursued avidly by Whalen who preferred co-operation rather than confrontation with the workforce. Proper training schedules were introduced as were induction programmes. Furthermore, he ended the distinction between blue- and white-collar staff introducing a single status. Workers arriving a few minutes late no longer had their pay docked. Similarly, pay was not deducted for attending medical appointments during working hours, with sick pay being guaranteed for six months as was full pay when workers were laid off through no fault of their own, and on retirement workers received two months of their final salary. In Whalen's own words, 'I've tried to treat the workforce as adults'.[39]

Over the course of its first decade in Coventry, Peugeot sustained losses of almost £300 million and struggled to maintain a market share of 6 per cent. In 1986, for instance, pre-tax losses stood at £15 million but this was followed by a pre-tax debt of £10 million the following year. Symbolic of this upturn was the decision to assemble the Peugeot 405 at Ryton alongside the 309, even though the latter did eventually revert to France. Such developments allowed the launching of a second shift at Ryton in 1988 and for the first time in twelve years output rose to over 80,000 units with 60 per cent of production being exported to Europe. The success of this became clear in 1989 when the firm recorded its best ever profit level of £135.3 million.[40]

The early 1990s brought more optimism to Ryton with capital injections of £350 million to facilitate the introduction of yet another new vehicle, namely the Peugeot 306 which was expected in 1993. The new investment was to comprise of a new paint shop, assembly tracks and a limited amount of automation. With the advent of the new vehicle, 405 production was switched back to France, again leaving Ryton as a one-product entity. Peugeot France's attitude, though, continued to be supportive, especially as market share began to rise, reaching 7.67 per cent in 1994 with pre-tax profitability, too, showing an upward trend to £9 million in the same year.[41] This momentum was kept going with the announcement that the TI206 would be built at Ryton from 1998, the first time that a new car had been produced simultaneously in France and the UK. In preparing for this a further £100 million in new investment was promised, and between 1996 and 1998 this totalled £66 million to substantially improve paint-shop facilities and automation levels, causing the number of robots to increase from the thirty-six used in 306 production to sixty-two for the TI. Added to this was equipment for understructure checking, an on-line laser check for the framed body as well as new assembly-line facilities including lineside equipment for brakes, air conditioning, oil fill and laser tracking. Significant training activity was undertaken to ensure that the workforce was capable of delivering the product at the appropriate quality.[42] The advent of the new car with projected increased output led to the creation of a third shift to begin in 1999. The new jobs came with a sting. All the work would be done over a long weekend. In return for weekend working, however, the weekend worker would work 439 hours fewer than those on the other two for the same pay. Overall 900 new jobs would come about with the help of a £2 million aid package from the British government, provided the workers were recruited from the ranks of the long-term unemployed.[43] At the time of writing Peugeot announced a profit of £36.5 million, an 8 per cent market share, the highest in over twenty years, with the intention of upping output to 150,000 units a year.[44] Overall, Peugeot's decision to persevere with its filial appears to have paid off in the medium term even if Paris continues to dictate policy allowing comparatively little local autonomy except in marketing and in limited local purchasing. For the next few years Ryton's future seems assured, but at the end of 1997 Peugeot established future projects for its main French plants and also its Spanish plant in Vigo. Ryton's name was absent from the list.

Jaguar's fate in the late 1970s and early 1980s has already been alluded to, but so important to Coventry's economy is the company that greater in-depth analysis is required. When John Egan assumed control of the company his options were either to make a go of it or to close it down. He recognised that Jaguar suffered from the British disease of low levels of output, productivity and quality, problems that could not be tackled overnight. Apart from their poor physical characteristics the vehicles were as much a product of years of low investment and neglect, the lack of a confident senior management team, proper accounting, marketing and sales departments as well as a demotivated workforce.[45] Resolution of such difficulties required a great deal of managerial acumen. In 1980 sales stood at only 13,000 vehicles a year and could be produced in only three colours, red, white or yellow, and capital was haemorrhaging out of Brown's Lane at a rate of £3 million a month or £47.3 million a year. This was transformed into a £50 million profit only four years later when the firm was privatised.[46]

Initially, Egan had little choice but to try to gain the support of existing management and workers. Symbolic of this was the restoration of the 'big cats' to their dominant position at the factory gates, having been previously removed by BL and in changing the telephone response of switchboard operation to 'Jaguar Cars' rather than 'British Leyland Large Saloon Cars No. 1 Factory'. Much more important, though, was the putting together of a credible senior management team with Ken Edwards heading up personnel, Mike Beasley as manufacturing director, John Edwards in finance and Neil Johnson in marketing. The prime task of the group was to identify product markets and to wrest control of finance from BL so that a full set of meaningful accounts could be realised. Labour productivity was appallingly low and Egan swiftly set about reducing the workforce by 40 per cent bringing it down to around

7,000 by 1982 only for it to rise again to 9,000 two years later. The difference though was that in 1980 only 14,000 units were produced but this figure had increased to 22,000 two years later, and then to 33,000 in 1984. Profitability also improved going from a loss of £48 million in 1980 to a profit of £91 million four years later.

There is no doubt that this was a dramatic turnaround for a company that had been lurching towards extinction. Simply putting together a senior management team and slashing labour, though, does not tell the whole story. In dealing with the shop floor Egan knew that he had to establish a two-way communication system with the workers as well as winning their hearts and minds. The first stage was to include workers in problem solving and encourage them to take a pride in working for 'the Jag'. It was only by these means that productivity and quality could be raised as there was precious little capital available for reinvestment. A start was made through the introduction of quality checks on a voluntary basis to create awareness of the cost of quality. An internal communication system was set up with weekly communication bulletins and team briefings for shop-floor workers. For management there were monthly and quarterly conferences. Training courses were professionalised under a much revamped personnel or Human Resource Department as it was renamed. The emphasis was on creating an environment where people felt they were being developed for the future. Running through much of this was a sense of accountability at all levels, even among the much de-layered management cadres who became subject to appraisal and performance measures. The hearts and minds side was not neglected. Open days were held for families as were fun runs, race meetings, pantomines and an evening cabaret with Pamela Stephenson. Finally, the crude BL Measured Day Work System of payment was abandoned and a bonus system reintroduced.

Quality problems needed identification and so questionnaires were sent to all Jaguar owners, who commented somewhat acidly. Once the top 200 faults were identified, it was clear, according to Ken Edwards, that around 50 per cent of those originated with suppliers. The outcome was that suppliers were held responsible for all rectification costs including parts and labour. Added closely to this drive for improving customer satisfaction was a reduction in the number of dealerships and a move to Jaguar-only dealerships so that Jaguar's revamped image would not suffer from having its products sitting beside those of BL on garage forecourts. Besides being wooed, British and American dealers agreed to reduce their margins from 18 to 15 per cent. Overall, the dealership network was pruned with only the best being retained. The result was that Jaguar slowly turned round and a major reason for this was renewed growth in the American market. Apart from the poor quality of the vehicle, American sales between 1980 and 1982 were hindered by the high levels of sterling against the dollar, even allowing for Jaguar's hedging policy. In 1982, however, the pound dropped significantly and undoubtedly this facilitated transatlantic sales.

From the first day in office Egan, in line with government thinking, hoped to privatise Jaguar through floatation on the Stock Exchange. This duly happened in 1984 in a £2.5 billion scramble with a substantial number of shares falling into American hands. Indeed, by 1986, 65 per cent of these were owned by Americans. Perhaps this was no accident as Jaguar was overdependent on the US market.[47] After privatiszation the drive for increased output continued, reaching 48,000 in 1987, and important in this was the successful launch of the XJ40 whose development necessitated the hiring of nearly 500 new engineers. Jaguar appeared to be on a roll. The Whitley Engineering Centre was purchased from Peugeot which led to subsequent investment of £55 million. The capital investment programme preceded apace with £140 million-worth being made available in 1988, and the training budget was increased to 2 per cent of turnover compared to 0.5 for the UK industry average. Underneath this impressive record, however, Jaguar remained weak in international terms. Its productivity was only two-thirds that of Mercedes and it was producing only 1,150 units a week which was far too low by international standards if Jaguar was to compete against BMW and Mercedes. Moreover, the firm was running short of cash. Profits fell from £97 million in 1987 to £47.5 million in 1988, with reserves dropping to a mere £79 million at the end of the same year against £150 million the previous year. The causes of the cash-flow problem proved easy to identify. The slump in US sales caused a £30 million sag in profits, a problem exacerbated by the strength of sterling which meant that 'every cent on the dollar pound exchange rate cuts upward of £3 million from profits and the strength of the pound against European currency £10 million'. Depreciation increased by another £15 million to £59 million, and research and development cash was up by £5 million to £56 million. Egan freely admitted the problem of low productivity. The hype surrounding Jaguar was over. The company and its shareholders had been brought down to earth with a bump. Dramatic improvements in levels of production, productivity and, less so, quality, had been achieved but by international standards the company still remained a poor performer. Jaguar had tried to grow quickly, rather too quickly, from a very slender resource base and still found itself a tiny player in a giant's playground, rendering it highly vulnerable to a takeover bid by a predator. Ford was on the prowl.[48]

In 1989 Ford signalled its interest and surprised the City when it declared it wanted a 15 per cent stake in Jaguar with the view of becoming a major shareholder. Immediately, the share price rose by 62p to 467p with analysts predicting that Jaguar could fetch a billion if Ford and GM went head to head over Jaguar. Lindsay Halstead, chairman of Ford Europe, duly wrote to the Secretary of State for Industry, Nicholas Ridley, informing him of the company's interest, offering to hold talks on Ford's plans for Jaguar's future. Jaguar, though, was seemingly protected by the government's 'golden share' which meant that no one could own more than 15 per cent of Jaguar and, under the conditions of the golden share, Jaguar could not be sold until 1990, but this could be relaxed by agreement between the company, shareholders and the Secretary of State who had the power to overturn the protective shield.[49]

Egan's preference was to remain independent, but if a partner had to be acquired his preferences were for GM or a European company rather than Ford. Yet a link with Ford would have helped in the US market and brought long-term financial security with low dependency on the variation of the exchange rate. Jaguar was in a weak position. The City was less than enthusiastic about its failure to pay dividends in 1988, considered it too small to survive independently, and saw in Ford the opportunity to be more dynamic in global markets. With this view so prevalent, Jaguar's days as an independent were numbered.[50]

Egan's preferred partner, GM, through its chairman Roger Smith, entered the fray and announced that it preferred to collaborate with Jaguar if it could acquire 15 per cent of the shares, and that it was prepared to pump £100 million in new investment into Brown's Lane and Radford to promote new model development in a mid-range executive car to compete with the lower end of the BMW and Mercedes range. Besides being designed to stop Ford, the intention behind this was to protect Jaguar beyond the expiry of the golden share at the end of 1990 and to bring it under GM's wing in component purchasing and market development. Jaguar's view of this was that GM would co-operate, Ford would dominate.[51]

Battle had commenced. The share price rose to 581p with Philips and Drew estimating that it could go up as high as 1,000p a share. Jaguar looked at possible ways of avoiding Ford, such as linking up with GKN or Lucas, but neither was interested. Ford was anxious to get hold of Jaguar for several reasons. It needed a luxury car in the European market, as the Scorpio model had failed to make an impact and acquisition of Jaguar offered an alternative route. It was argued that as a company it had solid UK credentials given the length of time it had been in Britain and so could offer access to its own well-established European research facilities which, it claimed, were superior to GM's. The bottom line, though, is that Ford knew, as did GM, that Jaguar badly needed a credible partner as its capacity to remain independent was fading rapidly.

When the negotiations between the two companies began, between Morgan Grenfell for Jaguar and Goldman Sachs and Warburgs for Ford, Egan wanted 900p a share where Ford were not prepared initially to go beyond 800p. The negotiations were tortuous but the outcome was obvious once GM made it plain that it would not go above 750p a share; the road was clear for Ford. Egan tried to hold out for 875p a share, dropping 25p from his opening position, but in the end had to settle for 850p. Ford, however, paid £1.6 billion for Jaguar and acquired an ailing company at a premium of £1.3 million over its book price. The whole exercise, though, was made much easier for Ford because Ridley decided to drop the golden share practically before negotiations had begun and virtually forced Jaguar into Ford's arms, much to GM's fury. Why had Ridley acted so? Ridley, a 'politican of consumate contradications', was a firm believer in mergers and takeovers based on market forces and saw the golden share as hindering Jaguar's long-term best interests and being a right-wing free-marketeer simply followed his logical instinct and political dogma. Jaguar was now in American hands with Egan being all but abandoned by the government that for years had lauded him.[52]

Ford executives were somewhat shocked when they visited Jaguar's premises after the takeover with Bill Hayden, the tough Eastender boss of Ford UK, allegedly commenting that he had not seen a factory as antiquated as Brown's Lane outside of Gorky. Within a year of take over Jaguar lost close on £100 million due to a collapse of both the US and UK markets. Sales fell from 49,494 in 1988 to 22,478 in 1992 at the nadir of the depression before recovering almost steadily to over 50,000 per annum in 1998 when Ford is reported to have made an operating profit of £250 million. On taking over it is clear that Ford faced very serious problems and well realised that it would take years to turn Jaguar round, as subsequent events proved. Indeed, between 1990 and 1994 Ford lost $1.2 billion and survived only with heavy subsidies from Detroit after which date no more subsidies were forthcoming. Over the same period investment in modernising the plant totalled $4 million US dollars and the workforce was halved from 12,000. Essentially, apart from absorbing lay-off charges Ford spent its money in modernising the plants to raise productivity and quality and Jaguar actually showed a small profit in 1995 before going into deficit again in the following year.[53] Crucial to the long-term recovery of Jaguar was Ford's decision to involve its own management team under Nick Scheele, and to pursue a policy of integrating Jaguar into Ford's systems of operations and purchasing of components. More attention was also paid to the requirements of individual markets to ensure that products were tailored to suit. For example, this involved targeting sports models at the German market and ensuring that cars destined for France had air conditioning and soft suspension. Above all there has been an increased emphasis on quality, reflected in fewer faults in cars coming off the line with one car in ten being thoroughly checked. In 1994, for instance, faults stood at 12.5 per vehicle, but have since fallen to 3.7.[54]

Not all of Ford's development has been concentrated on Coventry. The new X400 saloon will be built at Halewood on Merseyside, and the XS type was launched in 1998 at the Castle Bromwich complex which had been redeveloped partly thanks to government funding. This new compact vehicle was developed jointly between British and American engineers with much of the engine design and development being carried out in Detroit. Yet its styling and appearance emphasised its Britishness. In essence the spreading of work to other plants gave Jaguar wider options in its attempt to increase output with the X400 coming on stream in 2001. Overall, these moves will nearly quadruple Jaguar's production to 200,000 units, which it needs to meet spiralling development costs and future survival.[55]

Postscript

At the time of writing the original text, it appeared that with the granting of state aid by the British government Longbridge's future had been secured. Since then, however, much has changed. Rover has been broken up, dismembered and sold off by BMW. The Longbridge plant has been sold to Alchemy, a venture capital company. The Land Rover Solihull complex has been bought by Ford, but BMW has retained control of the Cowley Plant at Oxford and the Ham's Hall engine plant. The situation remains fluid as both the UK government and the trade unions are trying to persuade BMW to change its mind, so what follows is by no means definitive and may well be out of date by the time that this book appears.

BMW has given a plethora of reasons for its decision to offload Rover citing uncertainty of whether or not the EU would approve of the package agreed with the UK government, the effect of the high level of sterling, mounting financial losses, falling market share, brand weakness and a seeming lack of commitment by the UK government to join the euro or to run down the exchange rate. Despite this catalogue of reasons the whole exercise was badly handled by BMW which until early March continued to emphasise its commitment to Rover as part of its core business as a full line producer of cars. Throughout all of this it became apparent that the company, unbeknown to the British government, had been negotiating secretly with Alchemy from October 1999.

In November 1999 the European Commission announced that it was to launch a formal inquiry into whether or not UK aid conformed to EU rules. Mario Monti, the commissioner responsible, raised doubts about whether Rover faced a genuine challenge for the proposed investment from a Hungarian greenfield site as claimed by BMW. Though both the company and the UK government asked for a swift resolution, Monti indicated that no decision could be expected before summer 2000. Matters were then further complicated in February 2000 when BMW's German rival, Porsche, lodged a complaint in Brussels that any aid to BMW would distort competition in the market. Although Porsche does not compete directly with Rover's volume models, its forthcoming utility vehicle will rival Land Rover with Rover's MG being considered a low-cost competitor to Porsche's Boxster sports car. Though irritated by Porsche's intervention, the Bavarians did not seem unduly concerned and were confident that agreement could be reached with the EU even if the total package were reduced. However, they were later to say that the delay in reaching such a decision was a factor in their overall decision to pull out of the UK.[56]

It was clear in early January 2000 that all was not well with Rover as the previous year's sales figures showed that it had taken only 6 per cent of the market with overall sales tumbling to 143,000, a drop of 26 per cent on the 1998 figures. BMW, however, were insistent that recovery had begun and pointed to the launch of the R75 and the revamping of the 25 and 45 models even although sales of the R75 totalled no more than 511 units in December 1999. Behind the rhetoric, BMW continued to embark on its overhaul of the company by planning to reduce the workforce by a further 7,000 to 23,000, cutting projected spending on UK-sourced components by £2 billion a year over the following three years and by insisting that suppliers invoice in euros at DM2.70 to the pound, thereby placing the burden of the rising exchange rate firmly on the shoulders of Rover's UK suppliers. Additionally, Rover's sales and marketing operations were to be integrated with those of BMW at Bracknell in a search for greater synergy in those areas.[57]

By mid-February there came a hint that Rover could be on the market. The *Observer* reported that Volkswagen was thought to have approached BMW with a bid for Rover. BMW, however, refused to open talks until the outcome of the EU Commission was known, but there seemed to be the possibility that if the EU blocked the aid package then a sale might be possible and BMW would rid itself of a headache which by that time had earned the sobriquet of the 'English Patient'. It was also suggested that if VW acquired Rover then it would also assemble its Skoda and Seat models alongside Rovers. In return, VW reportedly offered BMW a stake in VW-Audi and strategic co-operation.[58] Towards the end of the same month, amid rumours that it was discussing the future of Rover with a consortium of both British and American venture capitalists who were prepared to acquire the group and operate Rover, Mini, MG and Land Rover as separate stand-alone businesses, the company issued a statement that 'The core message is that Rover is part of BMW Group's strategy to be a full-line supplier ... We are not in talks and there are no plans existing for a sale of our British brands'.[59]

Within three weeks of the above statement, Rover, a company that had been independent, merged, nationalised, denationalised and hawked around the market, had been sold unceremoniously by BMW to Alchemy and Ford, with only the Oxford plant being retained by the parent company. Almost immediately, BMW cited four reasons for its actions: the high level of sterling, accumulated losses, the uncertainty caused by delays in EU decision-making and the weakness of the Rover brand. For almost eighteen months BMW had complained bitterly about the high level of sterling which it said made it difficult to compete, a claim echoed by Honda. When it purchased Rover in 1994 the exchange rate stood at DM2.40 to the pound, but by January 2000 it had escalated to DM3.15 which the firm claimed was too high to allow it to compete internationally, and which in turn favoured imports. What made matters even worse, according to the Bavarians, was the UK government's vacillation over joining the euro. Some of this may well have been sabre rattling as several other overseas multinationals were hinting that unless Britain joined the euro they might have to reconsider further investment in the UK. Nevertheless, in early January the company was anxious about the level of sterling and in March 2000 a company spokesman iterated that 'We are watching the exchange rate almost by the day and this has important influences on future car decisions. We cannot deny that ... The basis for maintaining a manufacturing capability in Britain is deteriorating month by month.[60] While such protestations may have a ring of truth about them and may have also been an attempt to exert pressure on the government, BMW seemed to forget that under the same exchange rate it also benefited considerably. The rise in sterling allowed it to import large numbers of its premium brands into the UK and make a considerable profit on them. Equally, when BMW bought Rover it surely did not expect exchange rates to remain static and queries might be asked about its hedging policy. Simply to castigate sterling will not do. Other overseas car manufacturers such as Peugeot, GM and Ford continue to operate in Britain and Ford's purchase of Land Rover indicates that it regards the UK as still a viable place in which to make cars.[61]

The difficulties with the EU have already been alluded to, but listed among the reasons for sale were the weakness of the Rover brand and accumulated losses. In 1998 losses stood at almost £600 million and subsequently rose to £730 million in 1999. In effect, Rover was haemorrhaging capital at £2 million a day and, according to Joachim Milberg, this 'bitter reality' left the company with no choice but to break up the group.[62] In total, including the initial purchase price, BMW lost between £4.2 and £4.8 billion in its adventure with Rover, which does not include the time and effort devoted to Rover in attempting to turn it round. Such losses were heavy indeed, and it could be rightly argued that they were too high to be sustained in the medium let alone the long term. It appears that the Quandt family and several non-executive directors became impatient with Rover, fearing that its continued demise could have an adverse effect on the viability of BMW itself, making it vulnerable to a potential takeover bid, and so decided to sell. In fact, a small group of main board members, led by Heinrich Heitmann, wanted simply to close Longbridge entirely, arguing that this was a cheaper option than selling it because it would involve lower disposal charges. This was rejected by both Milberg and the Quandts because it would have been more politically damaging to BMW in the UK than selling the business to another buyer, thereby helping to conserve jobs.[63]

That Rover was a wounded or tainted brand there is no doubt, and BMW might well have overestimated brand strength when it bought the company. Rover had been losing market share for more than two decades. In 1994 market share was still in double figures, but by 1999 it had fallen to circa 6 per cent and continued to fall. To be fair, however, car sales generally in Britain were poor in the opening months of 2000 as consumers displayed a resistance to high prices compared to those in mainland Europe and, in many cases, were prepared to await the outcome of a government inquiry into new car prices in Britain in the hope that they would subsequently fall. In some instances consumers were prepared to import directly from Europe. BMW's dwindling market share was scarcely surprising simply because the models available throughout most of its stewardship of Rover were hardly appetising, with no new model appearing until 1998. The ageing Mini had become virtually a collector's item, the Metro was killed off, while the 200 and 400 series, both of which were given very late facelifts, had little market appeal and were at best Honda leftovers. Finally, as discussed elsewhere, the 600 and 800 series disappointed and were due to be phased out and replaced by the R75 in 1998. Sadly, the latter, whose launch was delayed due to production problems caused by BMW's drive for faultless quality, arrived too late on the market to arrest Rover's decline. Sales disappointed, and one wonders whether or not this was because the car was Rover badged and would have fared better if it had borne the BMW marque. Though new models such as the new Mini and a medium-sized car were promised, BMW did extremely little to enhance the Rover range over its tenure of six years, leaving itself with ageing vehicles which compared badly to those of Ford, Renault or Peugeot; yet the company went as far as blaming falling market share on the British consumer, for deserting it. It is worth recalling that for many years German and Japanese car manufacturers lived quite happily with overvalued currencies, because the efficiency and effectiveness of their production processes produced cars that people wanted to buy. BMW failed to replicate the Teutonic model in the UK and customers simply did not want to buy Rovers. Perhaps the company should have studied the relationship between its products, falling market share and successive losses before apportioning blame elsewhere.[64]

Finally, in citing the reasons for offloading Rover, BMW paid scant attention to the quality of management and its own responsibility for managerial quality. Elsewhere in this book it has been suggested that in its early days it tended to give Rover's underperforming management too much power and too little direction from Munich, and let it get on with the job. This in itself was a serious miscalculation and by the time that action was taken, the damage to Rover was irreparable; a potential turnaround seemed to disappear further into the horizon, and so BMW decided to exit. Indeed, Garel Rhys shrewdly observed in January 2000 that if BMW saw no prospect of recovery it would question seriously if there was any point in throwing good money after bad. Perhaps BMW would have emerged with more credit from the whole débâcle if it had simply admitted that it had tried its best to rescue Rover but had failed, rather than heap all the blame onto other factors.[65]

BMW's handling of its exit from Rover has been heavily criticised in the British press primarily for its secrecy and its failure to inform the government of its intentions. Throughout the months of January and February the firm publicly affirmed its commitment to Rover. Even at the Geneva Motor Show at the end of February, a smiling Joachim Milberg denied any plans to sell off Rover. On 10 March, however, the company did confirm in talks with Stephen Byers, the Minister for Industry, that it intended selling off peripherals. At the same time, it discussed plans to raise productivity through more overseas component sourcing, concentration on core businesses and reduced production of the Rover 25 and 75 which had been performing badly in the market, but denied that it intended selling off Rover as a whole: this despite the *Suedeutsche Zeitung* trailing the story of a possible Rover sell-off the same day.[66] Not for several days was any official announcement made and Byers only found out while travelling to a meeting with British Aerospace. Prime Minister Blair found out while watching the 9 o'clock news. BMW had, indeed, been economical with the truth when Byers had spoken to Werner Samann earlier, especially as it had been talking to Alchemy for no less than six months. Byers later made it clear that he thought that 'BMW had fallen below the standard expected of a major multinational company', whose response was that it had little alternative but to maintain secrecy for commercial reasons.[67] Though angry, the government tried to persuade BMW to change its mind and to find another main line car company to take over Rover, rather than Alchemy whose credentials for running a car firm seemed thin. Samann made it clear that there was no other buyer in the offing. BMW had approached Ford, General Motors, Toyota and Volkswagen, but not one would take on Rover without receiving a stake in BMW itself and this could not be countenanced by the board or by the Quandts.[68]

With hindsight it is easy enough to criticise the government for not picking up the signals that BMW intended selling Rover. Indeed, the company claims that it had sent out enough hints through its continuous criticism of the exchange rate level, but there is a difference between dropping hints which could be perceived as applying pressure on a particular issue and being up-front. If, however, Byers in particular is guilty, it is probably because while working so closely with BMW to secure EU's approval of the aid package he lost sight of the larger picture, which was not helped by BMW's secrecy.

The treatment of the trade unions, led by the calm, patient Tony Woodley of the TGWU and the experienced Duncan Simpson of the AEEU, was no less cavalier. Like Byers they, too, made the pilgrimage to Munich in an effort to get the parent company to change its mind and either to retain Rover or to find a suitable alternative buyer, but with no more success. BMW's attitude is perhaps best summed up by the fact that after giving the unions the manifold reasons for the sale, Milberg left the room only to return a few minutes later and said 'I forgot to tell you. We are also selling Land Rover, but I cannot tell you to whom.'[69]

What of the buyers, Ford and Alchemy? Ford was an obvious candidate. It had a cash mountain earning very low interest rates in American banks and knew that it could fit Land Rover products easily into its Premier Automotive Group of Jaguar, Aston Martin, Volvo and Lincoln. Having paid £1.85 billion for Land Rover, Ford's intentions are to boost Land Rover output to 250,000 per annum and to boost sales throughout the United States. Significantly, and perhaps ironically, it appointed Wolfgang Reitzle as chief executive at Land Rover. There is no reason to think that Ford will not be successful, but beyond that Ford has yet to comment on its future medium- and long-term strategies.[70]

Founded in 1997 by John Moulton, a chemistry graduate of Lancaster University who later qualified as an accountant at Coopers and Lybrand, Alchemy is essentially an equity company, specialising in turning round failing businesses such as the Fatty Arbuckle restaurant chain and Fads. Its record is laudable, but several analysts have reservations. After six months of discussion, BMW more or less paid Alchemy to take Rover off its hands with BMW taking responsibility for writing down the Longbridge plant. Under the terms of the agreement, Longbridge would continue to produce the R25, R45, old Mini and MGF models, with the R75 continuing to be made under licence by BMW at its Oxford plant where it would also produce the new Mini.[71] Being a venture capital company, Alchemy's interest in Longbridge appears to be limited. From the outset it spoke of selling on the business within seven years if successful, provoking the charge that it was simply an asset stripper – which it strenuously denied.

How, then, does it intend to make a success of its new entity? Essentially, Alchemy has to operate in both the short and medium term. Initially it intends running down eight months' existing stocks of unsold Rover cars by offering limited price cuts, at the same time pacifying Rover dealers, whose network it inherited. To facilitate this production cuts of 20 per cent were imposed on the R25 and R45 lines at Longbridge, which normally turned out 4,400 vehicles per week, and an extension of the three-day Easter break to five days was announced at the same time. Similarly, at Oxford output of the R75 was cut from 2,200 units a week to 1,000 and the night shift was axed. Nobody was made redundant or laid off and until further notice, shifts were scheduled to work alternate weeks.[72] Alchemy was initially coy about the medium-term future, except for announcing that it was dropping the name Rover and that the new entity would be known as the MG Car Company, in an attempt to develop a new image by reverting to a name that once denoted a quality brand even if that were only partly true. Within two years the Rover brand would disappear completely and all products would be badged as MGs. The firm announced that it intended to develop a sports version of the R75 as well as an MG variant, a policy not without risk as the R75 has yet to prove itself in the market and if it fails to do so, the chances of derivatives being successful may not be all that high. Finally, it is intended to produce a new sports saloon with an aluminium composite body.[73] Clearly, if total output is reduced the question arises as to where exactly Alchemy will position its vehicles in the market. As it does not intend being a volume producer it may well be forced to compete against premium brands such as Jaguar, Volvo, Mercedes and, ironically, BMW itself. Moreover, if its proposed new vehicle's output is in the region of only 10,000 units per annum as it appears to be, it is difficult to see precisely in which market segment it will compete. Finally, in an effort to try to allay the worst fears of the workforce and the dealers and show that it intended being a serious player in the auto industry, Alchemy announced that it had appointed Chris Woodwark, a former chief executive of Rolls Royce and a man with vast experience within the industry, as its chief executive and Brandon Gough, chairman of De la Rue's and Yorkshire Water as chairman of MG cars. Graham Halworth, an internal Alchemy official was appointed as finance director.[74]

There is no arguing that BMW's actions sent shock waves around the whole of the West Midlands. Almost immediately, speculation arose as to how many jobs would be lost. The figures quoted have fluctuated, but it seems likely that the break-up of Rover will lead directly to the loss of 9,500 jobs, including a minimum of 3,500 at Longbridge. This may well be an underestimate because if output is reduced to between 50,000 and 80,000 units a year then the scale of Longbridge job losses is likely to be far higher. There will be a further 1,500 job losses at Rover's Swindon pressings plant and 2,000 at its research and development centre at Gaydon, near Coventry. Other job losses extend to 1,000 at Rover's Warwick headquarters and 500 more at Oxford. At component supply companies the figures will be far higher with job losses of between 35,000 and 40,000 being quoted by local manufacturers. It is estimated that the overall impact of job losses could push unemployment in the Birmingham conurbation up into double figures. To try to ameliorate the situation, the government has set up a task force along with the local councils and chambers of commerce to try to attract new industry onto the Longbridge site and so alleviate the projected unemployment, and to this it has given an initial funding of £130 million.[75]

Did BMW have any other choice? Probably not. Rover was a company that had been in secular decline for well over twenty years. During this period it had received over £20 billion of investment from government, British Aerospace and BMW, to say nothing of what it gained from its collaboration with Honda. It singularly failed to develop a range of models that commanded a respectable showing in the market-place, and for every success there was Maestro, a Montego and a Metro. In the end, BMW probably felt that it had done everything it could and decided to cut its losses to conserve and preserve the parent company. Finally, as indicated at the beginning of this Postscript, what is written here may well be out of date by the time that this book appears, as this saga still has a while to run.

Notes

[1]   S. Smith, *Challenges and Opportunities for the Automotive Component Sector in Coventry for the 1990's* (Coventry City Council, Economic and Development Department, Coventry 1994), pp. 1–50.

[2]   Ibid.

[3]   Ibid

[4]   T. Kochan and R. Lansbury, *Employee Relations in the International Automobile Industry in an Era of Global Change* (IMVP, Washington, DC, May 1995).

[5]   Foreman-Peck et al., *The British Motor Industry*, pp. 217–19.

[6]   P. Willman, 'The Reform of Collective Bargaining and Strike Activity in BL Cars 1976 – 82', *Industrial Relations Journal*, vol. 15, no. 3 (1984), pp. 1–12.

[7]   Adeney, *The Motor Makers*, p. 325, K. Williams, C. Haslam, S. Johal, J. Williams, *Cars: Analysis, History, Cases* (Berghahn Books, Providence, 1994), pp. 161–5.

[8]   D. Faulkner, 'The Rover Honda Alliance' in *Exploring Corporate Strategy*, 5th edition, G. Johnson and S. Scholes (eds) (Prentice Hall, London, 1999), pp. 725–37.

[9] Ibid., R. Bertodo, 'Implementing a Strategic Vision', (privately distributed paper given at a Seminar at Warwick University Business School, June 1987.

[10] Foreman-Peck, et al., *The British Motor Industry*, p. 245.

[11] A. Wood, *Wheels of Misfortune, The Rise and Fall of the British Motor Industry*, (Sidgwick and Jackson, London, 1988), p. 214.

[12] Adeney, *The Motor Makers*, pp. 330–31.

[13] Foreman-Peck, et al., *The British Motor Industry*, pp. 246–7.

[14] Ibid.

[15] 'Business News from Rover Learning Business', August 1991; H. Kay, 'Lazarus goes to Longbridge', *Director*, October 1993, pp. 32–5.

[16] *Rover Tomorrow – The New Deal*, Rover 1992.

[17] *Total Quality Improvement, Suppliers Guide*, Rover 1992.

[18] 'The Purchasing Philosophy of the Rover Group', *EIU, Automotive Components Business*, March 1992, pp. 58–72.

[19] H. Kay, 'Lazarus goes to Longbridge', *Director*, October 1993, pp. 32–5.

[20] 'Strategic Update on the Rover Group', *EIU, European Motor Business*, March 1994, pp. 70–84.

[21] 'Rover taken over by BMW in £800m deal with BAe', 'Rover Unleashed', 'A Sudden Burst of Acceleration', Don't Cry Over Rover', BAe Flies Away From Rover With A Sackful Of Cash', *Financial Times*, 1 February 1994; T.C. Melewar, 'Putting the Brrrm back in Brum', European Case Clearing House, 596–049–8, 1994.

[22] 'Tom's New Car Company', *Car Magazine*, October 1996, pp. 47–9.

[23] 'A Marriage Made in Hell', *Car Magazine*, September 1996, pp. 50–54.

[24] 'The Shock of Absorption', *Financial Times*, 10 November 1996.

[25] 'High Pound Sends Rover Soaring', *Guardian*, 22 January 1996.

[26] 'Rover Joins Clamour For Fall in Pound', *Guardian*, 1 April 1998; 'Rover Blames 1500 Job Cuts On Strong Pound', *Financial Times*, 23 July 1998; 'Brown Blasts Rover Productivity', *Financial Times*, 24 July 1998.

[27] Rover Group Communication, 23 July 1998.

[28] 'Is It Over For Rover?', *Guardian*, 10 March 1999.

[29] 'Vote for New Deal or it's end of the road for Rover', *Observer*, 13 December 1998.

[30] 'Back from Munich: Rover Union Chiefs have won peace – for a time', *Financial Times*, 29 November 1998.

[31] 'More Agony for Rover', *Birmingham Post*, 1 February 1999.

[32] 'Brinkmanship may finish Rover', *Guardian*, 22 March 1999; 'Can aid keep our Rover in its kennel?', *Observer*, 14 March 1999.

[33] 'Rover plant on brink as BMW spurns aid deal', *Guardian*, 15 March 1999; 'Longbridge saved in £200m deal, *The Times*, 31 March 1999.

[34] 'Modest Profit Inspires Talbot', *Coventry Evening Telegraph*, 12 April 1983.

[35] Ibid.

[36] 'Talbot UK gives profit first in ten years', *Financial Times*, 9 September 1983; 'The Iranian Connection', *Coventry Evening Telegraph*, 8 January 1984; 'Talbot axes 275 Jobs after Iranian deal', *Guardian*, 28 June 1985.

[37] 'Talbot in the Tumbril', *Sunday Times*, 8 January 1984.

[38] 'Peugeot not for Ryton', *Guardian*, 28 February 1983.

39   'Peugeot Translated', *Guardian*, 17 September 1984; How Peugeot became the Pride of Coventry', *Financial Times*, 13 October 1988.

40   'Peugeot hits new Heights', Coventry Evening Telegraph, 19 April 1990.

41   Ibid., 20 April 1990; 'Return to profit with expectations of new model', *Guardian*, 22 April 1995.

42   'Right on Ryton', Coventry Evening Telegraph, 9 June 1998, Peugeot Plc, Annual Report 1998.

43   'Weekend sting at Peugeot', *Guardian*, 2 December 1998; '£2 m pump primer for Peugeot Jobs in Coventry, *Guardian*, 11 March 1999.

44   'Peugeot Profit Scheme Pays Out', *Guardian*, 26 March 1999.

45   'John Egan', 'The Money Programme', BBC 2, 27 February 1983.

46   K. Edwards, 'Jaguar' lecture given at the Centre for Business History and Business Policy, Coventry Polytechnic, 12 November 1987. Much of what follows immediately is based upon Mr Edwards's lecture and also on the case study 'Jaguar, Managing Survival, Regimentation and Growth'. This case was given to me in typescript copy by a colleague, but neither he nor I have been able to discover the identity of the author. Our debt to this so far unknown person is fully and freely acknowledged.

47   Ibid., 'Jaguar in the fast lane with bumper profits', *Guardian*, 22 February 1984; 'Americans capture Jaguar', *Sunday Times*, 18 February 1986.

48   K. Edwards, 'Jaguar'; Case Study, 'Jaguar Managing Survival, Regimentation and Growth';'Jaguar In The Fast Lane', *Guardian*, 22 February 1984; 'Jaguar launch of XJ40 puts brake on growth', *Guardian*, 19 August 1986; 'Jobs Warning at Jaguar as Profits Slide', *Independent*, 12 March 1988.

49   'Ford Signals Battle to Control Jaguar', *Independent*, 20 September 1989.

50   'More than just a car – more a way of life', *Guardian*, 20 September 1989.

51   'General Motors set to unveil Jag deal', *Observer*, 22 October 1989.

52   'How Ford trapped Jaguar', *Observer*, 5 November 1989; 'Jaguar threatened by US take-over', *Guardian*, 3 November 1989; 'Jaguar, Mr Ridley and a case of Weasel Words', ibid., 'Ford buys Jaguar', ibid., 3 November 1989; 'Ridley accused of selling out Jag work force', *Coventry Evening Telegraph*, 3 November 1989.

53   'Jaguar soars in £50 m profit', *Observer*, 7 March 1999; 'New model puts Jaguar back in Jobs Market', *Guardian*, 13 February 1999.

54   'Comment Ford a mis un tigre dans Jaguar', *Le Nouvel Economiste*, 3 November 1997.

55   'Jaguar', Midlands Report, BBC 2, 22 October 1998.

56   'EU to crack down on aid to car firms', *Guardian*, 25 November 1999; 'Porsche tried to halt Rover aid package', *Financial Times*, 7 February 2000.

57   'BMW to launch new shake up at Rover', *Financial Times*, 11 January 2000; 'BMW's problem child', *Financial Times*, 27 January 2000; 'Rover staff in BMW shake-up, *Financial Times*, 4 February 2000.

58   'VW bids to take a stake in Rover', *Observer*, 13 February 2000.

59   'BMW reaffirms backing for Rover', *Financial Times*, 27 February 2000.

60   'BMW to launch new shake up at Rover', *Financial Times*, 11 January 2000; 'BMW's problem child', *Financial Times*, 23 January 2000; 'Rover's six year struggle for survival', *Birmingham Post*, 15 March 2000.

61   'Blaming the pound is no answer', *Independent*, 18 March 2000.

[62] 'BMW boss blames bitter reality of £2m a day loss for Rover sale', *Independent*, 29 March 2000.

[63] 'Secret meetings sealed car group's fate', *Financial Times*, 17 March 2000.

[64] 'Blaming the pound is no answer', *Birmingham Post*, 15 March 2000.

[65] 'A difficult road ahead', *Financial Times*, 16 March 2000.

[66] 'Rover goes to scrapheap', *Sunday Times*, 19 March 2000; 'Minister battles to clear his name over BMW fiasco', *Independent*, 31 March 2000.

[67] 'BMW admit lying over Rover sale', *Independent*, 19 March 2000.

[68] 'Four car groups rejected Rover', *Independent*, 30 March 2000.

[69] 'Ex BMW boss seen as white knight', *Sunday Times*, 19 March 2000.

[70] 'Ford appoints ex-BMW chief to run Land Rover', *Financial Times*, 18 March 2000.

[71] 'The road to ruin', *Sunday Times*, 19 March 2000.

[72] 'Rover begins cuts at two main factories', *Independent*, 22 March 2000.

[73] 'Ex BMW boss seen as Rover's white knight', *Sunday Times*, 23 March 2000.

[74] 'Sale of Rover could cost up to 45,000 jobs', *Independent*, 23 March 2000.

[75] 'Sale of Rover could cost up to 45,000 jobs', *Independent*, 23 March 2000.

Bibliography

Records in public depositories

Bishopsgate Institute, London
    Reform League Report on Coventry 1868.
Coventry Record Office
    Acc 926 Alfred Herbert.
    Acc 985 Alvis.
    Acc 1060 Armstrong Siddeley.
    Acc BA/C/Q/12 City of Coventry, Enrolment of Indetures.
    Acc 594 Daimler.
    Acc 1040 ML Magneto.
    Acc 634 Smith's Stamping, Directors' Minutes.
Coventry Technical College
    Coventry Technical Institute, Annual Reports 1891–97.
Essex County Record Office
    Hoffman Mss.
Imperial War Museum
    Mss EMP 45. 7. Advisory Committee on Women's War Employment.
    Report on Industrial Conditions in Coventry, November 1916.
Museum of British Road Transport, Coventry
    Rootes at War Manuscripts and Reports.
    Hillman Division.
    Humber Division.
    Humber Spares.
    Nos 1, 2, 3 and 4 Shadow Factories.
    Rootes Securities.
    Special Division.
Public Records Office, Kew
    AVIA 15/320 Alvis.
    BT 31/15/15146/33732 Arden Motor Company.
    BT 31/9923/33732 Clarendon Motor Company.
    BT 31/7804/55841 Endurance Motor Company.
    BT 31/75146/33732 Rex Motor Company.
    ED 53/338 Board of Education, Area Records of Secondary
        Education in Coventry.
    MUN 5/214 Ministry of Munitions Reports.
    MUN 1962/3 Ministry of Munitions Reports.
University of London: Senate House Library
    Mss P/8/147 Pollitt Papers.

Mss 16/2 Simms Papers.
University of Warwick: Modern Records Centre
Mss 66 Coventry and District Engineering Employers Federation.
Mss 226/RO Rover Motor Company.
Mss 226/ST Standard Motor Company.

Records held by companies

Bluemel Brothers, Wolston, Coventry
Directors' Minutes.
Coventry Motor Panels Ltd
Directors' Minutes 1922–39.
Chairman's Annual Reports 1923–39.
Jaguar Cars Ltd, Coventry
SS Cars Ltd, Directors' Minutes.
Annual Reports and Accounts 1945–67.
Swallow Coachbuilding Company, Directors' Minutes.
Lloyds Bank Archive, London
Coventry District, daily journals, LBA B379a.
Midland Bank Archive, London
Coventry District, daily journals, MBA 358.
Peugeot Talbot Motor Co. Ltd
Miscellaneous Records and Accounts belonging to Rootes, Chrysler
and Peugeot Talbot Ltd.

Trade association and trade union records

Amalgamated Union of Engineering Workers
Minutes of the Coventry Branch.
Minutes of the District Committee.
Coventry and District Engineering Employers Association
Minutes of the Executive Committee.

Interviews

Coventry University
Audio History of the Coventry Car Industry, 1918–83:
Alick Dick
Jack Jones
Sir William Lyons
Eddie McGarry.

Theses

B.J. Beaven, 'The Growth and Significance of the Coventry Car Component Industry, 1985–1939' unpublished PhD thesis, De Montfort University, 1994.

F. Carr, 'Engineering Workers and the Rise of Labour in Coventry', unpublished PhD thesis, University of Warwick, 1978.

A. Holme, 'Some Aspects of the British Motor Manufacturing Industry during the years 1919–1930', unpublished MA thesis, University of Sheffield, 1964.

H. Perkin, 'The History of the Cycle Industry in Coventry 1896–1914', unpublished project for the Degree of BA (Hons) Modern Studies, Coventry Polytechnic, 1979.

R.F. Prosser, 'Coventry: A Study in Urban Geography', unpublished MA thesis, University of Birmingham, 1955.

Government publications

Central Policy Review Staff, *The Future of the British Car Industry* (HMSO, London, 1975).

Parliament (Commons), *Royal Commission on Motor Cars*, P.P. 1906, Vol. XLVIII (HMSO, London, 1906).

Parliament (Commons), *Committee of Inquiry into Industrial Unrest, Report of the Commissioners for the West Midlands Area 1917* (HMSO, London, 1917).

Parliament, (Commons), *Report of the Committee on Women in Industry 1919*, (HMSO, London, 1919).

Parliament, (Commons), *Fourteenth Report of the Expenditure Committee 1974–75: The Motor Industry* (HMSO, London, 1975).

Parliament, (Commons), *Eighth Report of the Expenditure Committee 1975–76: Public expenditure on Chrysler (UK)* (HMSO, London, 1976).

Books

M. Adeney, *Nuffield: a biography* (Robert Hale, London, 1993).

Anon., *Coventry Facts and Figures* (Coventry City Council, Coventry, 1997).

Anon., *Coventry Car Factories: A Centenary Guide* (Coventry City Council, Coventry, 1995).

P. Andrews and E. Brunner, *The Life of Lord Nuffield* (Blackwell, Oxford, 1959).

Armstrong Siddeley Motors, *The Evening and the Morning* (the company, Coventry, 1956).

K. Atkinson, *The Singer Story* (Veloce, Godmanstone, 1996).

R. Bacon, *From 1900 Onwards* (Hutchinson, London, 1940).

W.O. Bentley, *An Autobiography* (Hutchinson, London, 1958).

K. Bhaskar, *The Future of the UK Motor Industry* (Kogan Page, London, 1979).

K. Bhaskar, *The Future of the World Motor Industry* (Kogan Page, London, 1980).

A. Bird and F. Hutton Scott, *Lanchester Motor Cars* (Cassells, London, 1965).

G. Braybon, *Women Workers in the First World War* (Croom Helm, London, 1981).

P. Brendon, *The Motoring Century. The Story of the Royal Automobile Club* (Bloomsbury, London, 1977).

J. Bullock, *The Rootes Brother* (Patrick Stephens Ltd, Yeovil, 1993).

C.F. Caunter, *The History and Development of Light Cars* (HMSO, London, 1957).

R. Church, *Herbert Austin: The British Motor Industry to 1941* (Europa, London, 1979).

R. Church, *The Rise and Decline of the British Motor Industry* (Macmillan, London, 1994).

E.V. Cooper, *Fifty Years Reminiscences* (the author, Coventry, 1928).

C. Clutton and J. Stanford, *The Vintage Motor Car* (Batsford, London, 1954).

B. Crick (ed), *Unemployment* (Methuen, London, 1981).

R. Croucher, *Engineers at War* (Merlin Press, London, 1982).

M. Davis, *Every Man His Own Landlord* (Coventry Building Society, Coventry, 1985).

J. Davy, *The Standard Motor Car 1903–63* (Sherbourne Press, Coventry, 1964).

K. Day, *Alvis: the Story of the Red Triangle* (Gentry, London, 1981).

C. Dewar, *The Great Munitions Feat* (Constable, London, 1921).

P. Dunnett, *The Decline of the British Motor Industry* (Croom Helm, London, 1980).

M. Edwards, *Back From The Drink* (Collins, Glasgow, 1983).

J. Ensor, *The Motor Industry* (Longman, London, 1971).

R. Floud, *The British Machine Tool Industry 1850–1914* (Cambridge University Press, Cambridge, 1976).

J. Foreman-Peck, S. Bowden and A. McKinlay, *The British Motor Industry* (Manchester University Press, Manchester, 1995).

A.L. Friedman, *Industry and Labour* (Macmillan, London, 1977).

G.H. Frost, *Munitions of War* (BSA and Daimler, Birmingham and Coventry, ND).

J. Hasegawa, *Replanning the Blitzed City Centre* (Open University Press, Buckingham, 1992).

J. Hinton, *The First Shop Stewards Movement* (Allen and Unwin, London, 1973).

SP. Inman, *Labour in the Munitions Industries* (HMSO, London, 1957).

D.T. Jones, *Maturity and Crisis in the European Car Industry: Structural Change and Public Policy* (University of Sussex, Sussex, 1981).

B. Lancaster and T. Mason (eds), *Life and Labour in a 20th Century City: The Experience of Coventry* (Cryfield Press, Coventry, 1986).

J. Lane, *A Register of Business Records of Coventry and Related Areas* (Coventry Polytechnic, Coventry, 1977).

R. Langworth and G. Robson, *Triumph Cars* (Motor Racing Publications, London, 1979).

C.H. Lee, *Regional Economic Growth in the UK Since 1880* (McGraw Hill, Maidenhead, 1971).

W. Lewchuck, *American technology and the British Vehicle Industry* (Cambridge University Press, Cambridge, 1987).

A. Maxcy and A. Silberston, *The Motor Industry* (Allen and Unwin, London, 1959).

S. Morewood, *Pioneers and Inheritors: Top Management in the Coventry Motor Industry 1896–1972*, (Coventry Polytechnic, Coventry, 1990).

A. Muir, *75 Yeras* (Smith's Stamping, Coventry, 1958).

A.E. Musson, *The Growth of British Industry* (Holmes and Meir, New York and London, 1978).

E. Neufield, *A Global Corporation: A History of the International Development of Massey Ferguson Ltd* (University of Toronto Press, Toronto, 1969).

H. Nockolds, *Lucas: The First Hundred Years*, vol.1 (David and Charles, Newton Abbot, 1976).

R.J. Overy, *William Morris, Viscount Nuffield* (Europa, London, 1976).

S. Pollard, *The Wasting of the British Economy* (Croom Helm, London, 1982).

B. Price, *The Lea Francis Story* (Batsford, London, 1978).

E.H. Reeves, *The Riley Romance* (the company, Coventry, 1930).

B. Reynolds, *Rudge* (Haynes and Co., Yeovil, 1927).

G. Rhys, *The Motor Industry: An Economic Survey* (Butterworth, London, 1970).

K.E. Richardson, *Twentieth Century Coventry* (City of Coventry, Coventry, 1972).

K.E. Richardson, *The British Motor Industry 1896-1939* (Macmillan, London, 1976).

S. Ritchie, *Industry and Air Power: The Expansion of British Aircraft Production 1935–1941* (Frank Cass, London, 1997).

B.E. Smith, *The Daimler Tradition* (Transport Bookman, London, 1972).

D. Thoms, L. Holden and T. Claydon (eds), *The Motor Car and Popular Culture in the 20th Century* (Ashgate, Aldershot, 1998).

D. Thoms, *War Industry and Society: The Midlands 1939–45* (Routledge, London, 1989).

C. Trebilcock, *Vickers Brothers: Armaments and Enterprise* (Europa, London, 1977).

B. Tripp, *Renold Chains* (Allen and Unwin, London, 1956).

26 BIBLIOGRAPHY

A. Whiting, *The View from Cowley: The Impact of Industrialisation upon Oxford 1918–39* (Claredon Press, 1983)
A. Whyte, *Jaguar: The History of a Great British Car,* (Jaguar Cars, Coventry, 1983)
K. Whyte, *Company Heritage* (Chrysler UK, Coventry, 1979).
S. Wilkes, *Industrial Policy In The Motor Industry* (Manchester University Press, Manchester, 1988).
K. Williams, J. Williams and D. Thomas, *Why are the British Bad at Manufacturing* (Routledge, Kegan Paul, London, 1983).
K. Williams, C Haslam, S. Johal, T. Williams, *Cars: Analysis, History, Cases* (Berghahn Books, Warwick 1994).
G. Williamson, *Wheels Within Wheels* (Geoffrey Bles, London, 1966).
J. Womack, D. Jones and D. Roos, *The Machine That Changed The World* (MacMillan, London, 1990).
J. Wood, *Wheels of Misfortune* (Sidgwick and Jackson, London, 1988).
S. Young and S. Hood, *Chysler UK: A Multinational in Transition* (Praeger, New York and London, 1977).

Articles and book chapters

B. Beaven, 'Re-constructing the Business Community: the Small Firm in (Coventry Polytechnic, Coventry, 1977) the Coventry Motor Industry, 1896-1939', *Business Archives: Sources and History,* No. 72 (1996).
B. Beaven, 'The Growth and Significance of the Coventry Car Component Industry, 1895–1914', *Midland History,* vol. 18, (1993).
W. Brown, 'Pieceworking in Coventry', *Scottish Journal of Political Economy,* vol.18 (February, 1971).
R. Church, 'Nineteenth Century Clock Technology in Britain, the United States and Switzerland', *Economic History Review,* 2nd Series, vol. XXXVIII, No. 4 (1975).
R. Church, 'Markets and Marketing in the British Motor Industry before 1914', *Journal of Transport History,* vol. 3, (1982).
T. Donnelly and D. Thoms, 'Trade Unions, Management and the Search for Production in the Coventry Motor Car Industry', *Business History,* vol. 31 (1989).
J. Foreman-Peck, 'Tariff Protection and Economies of Scale: the British Motor Industry before 1939', *Oxford Economic Papers,* New Series, vol. 31 (1979).
J. Foreman Peck, 'Exit, Voice and Loyalty as Responses to Decline: the Rover Company in the Interwar Years', *Business History,* vol. XXIII (1981).
J. Foreman-Peck, 'Diversification and the Growth of the Firm: The Rover Company to 1914', *Business History,* vol. XXV (1983).
A.E. Harrison, 'The Competitiveness of the British Cycle Industry', *Economic History Review,* 2nd Series, vol. XXII, No. 2 (1969).

A.E. Harrison, 'Joint Stock Company Flotation in the Cycle, Motor Vehicle and Related Industries', *Business History*, vol. XXIII (1981).

R.A. Hart and D.I. MacKay, 'Engineering Earnings in Britain 1914-68', *Journal of the Royal Statistical Society*, vol. 138 (1978).

D.T. Jones and S.J. Prais, 'Plant Size and Productivity in the Motor Industry: Some International Comparisons', *Oxford Bulletin of Economics and Statistics*, vol. 40 (1978).

G. Jones, 'The Growth and Significance of British Multinational Firms Before 1914: The Case of Dunlop', *EconomicHistory Review*, 2nd Series, vol. XXXVII (1984).

T.H. Kerr, 'The Effect of the Automobile Industry on the Midlands', *Proceedings of the Institute of Mechnical Engineers*, Pt. 3, June 1927.

K.G.C. Knowles and D. Robinson, 'Wage Movements in Coventry', *Bulletin of Oxford University Institute of Economics and Statistics*, vol. 51 (1969).

J. Lane, 'Technical Training of Young Persons in Coventry and the Midlands', *SSRC Report* (Lanchester Polytechnic), 1977.

C.H.D.E. Leppington, 'The Evolution of an Industrial Town', *Economic Journal*, vol. 17 (1907).

C. O'Gallagher, 'Payne and Bates of Coventry: Pioneer Motor Manufacturers', *Warwickshire History*, vol. 5 (1974).

S.B. Saul, 'The Motor Industry in Britain to 1914', *Business History*, vol. 5 (1962).

A. Shenfield and P.S. Florence, 'Labour for the War Industries: The Experience of Coventry', *Review of Economic Studies* (1943–45).

A. Shenfield and P.S. Florence, 'The Economies and Diseconomies of Industrial Concentration: The Wartime Experience of Coventry', *Economic Studies* (1943–45).

A. Silberston, 'The Motor Industry 1955–64', *Oxford University Institute of Economics and Statistics*, vol. 27, (1965).

S. Tolliday, 'Militancy and Organization: Women Workers and Trade Unions in the Motor Trades in the 1930s', *Oral History Journal* (Autumn, 1983).

Index

For Product Safety Concerns and Information please contact
our EU representative GPSR@taylorandfrancis.com Taylor & Francis
Verlag GmbH, Kaufingerstraße 24, 80331 München, Germany

T - #0108 - 160425 - C0 - 216/148/14 - PB - 9781138739000 - Gloss Lamination